JEFFREY L. RODENGEN

Also by Jeff Rodengen

The Legend of Chris-Craft

*IRON FIST: The Lives
of Carl Kiekhaefer*

*Evinrude-Johnson and
The Legend of OMC*

*Serving The Silent Service:
The Legend of Electric Boat*

The Legend of Dr Pepper/Seven-Up

The Legend of Honeywell

The Legend of Briggs & Stratton

The Legend of Ingersoll-Rand

*The Legend of Stanley:
150 Years of The Stanley Works*

The MicroAge Way

The Legend of Halliburton

The Legend of York International

The Legend of Nucor Corporation

*The Legend of Goodyear:
The First 100 Years*

The Legend of AMP

*Applied Materials:
Pioneering the Information Age*

The Legend of Cessna

The Legend of AMD

The Legend of Amdahl

The Legend of Echlin

The Legend of Pfizer

The Legend of Inter-Tel

The Legend of American Standard

The Legend of Rowan

The Legend of Ashland

The Legend of Federal-Mogul

Publisher's Cataloging in Publication

Rodengen, Jeffrey L.
    The legend of VF Corporation/Jeffrey L. Rodengen.
    p. cm.
    Includes bibliographical references and index.
    ISBN 0-945903-38-3

    1. VF Corporation 2. Clothing trade—United States. I. Title

HD9940.U4R64 1998   338.7'687'0973
                               QBI97-40429

Write Stuff Enterprises, Inc.

1515 Southeast 4th Avenue • Fort Lauderdale, FL 33316
1-800-900-Book (1-800-900-2665) • (954) 462-6657

Library of Congress Catalog Card Number 96-61246
ISBN 0-945903-38-3

Completely produced in the United States of America
10 9 8 7 6 5 4 3 2 1

TABLE OF CONTENTS

INTRODUCTION

"WE'RE GOING to start an outlet complex and I want you to tell me how much it will cost and what kind of volume we'll do," M.O. "Whitey" Lee told his startled managers one day in 1970. "I'm coming back at 3 o'clock and you'd better be ready."

With the absolute determination that would mark his entire career, "Whitey" Lee plunged into the outlet business. When he came back that afternoon, "We had crunched the numbers," recalled VF Corporation's Richard Lamm, "and quoted him some conservative figures. He grabbed my shoulder and said, 'Darn you, kid! I'm going to teach you to think big!'"

Thinking big is a hallmark of VF Corporation, the clothing giant that not only dominates the world of blue jeans, but has brought fundamental changes to the apparel industry itself. VF's outlet chain now embodies a large network of modern stores that sell not only VF products but designer lines like Perry Ellis, Jones New York and Etienne Aigner.

Just as VF's outlet stores changed the way America shops, its Market Response System has changed the way retailers stock their shelves. At the dawn of the computer age, VF analysts, determined to discover what customers were buying, when and why, set about collecting this information and using it to predict market trends. What began as a simple punch card system has evolved into a sophisticated point-of-sale control that automatically transfers information on each garment sold back to VF factories. Customers get the merchandise they want and merchants know they will be able to stock the most popular styles, finishes, colors and sizes.

The Legend of VF Corporation is a story of just such innovation and leadership. Within 100 years, VF Corporation evolved from a small Pennsylvania producer of gloves and mittens into a multinational manufacturing giant with sales of more than $5 billion.

One-third of all the jeans worn in America today, including the best-selling Lee and Wrangler

brands, are produced by VF Corporation. But millions of people around the world wear or use VF products every day, whether they know the name or not. The toddler buttoned within a Healthtex romper, the street athlete wearing Pipes shorts, the housewife in Spain slipping into a Belcor robe, the airline ground crew stacking luggage in their Red Kap uniforms, the student shouldering a JanSport backpack, and the bride-to-be shopping for Vanity Fair lingerie — all are acquainted with VF Corporation.

The company began as entrepreneur John Barbey's ambitious dream. At the dawn of the 20th century, Barbey, son of German immigrants who owned a thriving beer company, founded Schulykill Silk Mills in Reading, Pennsylvania, near Barbey Brewery. The business flourished along with the fast-growing Pennsylvania town.

In 1919, the name Schulykill Silk Mills was dropped in favor of Vanity Fair Mills, and the business grew steadily across the nation. But like most American businesses, Vanity Fair felt the bite of the Great Depression. The company weathered the storm, however, and was able to add a new stocking factory. This was due in no small part to the efforts of J.E. Barbey, son of John Barbey. At the helm of Vanity Fair now, he worked tirelessly against grim economic times to keep the company afloat.

As the nation's economy recovered, Vanity Fair showed its leadership within the industry, introducing nylon, a new product that would forever alter the apparel industry. Acclaimed Vanity Fair designer Nancy Melcher introduced colors that had never been realized in nylon before, but it was J.E. Barbey who saw the true significance of this new fabric. "He knew that nylon could bring in color," noted Peter Velardi, who would rise to Vanity Fair Mills division president. "So all of a sudden we changed from a commodity business to a fashion accessory business, commanding higher margins and higher profits."

During World War II, nylon fell into short supply, along with silk and elastic. Vanity Fair converted its factories to wartime production, turning out parachutes, mosquito netting, camouflage tents and other products to help ensure the Allied victory. It was during World War II that Whitey Lee would join Vanity Fair as a night foreman. The man who would eventually lead the company with vigor and vision had wanted to be an aviation mechanic, but the Depression derailed his plans. Fortunately, he found his niche in the growing apparel company, where he would remain for the rest of his life.

One of Lee's innovations was the 1953 introduction of the zebra print, still popular today. Vanity Fair's colorful, casual clothes enjoyed overnight success with war-weary Americans as the nation returned to prosperity after World War II.

Vanity Fair continued to grow through the tumultuous 1960s, introducing new fabrics and forming an International Division to explore foreign markets. In 1966, Vanity Fair Mills was listed on the New York Stock Exchange, a pivotal moment for the company. Ever on the forefront of leadership, Whitey Lee purchased the first 100 shares, which sold for $37 each. The sixties was a decade marked by change: in April 1969, Vanity Fair Mills would become VF Corporation, and four months later it would acquire the legendary H.D. Lee Company, a leading jeansmaker. When the blue jean revolution exploded in the 1970s, VF would be well-positioned to claim a strong market share.

Fueled by the extraordinary success of Lee jeans, VF moved confidently into the 1980s. "Whitey" Lee launched a sweeping capital improvements program and declared war on waste, investing in an array of computerized cutting machines that would saves millions of yards of denim each year. He soon encountered a new enemy, however. Lee was diagnosed with cancer early in the decade and lost his battle to the disease on March 5, 1982. The man who, even at the height of his career would visit the factories, roll up his sleeves and help out on the floor, was no longer at the helm after 40 years with VF Corporation.

His successor, Lawrence Pugh, assumed leadership at a pivotal time for VF: in 1983, sales exceeded $1 billion for the first time in the company's history. Pugh called it the "Billion Dollar Beginning."

True to his prediction, the acquisition of the Blue Bell Companies loomed in the immediate future. The $762 million purchase, the most sig-

nificant single event in the company's history, would double the size of the company and establish it as a global presence. With the stroke of a pen, VF Corporation was in the swimwear (Jantzen), backpack, (JanSport), and uniform (Red Kap) businesses. Its jeans line expanded to include both Rustler and the fabled Wrangler brand, which enjoyed a long and romantic association with the American West. Pugh had taken the company from $1 billion to $2.57 billion in market value sales in the process.

It was from within the Wrangler ranks that VF's next leader would emerge. Mackey McDonald, who has served as president of Lee and executive vice president of Wrangler, became president of VF Corporation in 1993. Pugh, who would gradually hand over the reins to McDonald during the 1990s, engineered growth on several fronts for VF. The corporation would again lead the industry, building plants in Mexico, acquiring European lingerie lines and forging a working partnership in China.

McDonald, whom Pugh describes as "one of the most respected leaders in the apparel industry today," outlined a handful of goals as he took the helm of VF Corporation. He created a new organizational structure that consolidated the corporation's 17 divisions, allowing them to share services and supply chains. But chief among his goals is consumerization.

"It's reorienting everything we do — manufacturing, product development, systems — toward fulfilling the needs of specific consumers." Instead of following one or two trends that steer the market, today's consumer wants to express individuality, he said. Consumerization will ensure that VF responds.

At the end of the 1990s, "We've got brands that are known worldwide," Mackey McDonald says. "We've got demand for the products we offer, and we're much more focused. Consumer research, product development and marketing will continue to increase our market share."

VF Corporation, with a market value of $4.3 billion, continues to enjoy steady growth. Having set new, industry-wide standards in responsiveness, with its diverse brands positioned across all distribution channels, and with a new blueprint for leadership in its consumerization initiative, VF can look confidently forward to the 21st century.

ACKNOWLEDGMENTS

RESEARCHING and writing *The Legend of VF Corporation* would not have been possible without the help of many individuals.

The archival research, gathering of relevant artwork and development of historical timelines was accomplished in large part by my resourceful and industrious research assistant, Susan Shelly. Her careful and diligent work made it possible to publish much new and fascinating information about the origins and evolution of one of the world's foremost apparel companies.

The candid insights of VF executives, both current and retired, were of particular importance to this project. I am especially grateful to Chairman Lawrence Pugh and President and CEO Mackey McDonald, who graciously shared their time and unique perspectives with me.

It would have been impossible to produce this book without the help of Cindy Knoebel, director of Investor Relations, and Marilyn Bean, administrative assistant to the Chairman. Their patience in answering questions, helping to locate artwork and supplementing our research proved invaluable.

I am immensely grateful to Edwin Barbey, who shared memories of his father, J.E., and of the corporation's early days with me; to "Mister Wrangler" Bill Hervey, who added to the already dramatic Wrangler story; and to Arthur McArthur, official historian at Jantzen, and JanSport founder Skip Yowell, both of whom contributed artwork and helpful advice. Tim Zeigler generously shared his high-tech expertise in the section on the "cutting edge" machines VF uses. Grace Fidler, Gladys Knight and Andy Kress, loyal former VF employees, contributed their memories and their insights, which enriched the book immeasurably.

Hearty thanks are also due the VF corporate officers and employees who graciously agreed to be interviewed, in person or over the telephone, sometimes at short notice. They include Brad Bean, director of Operations for VF Factory Outlet; Marilyn Bean; Prakash Bhatt, president of VF Outlet; Mark Clift, president of DJ Industries, a VF division; Bob Coppage, president of VF Europe Jeanswear; Bob Cordaro, president for VF Asia/Pacific; Paul Delorey, president of JanSport; George Derhofer, president of VF Knitwear; Roger Eichlin, VF former assistant vice president for Risk and Real Estate Management; Louis Fecile, VF vice president for Employee Benefits; William Foulke, former VF Corporation director; Richard Francis, VF corporate accountant; Steve Fritz, president of Jantzen; John Jackson, former vice president of operations for VF Outlet; John Johnson, former president of VF International Group; Michel Jonchere, president of VF Diffusion; Cindy Knoebel;

Timothy Lambeth, vice president & president of European & Asian Operations; Richard Lamm, former executive vice president of The Lee Company; Donald Laws, president of Wrangler Westernwear; Terry Lay, president of Lee Apparel; Angelo Legrega, president of Mass Market Brands for Wrangler; Steve Lehmann, vice president for Administration, VF Factory Outlet; Steve Ludeman, executive vice president of Jantzen; Mike Martin, VF manager of Corporate Real Estate; Robert Matthews, president of Red Kap; Dan MacFarlan, VF vice president and chairman of Knitwear, Playwear & Intimate Apparel coalition; Harold McKemy, VF former vice president for Treasury and Financial Services; Sandy McMullen, VF administrative assistant; Scotta Miller, former secretary to M.O. Lee; Tom Payne, president of VF Services; Janet Peters, VF senior vice president for Intimate Apparel Product Design; Bill Pike, member of the VF Board of Directors; Pere Prat, VF International Intimates Coalition chairman; Vanessa Price, manager, VF Pension & Benefits Administration; David Reklau, VF financial controller; John Schamberger, vice president and chairman for North and South America Jeanswear coalition; Gary Simmons, president of VF Playwear; Lori Tarnoski, former vice president and corporate secretary; Frank Urban, vice president of VF International; Peter Velardi, former chairman and CEO of Vanity Fair Mills, and Larry Weidenheimer, former vice president of VF International. For handling corporate travel arrangements graciously and with utmost competence, we thank VF's Barbara King and Joan Hemming.

My staff and I are very grateful to Barbara Gill and her fellow members of the Historical Society of Berks County, Pennsylvania; to Vallie Reich and the reference staff of the Reading Public Library in Reading, Pennsylvania, and to Charles Gallagher, managing editor of the *Reading Eagle/Reading Times.*

Finally, a very special word of thanks to the staff at Write Stuff Enterprises, Inc., including proofreader Bonnie Freeman and transcriptionists Mary Aaron and Christine Aniello, who worked quickly and efficiently to make sure this book met our high standards. Particular thanks go to Executive Editor Karen Nitkin; Associate Editors Alex Lieber, Catherine Lackner and Jon VanZile; Art Directors Sandy Cruz, Jill Apolinario and Kyle Newton; Production Manager Fred Moll; Jill Thomas, assistant to the author; Marketing and Sales Manager Christopher J. Frosch; Bonnie Bratton, Director of Marketing Research; Bookkeeper and Office Manager Marianne Roberts, Logistics Specialist Rafael Santiago and Project Coordinator Karine N. Rodengen.

Women, like these workers who matched seams, left their homes in record numbers to work in factories during World War I.

CHAPTER ONE

FOUNDATIONS

1748–1920

"All the textile mills at Reading are having an activity that is unusual. As a center of hosiery manufacturing this prosperous Penn'a city is enjoying a briskness that extends to all branches of the trade."

— *Reading Eagle*, 1911[1]

THE TOWN OF Reading, nestled in the Schuylkill Valley of southeastern Pennsylvania, was established in 1748 and quickly developed into a thriving agricultural and industrial community and a center of textile production in the United States. When Reading's first census was taken in 1751, the town had already grown to 378 inhabitants.[2] A courthouse was established in 1762, followed eight years later by a city jail, and the town's first bank opened in 1808.[3]

By the end of the 19th century, the requisite ingredients for a growing textile industry would come together in this bustling Pennsylvania town. Rich natural resources, a successful history as a railroad terminal and river port, a skilled workforce and the entrepreneurial spirit of its people would fuse to make Reading the founding home to one of America's best-known clothing manufacturers.

Hatmaking was among the earliest industries in the small but bustling community. Shortly after the town was founded, hatmakers produced about 40,000 hats a year, mostly from wool and felt. Perhaps the most popular local product was a fashionable black silk hat known as the Reading Tall Hat.[4]

Reading, which changed its status to a borough in 1783, also became an important market commu-

nity. The rich soil and favorable climate were ideal farming conditions, and thousands of surrounding acres were cleared by hand to raise such crops as rye, wheat, corn, oats and buckwheat for food, and flax for homespun clothing.

Ironmaking was another burgeoning industry. After rich deposits of iron ore were discovered, early ironmakers built forges along some of the creeks near Reading. During the Revolutionary War, these forges manufactured cannonballs, gun barrels and shot for the soldiers serving in the Continental Army. The iron industry helped turn Reading into a thriving industrial center. The Reading Iron and Nail Works, later known as the Reading Iron Company, was founded in the mid-1800s, and by the end of the century, it employed about 4,000 workers.[5]

The foundries, located along the Schuylkill River between Reading and Philadelphia, needed coal for their furnaces. Although coal was plenti-

---

Reading, Pennsylvania, a flourishing rail and river port, became a textile manufacturing center in the late 1700s. Vanity Fair, cornerstone of VF Corporation, got its start in Reading. (Photo courtesy the Historical Society of Berks County, Pennsylvania.)

The Schuylkill Valley was blessed with rich veins of iron, which kept its forges and foundries, such as Hopewell furnace, running at full capacity. (Photos courtesy of the Historical Society of Berks County, Pennsylvania.)

1748: First settlers come to Reading, Pennsylvania, where Vanity Fair will eventually be founded.

1898: Reading celebrates its 150th anniversary. The textile industry had become a force to be reckoned with.

1847: Reading incorporates as a city.

1899: John Barbey and seven partners form the Reading Glove and Mitten Manufacturing Company.

ful in nearby Schuylkill County, transporting it was a challenge. In 1824, the Schuylkill Navigation Company opened a 108-mile canal system to transport coal from Schuylkill County to the iron works along the Schuylkill River and as far away as Philadelphia.[6] A round trip journey could take several weeks, but it was still safer and more economical than using the wagon roads, which were narrow, muddy, rocky and plagued by bandits.[7]

The newly dug Schuylkill Canal, which ran the entire length of the river, brought many changes to the region. Out-of-the-way hamlets suddenly became important river ports. People used the boats to visit friends and relatives or to reach desirable picnic grounds. Reading, the home of the Schuylkill Navigation Company, became the busy center of the canal system, and by 1830 its population had grown to 5,631.[8]

The young coal industry needed a convenient shipping route, so the Schuylkill Navigation Company carved out a 108-mile canal system that allowed coal to be shipped to distant ports.

1906: The new company suffers a downturn when the price of silk climbs.

1913: John Barbey founds the Schuylkill Silk Mills.

1911: The Reading Glove and Mitten Manufacturing Company is disbanded. John Barbey buys its equipment and, with several partners, continues manufacturing.

1919: The company is renamed Vanity Fair Silk Mills.

The reign of the canal system was short-lived. In 1839, the Philadelphia & Reading Railroad, later known as the Reading Railroad, opened.[9] A great rivalry ensued between the railroad and the Schuylkill Navigation Company because both sought the revenues for hauling coal to the foundries downriver. Eventually, the railroad took control of the canal system and forced the Schuylkill Navigation Company out of business.

The railroad shaped the expansion and development of Reading for many years. Because railroad jobs required skilled labor, workers entered apprentice programs, where they were trained to become machinists and pipefitters. Later, these workers would provide skilled labor to many industries throughout the region.

Reading continued to grow and thrive, officially becoming a city in 1847. By 1900, an impressive brick structure a short distance from the center of town housed the railroad's main passenger station. Trains that either originated or connected in Reading traveled to such destinations as Philadelphia, New York, the New Jersey shore, Washington, D.C., Baltimore and Boston. By that time, however, both the iron and railroad industries were losing their dominance in the region. The once-venerated Philadelphia & Reading Railroad had been forced to declare bankruptcy twice in the 1880s. When officials declared bankruptcy again in 1893, a nationwide financial panic resulted.[10]

Throughout the nation, steel was replacing iron as the preferred metal for bridges, railroad rails and large buildings. The Reading Iron

Railroads were a dominant force in the region, and the canal system was abandoned when manufacturers found it more convenient to ship necessary goods by rail. (Photos courtesy of the Historical Society of Berks County, Pennsylvania.)

E 6870 P. & R. YARDS, OUTER STATION, READING, PA.

The citizens of Reading threw a gala week-long celebration when the city marked its 150th anniversary in 1898. The textile industry was firmly entrenched, creating jobs and prosperity in the thriving town.

Company struggled for survival. Forced to cut back or discontinue manufacturing iron for bridges and railroads, the company concentrated on preferred iron products such as underground pipes and tubing. Meanwhile, men of vision began to look toward textile manufacturing as the industry that would propel Reading and all of Berks County into the 20th century.

Dozens of textile shops and factories, large and small, were established in and around Reading.[11] When the iron and railroad industries faltered, former railroad workers with strong mechanical skills quickly learned how to build and operate sewing machines.[12]

In 1898, Reading celebrated its 150th anniversary with a week-long festival of parades, fireworks, bicycle races and boat regattas. By that time, 80,000 people lived in Reading, making it the third-largest city in Pennsylvania.[13] In speech after speech, local politicians lauded the expanding textile industry within the city and throughout Berks County. The people of Reading were optimistic about the future. New textile factories were being constructed and machine shops were springing up to provide the necessary manufacturing equipment.

Most of the mills produced hosiery in the form of seamless cotton stockings, as well as other articles of clothing. During the 1890s, consumers became more interested in fashion and more dependent on ready-made clothing. It was a time of growth for the garment industry, as elaborate store-bought ensembles and accessories became status symbols for women. High heels became stylish, and women began wearing make-up with more frequency. Hatmaking remained popular and in 1899, 25 hatmakers were listed in the Reading City Directory.[14]

The Reading Glove and Mitten Manufacturing Company

On October 31, 1899, eight local entrepreneurs met to discuss their plans for creating a textile manufacturing concern. By the end of the meeting, they agreed to form a corporation "for the manufacture of Silk and Cotton Gloves and Mittens."[15] They contributed $11,000 toward the venture.

The founders and amounts contributed were, John M. Archer, secretary/treasurer of the Wilkinson Shear Company, $2,000; John Barbey, a brewer and bank officer, $2,000; A.J. Brumbach, a manufacturer of woolen goods, bank officer and officer of the Reading Cold Storage Company, $1,000; and Ferdinand Goetz and Ferdinand Winter, who together ran a leather manufacturing company, each $2,000. Additional founders and contributors were John H. Maltzberger, a cashier at Keystone Bank, of which Barbey was president, $1,000; Christian H. Ruhl, a lawyer, $500; and Emil O. Spindler, superintendent of the Pennsylvania Knitting Mills, $500.[16]

Goetz, Winter, Barbey, Archer, Ruhl and Maltzberger were elected directors.[17] The new board called their fledgling company the Reading Glove and Mitten Manufacturing Company.[18] Goetz was elected president and Maltzberger as secretary/treasurer.

Spindler had experience as superintendent of the Pennsylvania Knitting Mills and was a natural choice to become the company's first superintendent, at a salary of $1,300 a year.

Getting Started

The company's first factory leased for $60 a month in 1900 and was only 320 square feet. The two-year lease agreement included an option to buy the building at 940-948 Spruce Street for $11,000 when the lease expired.[19] The company joined a large number of other textile concerns already in business within the city. In the first year of the new century, Reading was home to 17 hosiery mills, 28 hat manufacturers and various other textile businesses that produced everything from handkerchiefs to pants.[20]

Meanwhile, Emil Spindler returned from a buying trip in Germany with three men he had hired to set up and operate the machinery he had purchased.[21] One of the men, E. Richard Meinig, would later become a successful glove and hosiery manufacturer in Reading, with several large factories of his own.[22]

Although the company's original paperwork called for the production of knit gloves, mittens and underwear, only cotton gloves and mittens (which sold for $1.90 per dozen)[23] were produced in the first few years of operation.[24] The board considered adding hosiery to its line, but a committee recommended shelving this bold idea.[25]

On the Ropes

The directors were also cautious about expansion. The nation was emerging from a severe depression in 1896, the worst on record.[26] At the same time, workers and management throughout the country were locked in disputes as large, impersonal corporations took the place of smaller businesses. Even so, innovations continued. In October 1902, silk gloves were added to the product line, and Meinig, who became superintendent after Spindler resigned, had to buy new sewing machines and alter several existing ones to accommodate the new material. The silk operation started out small, but customer demand caused it to escalate rapidly.[27]

In October 1904, Ferdinand Goetz, who had been president of the company since it was founded, died unexpectedly during a trip to New York City. A.J. Brumbach became the next president of the Reading Glove and Mitten Manufacturing Company.[28] In December, Meinig resigned as superintendent to start his own company, and August Granz took over his job, for a salary of $1,200 a year.[29] These critical management changes foreshadowed difficult years for the company.

The company's downturn was linked in part to the unstable price of silk, purchased in 1,000-

pound lots. For example, the price per pound in September 1905 was $4.78, in November it was $3.95, and in February 1906 it was $4.60. By the end of 1906, the cost of a 1,000-pound lot had climbed to $5.20 per pound.[30]

Meanwhile, demand for gloves and hosiery began to decline. A special meeting of stockholders was held June 10, 1910, to discuss the serious problems of disappointing sales and fluctuating silk prices. Directors had already declared a moratorium on silk purchases, and they elected to continue operations until September, then evaluate the situation.[31]

When business did not improve by September, the stockholders voted to shut down the business and sell its equipment at a public sale.[32] One of the directors, however, thought the company was worth saving. John Barbey purchased the equipment from his partners for $5,600 and agreed to take over the lease for the building.[33]

The original company was disbanded March 3, 1911. A new company was formed, with John Barbey as president. His son, John Edward Barbey, known as J.E., was elected vice president. He began working at the company after he graduated from Yale with a degree in philosophy.[34] Howard L. Hoff, a clerk at Britton's Department Store, was named secretary/treasurer, and Max Winkler, a foreman at another Reading mill, was hired as superintendent.[35]

John Barbey

John Barbey was a successful and respected businessman. His Barbey Brewery, founded in 1860 by his father, Peter, was one of the largest beer companies within the blue collar city. John joined the family beer business in 1880 and had taken over as president following his father's death in 1897.[36] The father of six daughters and one son, John Barbey was also the longtime president of Keystone Bank and

Barbey, at center in lighter coat, bought his partners out and founded the Schuylkill Silk Mills in 1913. He had honed his business skills at his family's beer company, one of the most prominent in the area.

In the early 1900s, women traded in their corsets and bustles for slimmer, softer undergarments. Barbey responded by adding "undersilks" to the product line.

served on the boards of various other businesses and industries.[37]

Barbey bought out his partners at an opportune time, because the decline in sales of the last few years soon reversed. Just five days after the transaction, an article reprinted from *Textile American*, a Boston-based trade publication, appeared in the *Reading Eagle*, identifying Reading as an important textile town.

"All the textile mills at Reading are having an activity that is unusual. As a center of hosiery manufacturing this prosperous Penn'a city is enjoying a briskness that extends to all branches of the trade. Not only are the old establishments adding to their capacity, but several new plants are to be established during the spring or summer. Silk mills are running full tilt."[38]

The first full year of operation, in 1912, was a good one, with sales of $119,628 reflecting a $20,923 increase.[39] The following year, the Barbeys changed both the name and location of the growing glove and mitten company, calling it the Schuylkill Silk Mills and moving it to Gordon Street in Reading, near the Schuylkill River.[40] The new location was close to the Barbey Brewery, making it easy for John Barbey to keep his eye on both businesses. This proximity also gave mill workers a fringe benefit — free beer in a designated area of the brewery during lunch breaks.

To increase business, the Barbeys forged an agreement with the Topken Company of New York

City, paying 3 percent of the gross for every pair of silk gloves sold by Topken.[41] The market for silk gloves flourished because they were popular with both men and women. Even suffragists, considered radical by some because they believed women should be allowed to vote, wore gloves up to their elbows when they wore short-sleeved gowns.[42] After the excesses of the late 1800s, fashions had relaxed somewhat but had not yet reached the elegant simplicity of the coming flapper look of the 1920s.

The Underwear Business

As called for in the original company's 1899 charter, underwear was added to the product line in 1914.[43] In response to ongoing transformations in fashion, underwear styles were changing rapidly. Slimmer, more casual clothes meant the demise of huge rustling petticoats. Comfortable brassieres replaced restrictive garments reinforced with bones (which shaped the upper body). Corsets, which cinched women's waists to unnatural proportions, also fell out of favor.[44] Coming into vogue were knickers, combination knickers and camisoles, and chemises, all in soft, feminine styles.[45]

Determined to build a strong identity for the company's products, J.E. Barbey launched aggressive marketing campaigns. In 1917, he sponsored a contest to choose a brand name, and Vanity Fair was chosen. The winner, whose name is lost to history, was paid $25 for his or her suggestion.[46] Once the name was selected, J.E. promoted both the name and the products with an extensive advertising campaign. With an advertising budget of $15,000, he hired the Philadelphia advertising firm of N.W. Ayer and Son.[47]

J.E.'s strategy was to demonstrate that underwear could be pretty as well as practical. Prestigious publications such as *Theatre Magazine* and *Garment Weekly* carried full-page advertisements featuring the Vanity Fair Sextette, a group of young, attractive women who modeled various styles of underwear, much of which reached only to above the knee. Other advertisements featured the Dolly Sisters, who modestly lifted their dresses above their knees so the ankle-

length Vanity Fair Pettibocker (a combination knicker and petticoat ensemble) could be glimpsed underneath.

Starting in 1917, the Barbeys sold directly to select retailers, bypassing the "jobbers," the middlemen who traditionally distributed the goods while diverting a considerable portion of the profits.[48] Partly because of these reforms, the company enjoyed total sales of $768,258 in 1917, a net gain of $124,263.[49]

It was J.E. Barbey's philosophy that a garment must look as good on the inside as it did on the outside. Frequent inspections assured this.

Inset: During World War I, Vanity Fair Mills workers produced electrically heated gloves, among other things, for troops overseas.

Below: When young men were called away to war, women, like these Vanity Fair employees, became a major part of the work force for the first time.

World War I

Meanwhile, America joined World War I on April 6, 1917, despite President Woodrow Wilson's vehement efforts to keep the United States from becoming involved in the European conflict. During the war, the company produced electrically heated gloves for Army aviators, who flew in chilly, open cockpits.[50] J.E. Barbey's vital role in the business was put on hold while he served as a captain in the United States Air Force during part of 1917 and 1918.[51]

The war spurred a profound change in women's fashions. For the first time in history, large numbers of American women filled the floors of the nation's factories, taking the places of young men who were fighting overseas. The long Victorian-style skirts worn by these women interfered with the serious business of wartime production. The skirts could catch in rotating machinery and belts, at best slowing production and at worst leading to serious injury. Women began to don "bloomers," pants-like garments originally designed to be worn under clothes. They also sported pants and overalls, when available. Vanity Fair's Pettibocker, while described as "dainty and dressy," also was touted as a "sensible utility garment," especially appropriate for women who were working during the war.

After the war, J.E. Barbey returned to a rapidly expanding company. Striving for greater continuity and name recognition, the Barbeys changed the company's name to Vanity Fair Silk Mills on February 24, 1919.

Soon after, in May 1919, the directors made plans to enlarge the factory. The production of underwear, or "lingerie," as J.E. preferred to call it, was becoming more important to the company than the glove and mitten trade. At the decade's end, the manufacture of gloves had decreased dramatically, and the Barbeys recognized that the company's future lay in the manufacture and marketing of quality underwear.[52]

When World War I ended, Vanity Fair returned to its profitable underwear business. By 1920, the company no longer made gloves, but concentrated on underwear.

CHAPTER TWO

EXPANSION AND DIVERSIFICATION
1920–1939

"Fashion, which for hundreds of years had lived by exaggerating in turn the main physical feminine characteristics, now set about eliminating these features. The ideal figure was a straight line."

— *Underwear, A History.*[1]

HE TWENTIES AND thirties were critical years for Vanity Fair, setting the stage for several trends that would define the company for decades to come. Women's fashions changed radically, from the boyish styles of the Jazz Age to the movie-inspired looks of the thirties. Always innovative, the company experimented with new fabrics, incorporating Silkenese and a revolutionary new product called elastic into its products. The company also opened its first facility in the South, another move with far-reaching consequences.

By 1920, Vanity Fair Silk Mills had abandoned the glove business altogether and was only manufacturing underwear made of glove silk. Business was so good that John Barbey and his son, J.E., expanded the Gordon Street factory to more than 50,000 square feet, doubling its size and making it the largest producer of glove silk underwear in the world.[2]

The expanded building was six floors high, with approximately 8,500 square feet on each floor. The factory made its own cloth and sold any surplus to other manufacturers. Underwear was produced in the same facility. Employees worked in areas such as the winding room, weaving room, warping room and cutting room.

The company was proud of its facility, describing it in promotional material as a "bright, cheerful, modern equipped plant." Management tried hard to make the factory attractive to female employees, who comprised the majority of Vanity Fair workers. A special "club room" was established on the fifth floor for the all-female Vanity Fair Club. The factory also had a cafeteria where "good wholesome food is served at cost," and a cooperative store that sold household staples at low prices. Other amenities included a library and a medical department, which contained a room in which female workers could retire for a rest.[3]

Vanity Fair actively recruited female employees.

Advertisements in the *Reading Eagle* promised "congenial work" for women at Vanity Fair Silk Mills. The ads, which appeared in January 1920, promised that jobs in the mills would not be overly tiring, and that employees would find it interesting to sew "dainty Vanity Fair silk garments." Steady employment, pleasant companionship and good wages were among the enticements offered.

As early as 1920, the directors extended the company's presence beyond the United States, registering the Vanity Fair and Pettibocker trademarks in Canada, Spain, France, Australia,

Above: Vanity Fair's Exotique underwear line was made of glove silk and advertised as being "cool as a summer breeze."

Bright, Cheerful, Modern equipped plant, having the largest production of glove silk underwear under one roof, in the world.

Advertisements promised women "congenial work" at Vanity Fair Silk Mills. At 50,000 square feet, it was the largest plant of its kind in the world.

1920: Vanity Fair Silk Mills abandons the glove business for underwear manufacturing.

1929: Vanity Fair builds a plant in New Holland, Pennsylvania, to produce women's stockings.

1925: J.E. Barbey marries Catharine E. Quier.

October 29, 1929: The stock market crashes, heralding the Great Depression.

South Africa, Norway, Denmark, Sweden, Greece, Brazil and Turkey.[4]

A New Level of Freedom

After decades of parades, speeches and protests, a constitutional amendment in 1920 finally granted women the right to vote. Perhaps inspired by this new power, American women began to rebel against the restrictive fashions of the past. Corsets, which emphasized the bust and hips by constricting the waist to inhuman proportions, were fast becoming historical artifacts. Barely able to breathe, women in corsets were prone to fainting and dizzy spells that may have seemed romantic in the movies but were inconvenient and dangerous in reality.

Gone were the long, full skirts that restricted movement and collected mud and debris as they brushed along the ground, posing a considerable safety hazard. Shorter skirts were the order of the day. Cumbersome bustles, which were worn under a woman's skirt to give the illusion of fuller hips and derrieres, were no longer considered necessary.

Hourglass figures were out and slim, flat-chested figures were in. This boyish "flapper" look

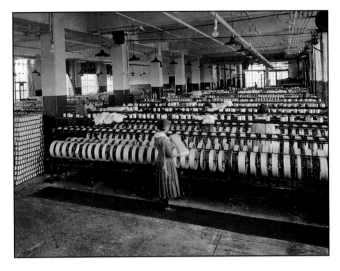

The company worked hard to keep its facilities bright and airy for its mostly female work force. Vanity Fair also provided a recreation room and company cafeteria for its employees.

was emphasized by a popular short hair cut known as the bob. "Fashion, which for hundreds of years had lived by exaggerating in turn the main physical feminine characteristics, now set about eliminating these features. The ideal figure

1931: J.E. Barbey becomes general manager in addition to vice president.

1939: Company builds its second plant, Clarke Mills, in Jackson, Alabama.

June 1937: Vanity Fair opens Monroeville, Alabama mill.

December 24, 1939: John Barbey dies. He is eulogized as a business and civic leader.

In the 1920s, Vanity Fair began to incorporate rayon and acetate, new yarns, into the fabric that was woven on huge looms.

was a straight line," noted Elizabeth Ewing's 1972 book, *Underwear, A History.*[5]

This new look called for modern undergarments, and Vanity Fair eagerly filled the need with soft, unrestrictive bloomers, bodice vests, bandeaux and chemises.

Vanity Fair actively began to search for new fabrics with which to manufacture its underwear. Rayon and acetate yarns were being perfected, and the company incorporated these new materials into its products, either alone or in combination with silk.[6] The availability of manmade materials was good news for Vanity Fair, which had depended largely on silk imported from Japan. While highly desirable, silk was expensive, and fluctuating prices made it difficult to price items and forecast margins.[7]

In 1923, Vanity Fair opened an office in New York City, at 295 Fifth Avenue, manned by one

employee, E. Joseph Belknap. The office was necessary because of an unusual law that barred the company from doing any business in New York unless an office was established someplace within the state.[8] Offices in San Francisco and Boston followed, and the company bragged about its ability to keep its retailers throughout the nation stocked with all the latest styles.

J.E. Barbey diverted his attention from the business long enough in June 1925 to marry Catharine E. Quier, a member of the locally prominent family that owned both the *Reading Eagle* and the *Reading Times.* Barbey's previous marriage, which had produced a daughter and twin sons, had failed. His second wedding, a small affair with only family and close friends in attendance, took place in the bride's home, during a record heat wave that was the topic of a front page story in the *Reading Eagle.*[9] Policemen were ordered to remove their coats, factories closed down early, and, in nearby Lexington, a 48-year-old cigarmaker shot himself while lying in his bed, supposedly because the heat had rendered him temporarily insane.[10]

Silkenese

By 1927, the company had salesmen in Reading, New York, Philadelphia, Boston, Atlanta, New Orleans, Minneapolis, Kansas City, Chicago, Dallas and Los Angeles. Starting in 1919, this scattered sales force was summoned to Reading every July for a convention. Meetings were held at the Vanity Fair plant, but the main event was a fancy dinner at the Berkshire Country Club, just outside of Reading.

The convention in 1927 was more festive than usual as officials celebrated the introduction of a new line of underwear made of Silkenese, a sheer fabric produced by combining silk and rayon. Tables were decorated in blue and yellow, the promotional colors for the new fabric, and the centerpiece of each was a miniature French mannequin dressed in Silkenese underwear. A special song promoting Silkenese was performed during the meal.

The *Reading Eagle* published a long article praising the new underwear. "Some garments are trimmed with real lace, others with touches of hand embroidery and all of them show the exquisite taste of the French designer who created them."[11]

Silkenese proved popular for many years to come. In a 1953 issue of *Top Drawer by Vanity Fair*, an in-house publication, L. William Dilts, vice president of Sales, explained how he convinced a reluctant Alabama store owner to stock Silkenese underwear:

"I was bound to sell that man Phillips on Silkenese — or else. ... Before he could go into action (and throw me out of the store), I whipped

Vanity Fair factory and office workers dressed up in their finest for this group photo, taken in the early 1920s. Every department, from the sewing room to the purchasing office, was represented.

out a pair of Silkenese bloomers I had hidden under my coat, and thrust them into his hand. I knew if I could just get him to feel this fabric he'd be sold. Automatically he took the bloomers. The 'feel' of Silkenese captured his attention where I had failed. He called in his buyer. They bought bloomers, vests and chemises in a range of sizes. That was the beginning of our Vanity Fair account with Burger Phillips."[12]

Showing Some Leg

Back when skirts reached the floor, hosiery had not been much of an issue. However, shorter hemlines created demand among women for full-fashioned stockings, which were made of silk or rayon and followed the shape of the leg, giving a smooth, close fit. These fashionable stockings had a seam running up the back of the leg. The forerunner of full-fashioned hose was a seamless cotton stocking that tended to bag around the ankles.

By the end of the 1920s, Reading had become a great hosiery manufacturing center. Half of the nation's hosiery knitting machines were manufactured within the borders of the Pennsylvania city.[13] The largest Reading hosiery manufacturer — in fact, the world's largest full-fashioned hosiery plant — was Berkshire Knitting Mills. By the end of the 1920s, the Berkie, as it was known locally, employed 6,000 people. Nolde & Horst, the next largest plant, employed 3,000.[14]

Though not the largest, Vanity Fair enjoyed a reputation as a leading manufacturer of high quality, fashionable undergarments, but company officials were eager to explore additional opportunities. They wanted a share of the hosiery boom, and in the summer of 1929 they built a factory about 30 miles from Reading in New Holland, Lancaster County, to produce full-fashioned women's stockings.[15] The factory was built on a

Silk, the raw material from which hosiery was made, was expensive and sometimes scarce, so Vanity Fair began to search for alternatives early in the 1920s.

four-acre plot purchased for $1 from David H. Styer. The Vanity Fair Stocking Company would last until 1950, when the area's full-fashioned hosiery industry began a downward slide toward obscurity.

Once spun, fibers were "creeled" onto huge bobbins by mill employees who worked late into the night.

The Great Depression

The decade which had been so prosperous for Vanity Fair and Reading industry in general was destined to end in economic disaster shortly after the Vanity Fair Stocking Company was formed.

On October 29, 1929, the bottom fell out of the stock market. Thousands of Americans lost everything they owned, and the value of most businesses dropped sharply. It was not long before the entire nation felt the effects of financial collapse. Unemployment shot up to a staggering 4 million. By 1932, 16 million people, one out of every four Americans, were out of work. Farmers let their produce rot in the fields because prices dropped so low that it was no longer worthwhile to bring it to market. Without income, desperate people lucky enough to have savings accounts raided them. As panic spread, 1,352 banks closed their doors in 1930. Once the banks started closing, more people pulled their money out, accelerating the crisis. In 1932, 3,646 banks went out of business.

The hosiery industry, the Reading area's top employer, was affected almost immediately. In

high demand during the carefree days of the prosperous Jazz Age, stockings were quickly deemed luxuries by women who were forced to become more cost-conscious than fashion-conscious. Sales of the less-expensive seamless cotton hose also dropped sharply during the early months of 1930.[16] Nationwide, production of full-fashioned hosiery fell from 20 million dozen pairs in 1929 to 17 million in 1930 and 15 million in 1931.[17]

Vanity Fair survived the crisis in relative comfort. Though profits dropped from $314,437 in 1929 to $112,986 in 1930 and to $6,107 in 1931,[18] the company continued to make money and even managed to expand during the depths of the Depression. Officials announced in August 1931 that an addition would be built onto the stocking company in New Holland, increasing its size by 50 percent. The stocking mill already employed more than 200 workers, and managers expected to hire even more after renovations were completed.[19]

J.E. Barbey, who in 1931 was named general manager of Vanity Fair Silk Mills in addition

Workers, like this employee in a Southern plant, checked fabric at many stages in the production process.

to his position as vice president, believed that aggressive advertising kept Vanity Fair profitable in the midst of widespread economic chaos. Barbey had been a strong advocate of advertising ever since he joined his father in the company in 1912, and had promoted the company in newspapers, radio and magazines. A bulletin posted in the silk mill plant in Reading underscored his philosophy.

"We have been fortunate in being able to keep our people employed in both our Reading underwear mills and our New Holland hosiery mill, even in the face of generally adverse conditions. Our rate of sales, of course, is the controlling factor. An analysis of our operations indicates that an important factor in this situation has been the proper timing of sales and advertising efforts. Our newspaper advertising is a year-round basic principle in our selling." [20]

Newspaper advertising may have been the company's mainstay, but radio was also important. Vanity Fair sponsored a weekly dramatic radio program serial, which aired every Sunday night at 6:45. *The Adventures of Barbara Wayne* starred Lucille Wall and Joe Bell, two popular radio artists of the day. Naturally, ads for Vanity Fair products were heard during commercial breaks.

However, the ads that ran in national magazines — *The New Yorker, Harper's* and *Vogue* — received the most attention. Vanity Fair's first *New Yorker* ad appeared in 1933, a time when underwear ads in magazines were virtually nonexistent. Underwear at this time was still considered utilitarian, but J.E. stressed in his advertising that it could be stylish, especially if made by Vanity Fair. The company's advertising reflected Barbey's concepts of grace and femininity, and the superior quality of Vanity Fair products was emphasized. [21]

Advertising or no, J.E. Barbey was putting in long, difficult hours to keep Vanity Fair afloat. "My father was never home, so I knew he was trying to turn a corner in the business," said his son Edwin Barbey. "Everybody was out on the street panhandling because of the Depression." Though he was only 8 years old, "I knew everybody was struggling," Edwin Barbey said.[22]

The elder Barbey had returned from World War I determined to make his mark in business and was well qualified to do so, his son said. "He was a true physical and mental genius. His associates worked like hell just to keep up. He was very, very, very, very demanding — which went along with his perfectionism — but he could out-think people."[23]

It is difficult to say whether it was J.E. Barbey's personal magnetism, the dollars spent on extensive advertising, or just the beginning of improving economic times that caused a return to profitability. After its worst year in 1932, with a loss of $96,078, the company's financial situation began to improve. In 1933, the company turned a profit of $49,788.[24]

During the Great Depression, many of Reading's smaller stocking factories closed or moved South in an effort to reduce production costs. Although Vanity Fair's stocking company operated in the red for most of the 1930s, its underwear division was profitable enough to sustain operations.

Fantastic Elastic

Even during the bleakest years of the Depression, Vanity Fair introduced new products, including girdles, panty girdles and brassieres that incorporated an innovative fine-gauge rubber-cored yarn.[25] This yarn, known as elastic, was underwear's major breakthrough of the decade, according to *Underwear, A History,* by Elizabeth Ewing.

"Alone and unaided, [elastic] created a new type of foundation which soon bore no resemblance whatever to the kind that had prevailed continuously. ... Fashion in the years since elastic came into general use in corsetry bears as little resemblance to what it was previously as does electric light to candles or the motor car to the horse carriage."[26]

Elasticized forms of rubber had been used for years in footwear and clothing. But uses were limited because of the material's properties. Latex, the milky sap of the rubber tree used to make elastic

Workers pressed and packed finished garments in an open-air facility where the heat of the irons could dissipate.

yarn, coagulated very quickly if not treated. As a result, it was shipped from rubber plantations in coagulated sheets which were reconstituted when they arrived in the United States. The sheets were then cut into strips and knitted together with various materials to give them elasticity. The resulting yarns, however, were very short in length, severely limiting their applications.

In 1930, however, a method was devised that prevented the latex from coagulating. Liquid latex was shipped in large drums aboard tanker ships. When it arrived at the factory, it was processed and then made to flow through small glass apertures into an acetic acid bath. The latex coagulated instantly in the acid, forming continuous lengths of round thread. The thread could be made in varying thicknesses, depending on the size of the aperture and the rate of flow.[27] This innovation revolutionized the underwear industry because the elastic thread could be woven or knitted as desired. The new elastic undergarments handily coincided with the advent of fashions requiring them.

American clothing fashions during the 1930s were largely dictated by movie stars. Movies were extremely popular during the Great Depression as people looked for a means of escape, if only for a few hours. When stars such as Marlene Dietrich and Katharine Hepburn first took to the screen in man-tailored pants and jackets, the audience was shocked and amused. Soon, however, women began sporting striped pullover shirts, the forerunners to today's T-shirts, and knit dresses. At the other end of the spectrum, a return to a more feminine style was evident in the soft, clingy dresses, especially backless evening gowns, that were also popular.[28]

These close-fitting shirts and dresses called for natural-looking foundations. Elastic made it possible for underwear makers to produce lighter, more comfortable garments. Refinements in bra design occurred when manufacturers realized that women with similar bust measurements needed different-sized cups.[29]

Not surprisingly, these changes were extremely well-received by women, as Ewing noted.

"The introduction of the new elasticized materials meant a new concept of corsetry. Figure control no longer depended upon boning, lacing and the imposition of a rigid kind of cage on the figure. Instead, support and control were created by means of the special tensions and 'pull' of the elastic in fabrics selected and used by the designer in such a way that they smoothed and molded the figure by a kind of persuasive action. Health, comfort and appearance all benefitted."[30]

In 1935, shortly after Vanity Fair Silk Mills started producing elasticized underwear, the company added Kneelast stockings to its product line. These stockings featured a decorative, narrow band of fine-gauge elastic yarn, which lengthened the life of the hosiery by providing elasticity near the point of greatest strain — the knee.[31]

The same year, a company called Bamaco, Inc., was formed to manage several of John Barbey's businesses, including the brewery, the silk mills and the stocking company. The men who served as the executive officers of Bamaco were also the executive officers of the other businesses. Bamaco, according to the agreement signed by officers of the participating companies on November 14, 1935, was intended to coordinate the management of the respective businesses so they could operate at peak efficiency and profitability.[32]

Going South

By 1933, the economic woes of Reading-area hosiery manufacturers were made worse

---

Above: Alabama Congressman Frank Boykin helped convince Vanity Fair to move to his state, which reaped tremendous economic benefits in the midst of the Great Depression.

Below: Hoping for jobs and prosperity, towns like Gulfport, Mississippi, courted the company aggressively, but ultimately the first plants opened in western Alabama.

by growing labor problems. President Franklin D. Roosevelt's National Industrial Recovery Act in 1933 set forth regulations regarding a minimum wage, a 40-hour work week and labor issues. It also guaranteed workers the right to unionize.

After the act was approved, sporadic attempts at unionization were made by small groups of Reading-area hosiery workers. At first, the new law was more of an annoyance to management than a serious concern. Although some of the smaller factories had already begun to move to the South, where unions were discouraged, wages were low and labor plentiful, there was no indication that larger companies would follow suit. Many must have considered the possibility, however, when organizers from the American Federation of Hosiery Workers in

Vanity Fair officials traveled throughout the South in 1936, searching for the perfect location for their plant. Daisey, Tennessee, above, and New Braunfels, Texas, at left, were among the towns which vied actively for Vanity Fair's presence.

Philadelphia set the stage for major labor problems in the Reading stocking mills.[33]

The big mills resisted workers' attempts to organize, prompting a walkout that shut down every mill in Berks County for nearly three months in the summer of 1933.[34] Over the next three years, almost every stocking factory in the county, with the exception of Berkshire Knitting, was unionized.[35] There is no account of labor unrest at either Vanity Fair Silk Mills or the Vanity Fair Stocking Company during the walkout, most likely because the stocking company was located in Lancaster County and therefore not among the Berks County mills targeted by the Philadelphia union organizers.

Shortly after the walkout, however, J.E. Barbey began traveling through the South, look-

ing for potential sites for a new mill. Those who knew Barbey said he would never allow a union shop. His decision later in the decade to move the bulk of his manufacturing facilities to Alabama was specifically in anticipation of labor problems in the Pennsylvania facilities. The move created no immediate layoffs in Pennsylvania; it was just Barbey's way of hedging his bets. He was quoted in 1938 as saying that it had been a mistake for Vanity Fair to build its stocking plant in the North 10 years earlier.[36]

Word had spread that Vanity Fair was planning to build an underwear factory south of the Mason-Dixon line. Officials and businessmen from various towns in Alabama, Texas, Mississippi, North Carolina, South Carolina, Georgia and Tennessee eagerly courted the company. Thomas W. Martin, president of the Alabama Power Company, even traveled to Vanity Fair to argue the merits of moving to his state.

"He was so direct, so sincere, so palpably a fine character that he made an impression on me," Barbey said in a speech he made in Monroeville, Alabama one year after Vanity Fair's factory opened there.[37]

Vanity Fair officer Howard "Pop" Snader had a memorable encounter with another Alabama booster. Snader, traditionally an early riser, was pacing the halls of the House office building in Washington, D.C., one morning in 1936, waiting to meet with his Pennsylvania congressman. Alabama Congressman Frank Boykin, also an early riser, saw Snader and told him he'd have a long wait for the Pennsylvania lawmaker, who usually didn't arrive until near lunchtime. The two started chatting, and before long, Boykin had Snader just about convinced that Alabama might be the spot for a Vanity Fair factory.[38] Though leaning toward Alabama, Vanity Fair officials continued to shop around. Barbey and other officials traveled through southern states by train and car in late 1936, eventually narrowing down possible locations to towns in Alabama, Georgia and Mississippi.[39]

When company officials visited Monroeville, a little town in the southern part of Alabama, they liked what they saw. They returned several weeks later with a proposal for the residents and businessmen of Monroeville.

Under the plan, the town would raise $40,000 to purchase and build on the land. Vanity Fair would contribute an additional $15,000.[40] Local promoters organized the Monroe Industries Corporation and sold bonds to raise the money. Bonds could be purchased for $25, $50, $100, $250 and $500, with buyers to be paid 6 percent interest.[41] The promoters worked hard, but money was scarce in the small town still reeling from the Depression. The community was able to raise only $35,000, but Vanity Fair purchased the remaining bonds in addition to its $15,000 commitment. The certificate of incorporation for the Monroe Industries Corporation was filed at the Monroe County Courthouse on March 9, 1937.[42]

J.E. Barbey eventually chose Monroeville, Alabama, as the site of the first Southern mill. Offices there, though simple, were set up for efficiency, as was the factory.

At the Monroe Mills factory, opened in 1937, machines were soon humming as workers turned out hundreds of garments. Though many earned less than $1 per hour, they felt fortunate to have jobs.

They began construction of a mill on 4.92 acres of land on South Alabama Avenue. Vanity Fair leased the land and building for seven years, with an option to renew the lease for five years. It agreed to quarterly payments totaling $3,565 a year.

The grand opening, on June 23, 1937, was a joyous affair in a town immensely grateful for jobs that would boost its sagging economy.

Alyne Sigler, who started working in the plant only a few months after it opened, remembered the town's gratitude. "We were glad we had jobs," Sigler said. "Not many people had jobs in the late 1930s. It gave people something to do and homes we wouldn't have had."[43] Another early employee, Frances Netles Carroll, remembered being hired in 1938 as an inspector and examiner of garments. She earned 16 cents an hour.[44]

During the one-year anniversary celebration of the mill's opening, Barbey promised the people of Monroeville that great things were still to come.

"I can see large things for this town, things I do not dare mention, but I can see very large things in store for this community, for Monroe County, for the counties surrounding it, in this venture, because I have unbounded faith in the future."[45]

His comments would prove correct, as Vanity Fair continued to expand in Monroeville and other Alabama communities. Each mill was named for the county, not the city, in which it was located.

And, although Vanity Fair still employed more than 1,000 people in the Pennsylvania silk mill and stocking factory, Barbey expressed his preference for the people of Alabama.

"I do not like for our operations to be in the big cities. I like to be out where folks are folks and where people are genuine and unsullied of too many city influences. The reason we are down here in Monroeville, as against being in Pennsylvania, is for that very same reason."[46]

The Vanity Fair-Alabama marriage was a good one, and in 1939 the first installment of Barbey's promise was fulfilled. Clarke Mills opened in the town of Jackson, one county east of Monroeville. Both mills were clean, modern and air conditioned. And also quite loud, according to Janet Peters, a one-time fit model and later the corporation's first woman vice president. Recounting her first trip to one of the southern manufacturing plants, Peters recalled Barbey's reaction when she commented on the noise:

"He said to me, 'Young lady, don't you ever call this noise. This is music — music to your ears, music

Above and below: In 1939, Vanity Fair opened Clarke Mills in Jackson, a town just east of Monroeville. As in Monroeville, townspeople helped raise money to build the factory.

to my ears. And if you don't hear that so-called noise that we call music, that means you don't have a job, and I don't have a job.' From then on, I knew when I

entered a manufacturing plant I'd better hear music or it means business is poor."[47]

Meanwhile, the Reading plant was operating at capacity. Vanity Fair had leased a large building in the city in late 1938, allowing it to consolidate both shipping and warehousing, and free up more of the main factory building for production.[48]

The last year of this financially troubled decade began with John Barbey's retirement as president. In his late 80s, Barbey was in ill health and ready to turn over the reins to his son. During a special meeting of the board of directors on February 1, 1939, John Barbey became chairman of the board and J.E. Barbey was named president. Howard B. Snader was elected treasurer, and W.E. Cusick was named vice president of sales. Harold G. Miller was named executive vice president and assistant secretary.

On Christmas Eve, 1939, John Barbey died in his home. He was buried December 28. During funeral services, Barbey was lauded as a great Reading business and civic leader.[49] The next day, a meeting of the directors of Vanity Fair Silk Mills was held to conclude business for the year. Profits were recorded at $63,624. But Vanity Fair's greatest years were still to come.

In the 1940s, Vanity Fair sold its lingerie from neatly appointed shops displaying the company's stylized cameo.

CHAPTER THREE

NYLON SHAPES THE WORLD

1940–1949

"In short, Vanity Fair was a typical American manufacturer, living and working in the American way. Surely there was no place for us in the great rearmament program — or was there? What of our machines, our skilled workers, our ability to produce the finest in knit fabrics? The manufacture of underwear and hosiery could not win a war, but the production of parachutes would help."

— *His Life in Our Hands,* published by Vanity Fair in 1944[1]

THE NATIONAL mood was apprehensive in 1940 as World War II entered its fifth month in Europe. Although America was not yet involved in the fighting, the nation was taking steps to prepare for war. The first peacetime draft in the nation's history was enacted, and industries began converting to wartime production in order to provide armaments and other supplies to Great Britain.

Officials at Vanity Fair Silk Mills were urgently concerned about the crumbling relationship between the United States and Japan. If the United States embargoed silk in retaliation for Japan's aggressions throughout the Pacific, the industry would lose access to its most important material. As relations between the United States and Japan deteriorated, manufacturers began looking for a material to replace silk.[2]

N-Day

The material that would revolutionize the industry was a synthetic fabric called nylon, created by the DuPont Company. Nylon had been exhibited at the New York World's Fair in 1939 and 1940, and samples were widely available in retail stores.[3] Berkshire Knitting Mills, the giant of the Reading mills and always a pioneer, had participated in

HIS LIFE IN OUR HANDS

DuPont's nylon production experiments in the late 1930s. In 1940, Berkshire converted some of its machines and made several batches of nylon stockings.[4] Following this lead, other manufacturers began to take nylon seriously. They especially liked the thermoplastic qualities of the material, which allowed nylon garments to hold their shape after they were treated with moist heat.[5] Nylon fibers clustered in orderly formations, making the material extremely pliable. Silk fibers, on the other hand, clustered randomly, making the material more difficult to process.

Skirts in 1940 were worn just below the knee, and hosiery was a vital accessory.[6] Consumers were nearly as concerned about the availability of silk as the men in charge of the hosiery and underwear manufacturing plants. When DuPont and the textile industry declared that May 15, 1940, would be "N-Day" (N, of course, being for nylon), a major stir occurred among the fashionable.[7] "Near hysteria" erupted

During World War II, Vanity Fair converted its factories for war production. The company published and distributed His Life in Our Hands to impress upon workers how important their efforts were. (Courtesy of the Historical Society of Berks County, Pennsylvania)

among shoppers who jammed stores to purchase their first pairs of nylon stockings.[8]

The same day, news arrived that the war in Europe had escalated. Holland had surrendered to Germany, and French and British troops were frantic to avoid the German onslaught. British Prime Minister Winston Churchill appealed to President Franklin Roosevelt to aid the beleaguered allied troops. Although the United States did not enter the war immediately, the government began drafting men away from their civilian jobs, while factories began preparations in earnest for war production.[9]

On July 26, 1941, the government froze the already dwindling supply of silk, reserving its use for parachutes and other war items, and nylon production escalated. By the time America entered the war, 30 percent of the nation's hosiery was manufactured from nylon.[10]

Vanity Fair Goes to War

On December 7, 1941, more than 360 Japanese warplanes swooped down on the unprepared U.S. Pacific Fleet, sinking or seriously damaging five United States battleships and 14 small-er ships. More than 2,000 United States Navy personnel were killed in the attack, along with more than 400 civilians. Within four days, the United States declared war on Japan and her Axis partners, Italy and Germany. America had joined the fury of world war.

Forced to temporarily abandon its line of brassieres and girdles due to a government ban on civilian use of elastic, the company turned its attention to producing items to aid in America's war effort.[11]

Vanity Fair contributed to the war effort by producing three types of parachutes: personnel chutes for paratroopers; cargo chutes to air-drop supplies and equipment ranging from food to tanks; and flare chutes, used for light flares that illuminated targets, making it possible to bomb enemy military and industrial installations that were too heavily protected during the day.[12]

Andy Kress oversaw the parachute shipping department at Vanity Fair's Reading factory during the war. "The chutes were made by Vanity Fair, assembled with accessories purchased from other companies by Vanity Fair, and were folded and packed by Vanity Fair," he said during a 1987

1939-40: DuPont introduces nylon at the New York World's Fair.

July 26, 1941: U.S. government freezes sale of silk, reserving it for parachutes and other military uses.

May 15, 1940: "N-Day," women buy first nylon stockings.

December 1941: After Japanese planes attack Pearl Harbor, America enters World War II.

interview. "And, out of all the Vanity Fair parachutes produced during the war and subjected to rigorous military testing, we never had a single one fail inspection." [13]

Vanity Fair also manufactured sails for life boats, mosquito netting, camouflage nets, protective tarpaulins, and jersey underwear and slips for women in the military. It participated in war research, helping find ways to make raincoats and engine covers more water resistant, and made improvements to heated suits for high-altitude flights. [14]

In 1944, Vanity Fair published a book describing its contribution to the national war effort. *His Life in Our Hands*, which was distributed to employees, listed the products manufactured by the company and gave insight into Vanity Fair's commitment to assist in the war effort.

"In short, Vanity Fair was a typical American manufacturer, living and working in the American way. Surely there was no place for us in the great rearmament program — or was there? What of our machines, our skilled workers, our ability to produce the finest in knit fabrics? The manufacture of underwear and hosiery could not win a war, but the production of parachutes would help." [15]

Business, however, was not restricted to war production. The company still maintained its manufacture of rayon stockings and underwear and, because the use of nylon was restricted during the war, converted back to rayon and worked to improve the fabric. The fabric, however, was considered less luxurious and desirable than silk or nylon.

Since girdles and other undergarments were in short supply during the war years, dresses and other garments were designed accordingly. Some dresses were given adjustable waists and busts, designed to fit with whatever undergarments were available. Buttons and other closures replaced zippers, which could not be produced due to a government ban on nonessential uses of metal. [16]

Women were told to "use it up, wear it out, make it do or do without," and they responded admirably. They took apart garments and made them over, turned old blankets into coats and jackets, and took to wearing overalls to the facto-

March 1942: Directors change the company name to "Vanity Fair Mills."

June 1948: J.E. Barbey announces the company will convert entirely to nylon in its hosiery and lingerie.

August 14, 1945: After the U.S. drops atomic bombs on Nagasaki and Hiroshima, Japan surrenders. World War II is over.

August 16, 1948: Vanity Fair closes the Reading plant after organizers stage an unsuccessful attempt to unionize.

ries where they performed what traditionally had been "men's work."[17]

Women even adapted to the war by changing their hairstyles. Some women working in factories had been badly injured when their long hair got caught in machinery. They were urged to, and did, have their hair cut short. The Victory Roll and Liberty Cut were the popular styles of the day. Even film star Veronica Lake relinquished her trademark cascade of hair that covered one eye. With great fanfare, she switched to an upswept style, and encouraged her fans to do the same.[18]

To improve morale among workers, directors began a pension program that included automatic retirement and a monthly income at age 70. The pension carried no guarantees but was to be continued for as long as the payments did not cause an undue financial strain on the company. The board noted that the pension program would be more than compensated for in improved morale and efficiency among workers.[19]

In 1941, Vanity Fair established Extacee, Inc., a subsidiary to handle the production and sale of junior-sized clothing. Government surveys indicated that 72 percent of all American women were 5-feet, 4-inches tall or shorter, and more than half of these women were proportioned for 9-to-15 "junior" sizes rather than the traditional "misses" sizes. It was considered revolutionary

Above and below: Vanity Fair opened its own showroom in Manhattan in 1942 and pioneered the use of live models rather than mannequins. Accomplished in good taste, it enhanced the company's image.

when Vanity Fair began presenting lingerie manufactured exclusively for women of junior sizes.

With its usual flair for marketing, Vanity Fair commissioned a statue called Extacee to represent this new line of garments. The statue was created by Mario Korbel, who had been called "the greatest sculptor of American womanhood." His works were displayed in major museums throughout the country, and his statue of St. Therese was housed in the Vatican.[20] Unfortunately, the junior concept proved to be ahead of its time, and Extacee, Inc., lasted only about a decade before it was dissolved.

In March 1942, the board of directors, noting that they were not using silk in their products and probably would not have silk for some time to come, voted to change the name of the company from Vanity Fair Silk Mills to Vanity Fair Mills.[21] The board also changed the Articles of Incorporation to read: "Said Corporation is formed for the purpose of manufacture, fabrication and sale of textiles, fabrics and similar materials, and of articles containing such materials." The articles had previously read: "Said Corporation is formed for the purpose of manufacturing and selling knit gloves, mittens and underwear."[22]

One month later, a wholly owned subsidiary, the Vanterial Corporation, was created in Pennsylvania to handle many of the company's war contracts.[23]

Also in 1942, the company made fashion news when it inaugurated its own show-room in Manhattan and began lingerie presentations with live models — a practice unheard of at the time. J.E. Barbey made sure the company adhered to its principle of good taste, and the shows enhanced Vanity Fair's sophisticated image and set it apart from other companies.[24]

Manford O. Lee

In October 1942, a young man named Manford O. Lee was hired as night foreman of the flare parachute department. Lee, who was paid $200 a month, would eventually become president, chief executive officer and chairman of Vanity Fair, guiding it through years of tremendous growth.[25] Lee, no relation to the H.D. Lee Company that Vanity Fair would later acquire, was born and raised in rural Nebraska. He left his home town of Stockville after high school and went to Lincoln to learn to fly and be an aviation mechanic.

Unfortunately, the Great Depression got in the way of his plans. Lee, who had been called "Whitey" since childhood and kept the nickname until he died, returned home and married his high school sweetheart, Rosalie Hakal. It is at this point that the Lee legend diverges.

Changes at home even as the war raged in Europe: Roger Morton, above, became executive vice president in 1943, and Harold Miller, right, became secretary and assistant treasurer.

An article about Lee that appeared in an Omaha newspaper in 1972 said Lee had signed up with the Agricultural Adjustment Administration in Stockville after returning from Omaha. After a few years he was transferred to Colorado. J.E. Barbey had a ranch in Steamboat Springs, Colorado, where he was noted for raising prize Angus cattle. Lee and Barbey met in 1940, according to the article, and Lee went to work for him two years later.[26]

Vanity Fair old-timers reveal more to the story. Lee was working near Barbey's ranch for either the electric or telephone company. He was up on a pole one day when Barbey came along, upset because service to his ranch had not been completed. Lee told him he would take care of it, and got the job done — right away. Barbey was so impressed with Lee's initiative that he hired the young man to work at Vanity Fair. Regardless of the circumstances under which he was hired, Lee served a long and distinguished career at Vanity Fair and was recognized as one of the top chief executives in the industry. He was chairman and chief executive officer of VF Corporation when he died in 1982, and for many years, a pair of lineman's spike boots was on display in the VF board room.

A Peaceful Lift

Although the United States avoided the worst hardships of war, citizens felt the impact of the battles raging overseas. Gasoline, food and clothing were rationed. Although certainly not one of the more serious problems facing society at the time, fashion — or the lack of it — was a cause of declining morale among American women. The scarcity

Suited up and ready for action, the Vanity Fair Men's Baseball Team practiced teamwork on the field and in the factory.

of stockings was especially troubling. Gone were the luxurious silks and nylons that women had prized before the war. Rayon, although improved, was still considered a poor sister to preferred fabrics, but even stockings made of rayon were in short supply.

Women responded to the shortage with characteristic creativity. They wore pants more often so stockings were unnecessary. When they wore dresses, they used Cyclax Stocking-less Cream or other forms of leg makeup, completing the illusion of stockings by using eyebrow pencil to draw "seams" down the backs of their legs.[27]

Company leadership changed in 1943. In June, directors elected Roger Morton executive vice president, replacing Harold Miller, who was named secretary and assistant treasurer, and Howard Hoff's title was changed from secretary to assistant secretary.[28]

The End of the War

Victory in Europe for the Allies finally came on May 7, 1945, when Germany surrendered unconditionally.

Fighting continued for several more months on the Pacific front. Since 1943, General Douglas McArthur and Admiral Chester Nimitz had been positioned to invade Japan, but it wasn't until the Allies dropped atomic bombs on Hiroshima and Nagasaki that Japan was brought to her knees. On August 14, 1945, Japan surrendered. World War II was over.

Four days later, on August 18, 1945, the government lifted its wartime production restrictions and Vanity Fair resumed manufacture of brassieres and girdles. The company also worked closely with the DuPont Company to increase its use of nylon.[29]

As America returned joyously to the pursuit of peace, Vanity Fair turned its attention to internal improvements. In 1945, the Vanity Fair Foundation was established in Monroeville as a charitable trust that provided recreational, social and cultural opportunities to area residents. The Vanity Fair Foundation-Clarke was formed soon afterward as a counterpart for the mill in Jackson. Machinery was upgraded in southern facilities and plans were made to expand the mills. In 1946, M.O. Lee was sent to Jackson as plant manager, and would soon became general manager of the company's entire southern operations.[30]

Expansion was not confined to the South. In February 1946, directors voted to purchase a mill in Denver, Lancaster County, for

$30,000. The company was already using the mill, and directors determined that it was more cost-effective to purchase it than to continue renting it.[31]

The third generation of Barbeys joined Vanity Fair Mills in December 1947 when John E. Barbey, Jr. was named assistant treasurer and a member of the board of directors. The younger Barbey was one of twin sons born to J.E. Barbey and his first wife. The other twin, Pierre, would die tragically at the age of 27.[32]

Closing the Reading Factory

For Vanity Fair Mills, the following year, 1948, was momentous. It was a period of great acclaim for the company, but also one of growing bitterness between workers and management at the Reading factory.

While still recovering from the war, American manufacturers experienced severe labor problems. Large numbers of workers joined unions, expecting increased job security and benefits. Many employers resisted the effort, fearing costs. The conflict led to strikes and walkouts that crippled many industries.

Grace Fidler, who worked in the Reading factory with four of her family members, vividly recalls the day the machines were stilled and the Reading factory closed.

A nationwide railroad strike was called, and coal miners walked off their jobs. Workers at the Reading factory of Vanity Fair Mills attempted to unionize in 1945, and the International Ladies' Garment Workers' Union returned to Reading in the spring of 1948 to try again.[33]

Just months after the second union attempt, on Friday, August 16, the plant closed without warning, leaving 475 workers jobless. A notice posted at the plant said the closing was due to economic reasons and would be for "an indefinite period," but did not rule out the possibility of reopening. "The cost of making merchandise here has steadily increased to a point where continuance of manufacturing in this plant is clearly impractical," it read. "Vanity Fair hopes that eventual reopening of the Reading mill may be found practical."[34]

The company's headquarters and warehouse in the city remained open. Workers claimed the closing was in retaliation for their attempts to unionize. A large, paid advertisement in the Saturday, April 17, edition of the *Reading Eagle* urged all workers to report to the Teamsters Building Hall the following Monday morning to discuss strategies to force Barbey to reopen the mill. "Barbey has violated the law by closing the mill. ... This is a lockout! ... An unfair labor practice under the law! Uncle Sam is on your side," the ad pronounced.[35]

Even if Uncle Sam was on their side, the workers were unable to have the mill reopened. Instead, each worker was issued a check for one week's pay, and workers had no choice but to look elsewhere for work.

Almost 50 years after the closing, former employees still vividly recall the event and the bitterness it caused. Grace Fidler, whose father, two sisters and brother were also employed by Vanity Fair, remembers the day the notice was posted.

"It was posted on a bulletin board at the back of the shop. There were 300 and some sewing machines in operation, and they just shut off down the line as the news spread. People figured they wouldn't even finish what they were working on. I sat there and listened as row by row, they all shut down. I'll never forget that sound."[36]

Gladys Knight, who started working for Vanity Fair in 1929 when she was 14 years old, also recalled the day. "It was one of the saddest days I've ever seen," Knight said. "Some of the girls wouldn't leave. They just sat at their machines until somebody came around and told them to go."[37]

Other former employees recalled that the machinery in the Reading factory was packed up and sent to Monroeville. They said that the garments still in production when the closing was announced were used to pack the machines for their trip south.

Casting about for an explanation, workers circulated dozens of rumors about the closing. Some believed that state officials in Alabama had bribed Vanity Fair into relocating. "We all heard that Alabama gave them free water and electricity when they moved down there," said June Miller, another former employee. "How could we compete with that?"[38]

Though bitterness toward the company, and particularly J.E. Barbey, lingered in Reading for a long time, old-timers said they remembered that the company treated its employees well. One woman who started in the pressing and packing department at Vanity Fair in 1937 recalled that she earned 35 cents an hour — 10 cents more than at the job she left at Luden's, a major candy manufacturer in Reading. An employee store offered discounts of 50 percent, and workers were permitted to purchase four garments a month. Detailed records were kept to assure no employee bought more than his or her share.

A group of women who worked in the factory when it shut down have gathered regularly once

Gladys Knight, 91 in 1996, joined Vanity Fair at age 14. She called the Reading plant closing "one of the saddest days I've ever seen."

a year for a get-together. By 1997, most were in their 80s, and some in their 90s. Each year the women claim that meeting will be their last.

As business was winding down in the North, it was picking up in the South. Vanity Fair had purchased 70 acres of land in Monroeville to be used for a community park. M.O. Lee moved from Jackson, where Clarke Mills is located, to Monroeville in 1948, and oversaw a community effort to establish the Vanity Fair Park. It was customary in Monroeville for many businesses to close down on Thursday afternoons and Lee organized community members to join Vanity Fair officials on Thursdays to help clear and clean up land for the park.[39]

The Wonder Yarn

Yet another significant announcement in 1948 brought widespread acclaim to Vanity Fair Mills. A full-page advertisement on June 8 in *The New York Times* announced that Vanity Fair was converting fully to nylon for its hosiery and lingerie. In the ad, Vanity Fair called nylon "the wonder yarn of our era, miraculously strong, yet delicate as gossamer."[40] The ad referred to the Vanity Fair mills as "jewel boxes" and said the change to nylon was a sign of the company's determination to keep its lingerie the favorite of American women.[41]

The news took the fashion industry by storm and quickly set Vanity Fair Mills apart from its competition. Some people in the industry were skeptical, and even Vanity Fair representatives were surprised. M.O. Lee, who was running the Alabama mills, said later that he had been shocked when he heard of the decision, since nylon was still somewhat scarce and cost about $4 per pound, compared to about $1 for rayon. [42] J.E. Barbey, however, was steadfast in his decision. The company's Reading plant had been working with the DuPont Company for several years, perfecting the complicated knitting process

OUR MESSAGE TO THE WOMEN OF AMERICA

Vanity Fair

CONCENTRATES ON NYLON LINGERIE

Above: When named executive vice president, Howard Snader immediately set about upgrading the company's factory equipment.

Right: An announcement that would alter forever the course of Vanity Fair and shake the American apparel world to its foundations.

Vanity Fair ANNOUNCES

LOWER PRICES THRU VOLUME ECONOMIES

Last year, the Vanity Fair Mills, in keeping with its tradition, became the first of the great lingerie makers to concentrate all of its facilities on the production of Nylon Lingerie.

This year the Vanity Fair Mills celebrate fifty years of leadership in the making of fine merchandise for American women. Through three generations, the owners have held to one concept – that Vanity Fair must at all times produce the finest lingerie of its kind in the world, not only exquisitely fashioned and in flawless taste, but also offering the utmost in quality and at reasonable prices.

AMAZING VALUES THRU VOLUME PRODUCTION

Today again, in keeping with its tradition, Vanity Fair becomes the first to pass on the economies earned through its specialized experience applied to volume production of nylon tricot lingerie. Following our deep obligation to America's fine stores ﹔﹕﹔ our active responsibility to so many thousands of women who prefer Vanity Fair when they shop for lingerie ﹔﹕﹔ we promptly pass on these economies which will make this superb merchandise available to a much greater number of your customers.

QUALITY AND FINISH FURTHER IMPROVED

Today, the quality, finish and styling are not only up to the precious standards of Vanity Fair in the past, but further improved. All the highly specialized Vanity Fair fabrics are finished with Vanitiset, an exclusive process, which assures you the best nylon tricot lingerie anywhere.

EXTACEE SIZE LINE CONTINUED

Vanity Fair is not only made in regular sizes and out-sizes, but now further adds Extacee (junior) sizes. Due to the persistent demands made upon Vanity Fair to take care of the 9 to 15 (junior) sizes, it has been decided to continue in the manufacture, sale and servicing of these sizes. There will be available, commencing with the Fall Line, a complete Junior Line of nylon tricot lingerie as previously supplied by the Extacee Division of this company.

This merchandise will come through with the added value of carrying the Vanity Fair label.

DELIVERIES

Due to a realignment of our production facilities, beginning with the August 1st delivery, Vanity Fair has enormously improved its ability to satisfy the demands made upon it by its customers.

Vanity Fair Mills, inc.
EXECUTIVE OFFICES: READING, PENNSYLVANIA

In May 1949, celebrating "50 years of leadership" in the lingerie business, Vanity Fair promised to pass along to consumers savings gained through volume purchasing and manufacturing.

---

for nylon. The experiments were moved to the southern facilities.[43]

Any lingering doubts about nylon were quickly dispelled in the face of its tremendous success. The fabric was given *American Fabric* magazine's award for textile achievement and was featured in the Metropolitan Museum of Art's "American Textile, '48" display.[44] According to Peter Velardi, a one-time Vanity Fair Mills division president who retired in 1994 after 44 years with the company, J.E. Barbey knew something his competitors didn't when he made the decision to convert fully to nylon. "He knew that nylon could bring in color," noted Velardi.

"So all of a sudden we changed from a commodity business into a fashion accessory business, commanding the higher margins and higher profits that a fashion accessory could."[45]

Although Vanity Fair led the industry in its conversion to nylon, other companies soon followed. The fall and pre-Christmas seasons were disappointing, and officials felt the company was losing the advantages it had enjoyed as the first major company to convert to nylon. The only way to keep ahead, declared J.E. Barbey during a special meeting of the board of directors on December 20, 1948, was to upgrade equipment and make the factories more modern and efficient.

A report to the board by Howard Snader, the company's newly elected executive vice president, identified the equipment needed and the approximate costs of the machinery. He recommended that the company purchase 10 Whitin tricot knitting machines at $10,000 each, and six FNF English-made knitting machines for $20,000 each. He also suggested the purchase of two Cascade warpers for $40,000 each, a boiler for $45,000, and miscellaneous other equipment. The board agreed to all the purchases and also approved improvements to the dyeing department and other areas of the factories. All told, the company prepared to spend between $500,000 and $600,000 in the coming months.

During the same month, John E. Barbey Jr., took over for Miller as secretary, retaining his title of assistant treasurer. Lee was named vice president in charge of operations. The following year Lee was named a member of the board of directors.[46]

Heights of Fashion

Vanity Fair continued its role as a fashion trailblazer, developing a method of permanently pleating nylon fabric in 1949. The company, led by its acclaimed designer Nancy Melcher, added new pastel colors to its lingerie, and offered new neutrals like beige and silver gray. Printed fabrics were introduced, along with rich, deep colors which were new to lingerie.

On May 26, 1949, full-page displays in *Women's Wear Daily,* among other prestigious fashion publications, announced that Vanity Fair would offer lower prices. Advertising was increased and became more glamorous. Selling underwear had never been taken quite so seriously.

At the insistence of J.E. Barbey, the Abbott Kimball agency was commissioned to help create a new image for Vanity Fair products. Barbey, who had always taken a strong interest in advertising, said he wanted to stress beauty and emphasize the product. This directive led to Vanity Fair's famous models, portrayed with covered faces, so as not to divert attention from the product worn. High-fashion leg model Joan Pederson was one of the models who posed for these striking advertisements. Fashion photographer Mark Shaw was recruited, and Vanity Fair's advertising reached new heights of sophistication.

The decade ended on a high note for Vanity Fair Mills. Sales rose from about $10.9 million in 1948 to $12.9 million in 1949. More significantly, earnings more than doubled, from $730,000 in 1948 to $2 million just two years later. After the cataclysmic social and economic changes of the 1940s, Americans looked forward with confidence to the 1950s. Consumerism would become firmly entrenched and Vanity Fair, like other manufacturers of consumer goods, would prosper.

The leopard print, introduced in 1953, was a favorite.

CHAPTER FOUR

A Decade of Progress

1950–1959

"An expert in the use of nylon tricot, Nancy Melcher knows what will best satisfy the dreams of American women — and gives it to them."

— *Christian Science Monitor*, 1960[1]

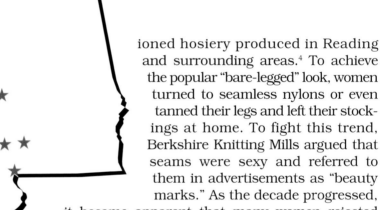

THE FIFTIES WERE a time of optimism and prosperity for America. Pent-up consumer demand from the Depression and war years, combined with a manufacturing prowess unmatched by any other nation on earth, fueled an economic boom that allowed Americans to pursue a culture of consumerism. Mass-produced suburban homes were quickly stocked with the very latest appliances. Television sets could be found in 1.5 million homes in 1950, and in 15 million the following year.[2] Fashion was a natural extension of a new desire to showcase the many luxuries that money could buy.

Vanity Fair grew rapidly during this period. While underwear production flourished in Vanity Fair Mills' Alabama facilities, stocking production was being phased out in the North. In January 1950, the Vanity Fair Stocking Company in New Holland was sold to Julius Kayser & Company, Inc., of New York City for $100,000. As part of the deal, Vanity Fair agreed not to manufacture, sell or distribute women's hosiery for five years.[3] Vanity Fair abandoned the stocking business at the perfect time. Pantyhose were replacing the traditional stockings that were attached to garter belts. Women who still wore nylons preferred them without the classic seams of the full-fash-

ioned hosiery produced in Reading and surrounding areas.[4] To achieve the popular "bare-legged" look, women turned to seamless nylons or even tanned their legs and left their stockings at home. To fight this trend, Berkshire Knitting Mills argued that seams were sexy and referred to them in advertisements as "beauty marks." As the decade progressed, it became apparent that many women rejected that notion.

Southern Expansion

Meanwhile, Vanity Fair was increasing its underwear production in Alabama and adding manufacturing facilities there. On January 12, 1950, the lead story of the *Demopolis Times* announced that Vanity Fair would locate its third mill, Marengo, in Demopolis. Area citizens purchased bonds, which Vanity Fair repaid over the years, to raise construction money.[5]

The community was extremely enthusiastic about having Vanity Fair in town. It had already

---

By the late 1950s, Vanity Fair had four Alabama plants: Monroe Mills in Monroeville, Clarke Mills in Jackson, Marengo Mills in Demopolis, and Escambia Mills in Atmore.

seen what the company had done for the towns of Monroeville and Jackson, both of which had benefitted not only from the boost to their local economies, but also from the Vanity Fair charitable foundations established there during the 1940s. The Jackson Community House had just been completed and was to become the center of a Vanity Fair Park that by the end of the decade would boast a swimming pool, tennis courts, playgrounds and a nine-hole golf course.[6]

A fourth facility, Escambia Mills, was constructed in 1951 in Atmore, Alabama, south of

Monroeville. Asked to raise $225,000 through the sale of bonds, residents reached the goal in only one hour.[7] The Alabama mills, all located within a 90-mile radius, were named after the counties in which they were located.

In 1950, the company also expanded the Monroe Mills in Monroeville in anticipation of future growth.[8] While Vanity Fair was expanding in the South, textile manufacturers throughout the nation watched anxiously as the United States became involved in an undeclared war with Korea that began in June 1950, when North Korean soldiers swept into South Korea. Still recovering from the rationing and conversion hardships of World War II, manufacturers wondered how another conflict would impact their businesses. The United Nations police action — which pitted American and South Korean forces against North Korean soldiers and Chinese "volunteers" — dragged on for three years. Although

Residents raised $225,000 in one hour as an incentive for Vanity Fair to build the Escambia plant in Atmore. The plant, built in 1951, only performed cutting and sewing operations.

1950: Vanity Fair gets out of the stocking business, selling its New Holland plant to Julius Kayser & Company.

March 19, 1951: Vanity Fair goes public, offering one-third of its shares to the public.

1950: A third mill, Marengo, is planned for Demopolis, Alabama.

April 1951: M.O. Lee, hired in 1942, becomes vice president.

Marengo Mills in Demopolis was built in 1950 as part of Vanity Fair's expansion in the South.

nylon was in short supply during the conflict, no rationing or government controls were imposed.[9]

Celebrated Styles

Vanity Fair Mills rejoiced in October 1950 when Nancy Melcher, the company's designer since 1937, won an American Fashion Critics' Award for her use of nylon tricot fabric in lingerie styling. She was honored at a party given at the Waldorf-Astoria Hotel in New York City.[10] The October issue of the *Vanity Fair News*, an in-house newsletter, described the event as a "gala party."

Melcher had won high acclaim within both the company and the fashion community for her innovative work with nylon tricot. She utilized permanent pleats, developed in the late 1940s, to create lingerie different from any that had ever been produced previously. Her work, which was feminine and easy to care for, was welcomed by women who were still recovering from the fashion deprivation of the World War II years. Women wanted clothes that were delicate and romantic looking. But Americans also were enjoying more sports and leisure activities and needed clothing that did not require constant maintenance.[11] Melcher's designs in easy-care nylon delivered both fashion and practicality.

The fashion editor of the *Christian Science Monitor* praised Melcher's creations.

"An expert in the use of nylon tricot, Nancy Melcher knows what will best satisfy the dreams of American women — and gives it to them.

1951: Alabama expansion continues with a fourth facility, Escambia Mills, in Atmore.

1953: Vanity Fair introduces the leopard print, which becomes an overnight sensation.

1952: Edwin Barbey, son of J.E. Barbey and grandson of founder John Barbey, becomes assistant treasurer.

October 21, 1956: J.E. Barbey dies at his Reading home.

Recognizing the extraordinary advantages inherent in this interesting fabric, utilizing its elasticity and dimensional stability, its unusual width and the wonderful opportunities for design in permanent pleats, a feature made possible by the laboratories of Vanity Fair Mills, Melcher found a new world of design at her slim fingertips."[12]

Melcher's work was a source of pride for Vanity Fair employees, who reveled in her talent and receipt of the Critics' Citation Award. "We are all proud and happy to know that Nancy Melcher's name will be inscribed along with the other great designers in The Hall of American Fashion Fame," the newsletter read. "What delightful designs of Vanity Fair loveliness will

Above: Award-winning designer Nancy Melcher was known for her innovative work with nylon tricot.

Below: Vanity Fair and Monroeville were justly proud of the 97-acre Vanity Fair Park, which boasted a five-acre lake, baseball diamond, tennis courts, picnic grounds and recreation areas.

be forthcoming from this versatile designer in the years to come remain, of course, in the realms of mystery. We cannot anticipate the exact form in which they will emerge, but that they will be distinctive, original, practical, wearable and exquisitely beautiful is neither speculative nor conjectural!"[13]

Becoming a Public Company

The new year brought significant changes to Vanity Fair. The company went public and accelerated its expansion in the South. On March 19, 1951, directors voted to offer about one third of its outstanding shares of stock to the public. All shares to be offered came out of the holdings of J.E. Barbey, who owned 5,980 of the company's 6,000 shares of common stock.[14] Before the stock was made public, its par value was $50 per share. Directors elected to recapitalize the company, creating one million common shares with a par value of $5 per share. Of those shares, 600,000 were offered to the public. Stockholders would receive a quarterly dividend of 30 cents per share.[15]

In April, M.O. Lee became vice president, replacing Howard Snader. Lee, who lived in Alabama, had served as vice president in charge of operations since 1948.[16]

In 1951, more plants were completed and put on line, including Escambia Mills in Atmore, Alabama. The Monroeville plant was significantly expanded to include a new dyehouse and improved finishing facilities and the Clarke Mills

Above: The centerpiece of Vanity Fair Park was the Community House, which included a ballroom, separate lounges for men and women and a kitchen.

Below: Workers dyed fabric before it was cut to assure even color distribution.

Residents raised $10,000 the first day. After three weeks, $16,215 had been accumulated, and the total amount was raised within seven months. The Community House included a ballroom, dining room, kitchen, civic room, entrance hall, separate lounges for men and women, a snack bar and bathhouse facilities for swimmers in the five-acre lake. The 97-acre park, which townspeople

factory was also enlarged. The same year, directors voted to contribute $26,000 to the Vanity Fair Foundation in Monroeville; $20,000 to the Vanity Fair Mills Foundation in Jackson; $20,000 to the Vanity Fair Mills Foundation in Marengo, where the Marengo Mills had opened in 1950; and $20,000 to the Vanity Fair Mills Foundation in Escambia County.

On December 11, 1952, the Community House in the Vanity Fair Park in Monroeville was dedicated in a ceremony attended by J.E. Barbey and other Vanity Fair officials, as well as 500 residents of Monroeville. Construction of the $100,000 structure had begun in March and was funded by contributions from Vanity Fair and Monroeville residents and businesses. Vanity Fair had issued a challenge to residents, offering to build the center if residents could raise $33,000.

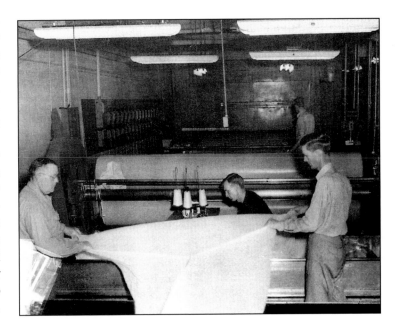

promoted as the finest in the state, also contained a baseball diamond with grandstand, two lighted tennis courts, a picnic and recreational area, playground, barbecue pits and a large pavilion with tables.[17]

By early 1952, a third generation of the Barbey family was made an officer in the company. Edwin Q. Barbey, a son of J.E. Barbey and his second wife, Catharine, was elected assistant treasurer of Vanity Fair Mills. He also retained his position as a company salesman.[18]

Before becoming assistant treasurer, Edwin Barbey had worked at the family ranch in Steamboat Springs, Colorado, at the hosiery mill in New Holland, Pennsylvania, and at the Reading factory.[19]

"I was on the knitting machine shift. I would also help out repairing sewing machines if somebody needed an extra hand. Having the Barbey name was a two-edged sword. It gave you absolution if you wanted to take advantage of it, but I was conscience-stricken and I probably didn't take enough advantage of it."[20]

The corporate philosophy was clear-cut: "Everybody covers up for everybody, but not for their errors," Edwin Barbey said. "Your errors are on the record. If you slip and fall, we'll pick you up, but don't ever make the same mistake twice."[21]

Directors recognized that the growing company needed a new corporate structure, and in 1953, the position of chairman of the board was established. The post was filled by J.E. Barbey, who continued to serve as president.[22] That year, the first Annual Report was distributed, showing that sales for 1952 were a record $20.7 million, and net earnings were $1.3 million.[23]

Innovations in 1953 included the launch of Shevelva™, a new type of light, velour-type nylon tricot fabric. The Vanity Fair Crest was also introduced. The design incorporated the cameo, the original symbol of Vanity Fair and a small Pennsylvania-German design, in recognition of the company's original location. Feathers

Above: Vanity Fair lingerie used DuPont nylon, a revolutionary new fiber.

Below: The Vanity Fair Crest, introduced in 1953, combined traditional symbols of femininity.

interlaced with ribbons and pearls, along with a stylized camellia flower, representing the full flower of the South. The center of the elaborate design contained the Vanity Fair monogram, and the company signature appeared at the bottom.[24] An in-house publication noted that the plumes at the top reflected the "consistent and tireless effort to achieve the Best and most Beautiful, and to do it with a light touch and a sense of drama."

The Height of Fashion

Vanity Fair continued to define the underwear industry with innovative designs that were in such demand that women stood in long lines to buy lingerie and loungewear. The leopard print, introduced with some trepidation in 1953, became an immediate success. Although some officials thought the exotic design would have limited appeal, J.E. Barbey was enthusiastic about it. A 1960 *Christian Science Monitor* article revealed that Barbey's instinct was correct. The article noted that the first samples were sent to the chic Henri Bendel store on 57th Street in Manhattan, which had mistakenly advertised that the pieces would be available the day before they actually arrived in the store. "That same morning there was a line of customers, ads in hand, demanding a look. Three times as many were ordered in the first hour as the store expected to sell in total. Fabrics had to be flown by air, printed, sent to plants, cut, sewn, and shipped. Leopard prints turned out to be the most sensational item for the entire season."[25]

Other popular prints introduced in the fifties included the mermaid, butterfly and zebra. These bold and unusual patterns helped Vanity Fair transform underwear from dull necessity to appealing fashion accessory.

Competition at this time was fierce and advertising was more important than ever. Vanity Fair advertisements continued to feature the striking image of a model with a covered or partially covered face. These compositions appeared in such fashionable publications as *Bride's Magazine*, *Mademoiselle*, *The New Yorker*, *Christian Science Monitor*, *Town and Country*, *Vogue*, *Glamour*, *Harper's Bazaar* and *Charm*.

Vanity Fair, which by that time had established itself as the standard-bearer of fashion and quality, began including the prices of its top-of-the-line merchandise in its advertisements while maintaining its value line of lingerie. The highest-priced items, referred to as "conversation pieces," were showcased to establish an aura of prestige. In 1955, for example, Vanity Fair offered a gold lamé nylon tricot nightgown that sold for $450. A Chicago department store displayed five of them in its front window, counting on the nightgowns to get customers excited about its merchandise.[26] The pricey items had a following — a certain class of women in the mid-1950s did not hesitate to pay $69.96 for a pleated gown or $125 for a sheer lacy gown.[27]

Vanity Fair pioneered the use of live lingerie models in its showrooms.

Of course, many more women purchased the mainstream items such as pettiskirts, briefs and lounging pajamas. Pettiskirts, which ranged from slim, plain designs to full circle skirts covered with polka dots, were sold in 1952 and 1953 at prices ranging from $4.95 to $14.95. They were advertised in styles such as rose-in-bloom, the classic with pleats, the sheath in taffeta and polka dots in taffeta. A pair of briefs in the then-popular zebra stripe sold for $2.50 in 1954. Lounging pajamas of the same print were priced at $16.95, and a dressing gown in zebra stripe was $29.95.[28]

John Barbey, who built the company from its infancy, died in 1956.

The End of Barbey Leadership

In 1955, John E. Barbey, Jr., J.E.'s son, stepped down from his posts as secretary and assistant treasurer of the company to devote his time to other interests. Frederic Eaton, Jr., became the company's new secretary. J.E. Barbey, who some old-time employees say was extremely demanding, especially of his children, was once again the only Barbey to serve as an officer of the company started by his father a half century before.

"Things moved so fast in his life that just keeping up with him was formidable," said Edwin Barbey, another of J.E.'s three sons. "It was devastating to be a son of his because he was so quick and so brilliant and so articulate." He was a demanding father who would brook no disagreement, his son said. "If you tried to rebut him, he would not negatively dissuade you, but he would give you very short logic on why your idea wouldn't work."[29] Edwin Barbey had left the company before John Barbey.

Another long-time employee, Treasurer Harold Miller, tendered his resignation in September, citing health considerations. The directors voted to establish a position of vice chairman of the board

of directors, and elected Miller. The new treasurer was Robert H. Andrews.

In October 1955, the company began a stock option plan for select officers and employees, giving them the opportunity to purchase shares of common stock. The plan stipulated that J.E. Barbey would choose the individuals to be granted the option, and determine how many shares of stock each would be offered.[30]

J.E. Barbey's tenure would not last much longer, however. The board meeting of December 28, 1955, would be his last. Shortly after, he learned he was dying of cancer and removed himself from day-to-day operations. After learning of his diagnosis, Barbey rarely set foot in his office, said his secretary, Scotta Miller. "I guess he didn't want people to see him after he got sick," she said. "He was a proud man, and somewhat vain. Once he got sick, he only came into the office once or twice. When he did come in, he'd go in and out of his office through a back door so no one would see him."[31]

Nonetheless, Barbey kept up-to-date with company business. He made and took phone calls from his home. Miller took mail to him a couple of times a week, and he would send messages back with her. Sometimes, however, he would tell her not to come. "Some days he just didn't feel like seeing anyone," she said.[32]

J.E. Barbey died late in the afternoon of Sunday, October 21, 1956, in his home on Golf Road in Greenfields, an affluent section of Reading. He was survived by his widow, Catharine, and four children. Barbey, however, lived alone in his large house, with only a housekeeper to help him care for the home. His wife was residing at the Tenacre Foundation, a Christian Science facility near Philadelphia; John E. Jr. had moved to LaJolla, California; and Edwin had moved to Needham, Massachusetts.

His daughter Mary had married DeWest Hooker and lived in Greenwich, Connecticut, while Helen lived in Wilmington, Delaware, having married Samuel F. du Pont, a fitting union considering the role the DuPont Company and its nylon fabric had played in the success of Vanity Fair Mills. (The couple later divorced.) Also surviving J.E. were nine grandchildren and two sisters. Neither sister lived in the Reading area, but both were stockholders of Vanity Fair Mills.

Barbey had been a member of the First Church of Christ, Scientist — a religion that he had apparently embraced after learning he had cancer. Acquaintances said he donated substantial sums of money to the church. Christian Scientists generally believe that illnesses are caused by mental error and can be treated and healed spiritually, without benefit of medicine. Scotta Miller believed Barbey never sought medical treatment for his cancer. "To my knowledge, he did not have any medical attention," she said. "I think he just went home and accepted that whatever was going to happen would happen."[33]

As stipulated by his will, two-thirds of Barbey's stock shares were placed in trusts for various persons and organizations. After selling one-third of his shares to the public in 1951, Barbey had placed a quarter of the remaining shares in trust funds for each of his children.[34]

The board of directors met the day after Barbey's death and authorized the closing of all plants and offices on October 23. Harold Miller reviewed Barbey's "long and brilliant" career, and expressed "great loss, sorrow and regret" on behalf of the board.[35]

At the November board meeting, Harold Miller was elected chairman, apparently having recovered from whatever health problem had prompted him to resign as company treasurer. (Miller lived to celebrate his 100th birthday in 1996). Neal Dow, vice president of Marketing, was elected president of Vanity Fair Mills; M.O. Lee, vice president of Manufacturing, was named vice president; and Robert Andrews, treasurer, was named to the board of directors. Lee also became a member of the board's executive committee.[36]

Above: Robert Andrews became treasurer and board member after J.E. Barbey's death.

Below: The 1950s saw the modernization of Vanity Fair's Alabama plants.

"Nobody talks about Harold Miller, but he's the hero, he made the transition after Dad died," said Edwin Barbey. "He had a mutual accord with my father about what Whitey Lee could do and couldn't do. And they both knew that he had to keep a thumb over him or he would try and take over everything."[37]

Vanity Fair reported record sales of $23 million for 1956, a 7 percent increase over the previous year. Net profits were $1.36 million, also up from the previous year.[38] Dow reported that sales would have been even higher, but the company lacked the manufacturing capability to meet demand.

New Frontiers

The company sought to remedy this production shortfall the following year, starting with a program of modernization at the Monroeville and Clarke Mills facilities. The plants were remodeled and relighted, and equipment was rewired and relocated.[39]

Employee benefits were also changed for the better with the introduction of a pension plan. Under the plan, an employee who had worked at least 15 years for the company would receive 35 percent of the average monthly salary earned for the 10 years prior to retirement. Employees who had worked for more than 10 years but less than 15 would be eligible for a lesser percentage of their average salaries. The payments would continue for the life of the retiree. Employees did not have to contribute to the plan, and the company could deduct its contributions from its income tax. The company had instituted a limited pension plan in 1940 for employees who reached a retirement age of 70. The new pension plan allowed employees to retire at 65.[40]

Sales of $24.9 million and net earnings of $1.6 million made 1957 another record year. Mass market consumers were becoming more fashion-conscious than ever, and eagerly bought sleepwear and lingerie in a wide variety of colors and patterns.[41]

In April, Neal Dow resigned as president and left Vanity Fair Mills. Peter Velardi, who joined Vanity Fair Mills in 1949 and retired as chairman and chief executive officer in 1994, believed that Dow's management background was not suited to the world of fashion. "It was very difficult for Mr.

Charles Burg, who had been with Vanity Fair since 1951, became vice president of Sales after J.E. Barbey's death.

Dow, who came from a professional management background, to come into a business that required a great deal of intuitive feel," he said. "Almost anybody who was going to succeed Mr. Barbey had to be very special because it was Mr. Barbey's company. It had his imprint. It had his taste level. He had a fabulous ability to look at something and decide if it would be fashionable."[42]

Harold Miller was elected president, adding to his duties as chairman of the board. Robert Derx filled Dow's seat on the board of directors. Derx, formerly vice president of Sales, was named vice president of Marketing. Charles A. Burg, who had been with the company in a senior sales capacity since 1951, became vice president of Sales. In the final years of the 1950s, the company focused more than ever on expansion. Escambia Mills was expanded in 1959, and talk had begun about building a second plant in Monroeville. Directors

M.O. Lee became Vanity Fair's next president in 1958.

also had complained about a lack of space in their New York showroom.

Expansion of product lines was an important element of the company's growth. A new, more modern line of foundation garments — brassieres, girdles and panty girdles — was developed to correspond with changes in fashion. In the 1950s, brassieres helped women achieve the unnaturally pointed look that was in vogue at the time. Calf-length full skirts were drawn tight at the waist and demanded lingerie that shaped the body more than in years past.[43] Two new nylon tri-cot fabrics, Ravissant and Arielle, were introduced in the latter part of the 1950s. They were sheer, but not as transparent as earlier fabrics.[44]

The company also began expanding beyond the United States. In 1958, Vanity Fair formed an agreement with Wolsey Ltd. of Leicester, England; Wolsey would manufacture and sell women's lingerie of Vanity Fair styling, design and specification under the name of Wolsey-Vanity Fair.[45] A year later, the company entered a similar agreement with the Australian firm of E. Lucas & Company Ltd. Both companies reported enthusiastic response from buyers.

At the directors' meeting in April, Harold Miller, who had been with the company since 1919, asked that he not be considered for the vacant post of company president. Elections were held, and M.O. Lee became president.[46] Lee's leadership style was marked by his strong personality. "He was kind of a gruff guy," said Richard C. Lamm, who began in the Vanity Fair Mills mail room in 1944 and rose to become executive vice president of Lee. (Lamm was also named chief operating officer in October of 1988, and in September 1989, his title was changed to chairman of Lee). "You could get along with him, but his word was the law. ... When he said something, he meant it. He was the boss."[47]

Peter Velardi noted that Lee, whose childhood in rural Nebraska and minimal education were very different from Barbey's Yale-educated background, nonetheless "came out of the same school from the standpoint of leadership and dynamics."[48]

As the decade came to a close, officials had reason to look to the future with optimism. Sales were at an all-time high of $27.7 million and net profits were nearly $2 million. A new president was in place, and consumers remained eager to purchase high-quality Vanity Fair garments available at more than 3,000 stores across the country.

Ombré tones: new   delicate shadings of color by VANITY FAIR

First Orchid darkens richly against Blue Star, heralding fashion's new mauve decade. Gown of our nylon tricot, satin sashed, pinned with a Parisian leaf of paillettes. 10.95   Vanity Fair Mills, Inc., 640 Fifth Ave., N.Y.

Richard Avedon

Vanity Fair launched luscious new colors for the stylish sixties.

CHAPTER FIVE

SUCCESS AT HOME AND ABROAD

1960–1969

"The listing will not only broaden the financial base of the company and facilitate expansion, but it also will increase exposure of the firm's name to consumers."

— M.O. Lee, regarding the addition of VF
to the New York Stock Exchange[1]

LED BY A CHARISMATIC president and glamorous first lady, the nation began the sixties awash in the glow of youth and optimism. But by the end of the decade, John F. Kennedy would be assassinated, the first in a series of tragic losses that would devastate the nation. The civil rights movement would turn violent and the nation would divide over America's involvement in the war being waged in the far-off jungles of Vietnam.

The sixties were tumultuous for the country, but for Vanity Fair, the decade would herald a time of tremendous growth and stability. The company introduced foundation garments and leisure wear, and began a policy of strategic acquisitions with the purchase of two remarkable companies, hosiery manufacturer Berkshire International and blue jeans leader H.D. Lee Company.

Early in the decade, fashions continued to evolve, though not as quickly or dramatically as they would a few years later. Mainstream dress still mirrored the tailored look of the 1950s. Soon, many women emulated Jacqueline Kennedy, who wore pillbox hats, simple dresses and elegant designer suits in sherbet colors. But young people began emulating the style of such renowned "beat" writers as Jack Kerouac and Allen Ginsberg, wearing black turtlenecks, sandals, tight black pants and black berets.[2]

Foundations were necessary regardless of the fashions. The company, which had entered the foundation garment business in the late 1950s, posted record sales in 1960. By the end of the year, foundation garments were available in all of the company's sales territories.[3] The decision to enter the lucrative bra business was a milestone in the history of Vanity Fair Mills. The company also introduced new shades with names such as gardenia, honeysuckle beige, leghorn straw, dawn pink, fresh peach, moongreen, aquarelle and heaven blue. Full page color advertisements in national magazines and newspapers promoted the colors as "not only flattering as cosmetics, they are as fashion conscious as a cable from Paris. Each one has an indispensable place with the season's apparel picture."[4]

The Age of Lycra

Vanity Fair's pioneering use of fabrics once again made industry news when it converted its foundation garment business entirely to Lycra, the new synthetic elastic fiber created by DuPont.[5] At first, Vanity Fair used both Lycra

The Beauty Clasp foundation garment combined femininity with practicality.

Jackson Mayor W.W. Andrews breaks ground for the Clarke Mills expansion. The project, launched in September 1962, was part of VF's program to build a new plant or expand an existing one each year.

full-page ad in *The New York Times* similar to the one it had run when it converted fully to nylon in the 1940s. The ad explained that Lycra was finer, softer, more sheer, more durable, and more resistant to body oils, perspiration and detergents than rubber.

"We are convinced that the era of rubber in foundations has passed, the era of Lycra is here. Everything rubber, or any other elastic-type fiber, can do in girdles and bras, Lycra does much better," the ad announced.

"From this day forward we will use no rubber, no conventional elastic in Vanity Fair girdles and bras — not one inch. To our concept of 'fit, function, fashion and flattery' we now add 'in Lycra and only Lycra.' We believe it is inevitable that other manufacturers will follow our lead in concentrating on Lycra, just as other lingerie makers followed us in concentrating on nylon. But as in nylon lingerie, Vanity Fair will set the pace. The age of Lycra is here and we are ushering it in."[6]

and rubber in its foundation garments, but the use of rubber was halted entirely in early summer of 1961. In November, the company ran a

By the end of the year, all merchandise containing rubber had been liquidated.[7]

1961: Vanity Fair begins using Lycra and completely phases out the use of rubber in its manufacturing.

July 5, 1962: Vanity Fair forms its International Division to develop new foreign markets.

July 1962: The company opens a second mill in Monroeville.

July 25, 1966: Vanity Fair Mills is listed on the New York Stock Exchange.

Expansion in the South

Early orders for 1962 were substantially greater than those for the previous year, and company officials recognized the need to add manufacturing capacity. Sales for the year would reach record levels, growing by over 18 percent to $38.7 million.[8]

Most of the expansion took place in the South. In July 1962, a 5,000-square-foot plant opened on Drewery Road in Monroeville, Alabama. The new facility, the second in Monroeville, was used primarily for dyeing, finishing, and warehouse space.[9] It cost $476,200 to build, $192,200 of which was raised by the community.[10]

In August, the company announced it would construct its seventh Alabama facility in Robertsdale, Baldwin County. The 35,000-square-foot plant would be used for the production of lingerie and foundations.[11] The South Baldwin Industries Corporation was formed almost immediately to sell bonds to finance the $350,000 project. Although some residents balked at having to raise the money, in general the community responded with enthusiasm. The mayor of Robertsdale, J.D. "Josh" Sellers,

Many Monroeville residents, like these who took the tour in 1968, wanted to see the how the mills worked and how the clothes were produced.

reminded residents of the many benefits that Vanity Fair brings to a community. "All of us are indeed thankful that Vanity Fair has chosen Baldwin County as the site of its newest operations because this company is one of the finest

1968: The company develops a computer stock replenishment program, forerunner to its Market Response System.

April 1969: Vanity Fair Mills changes its name to VF Corporation.

January 1969: In its first acquisition, Vanity Fair buys Berkshire International Corporation for $13.2 million.

August 1969: VF acquires The H.D. Lee Company, a major jeans producer.

Visiting company officials and guests stayed at the Monroeville guest house, nestled among majestic trees. Golf pro Henry C. Poe and his gracious wife, Lillian, presided over the guest house.

and most public-spirited firms in the nation," he said.[12]

Hosting a Vanity Fair facility had become a status symbol for these small towns, all located within a fairly tight radius in the southwestern part of Alabama. In addition to employment and taxes, Vanity Fair provided company-funded improvements such as parks, golf courses and community centers. Failing to raise the money to lure such a generous company would have been considered disgraceful. "The question is not whether the bonds can be sold, but how fast can it be done? To fail is unthinkable. Baldwin couldn't stand such a black eye," Sellers said.[13]

The plant opened in April 1963 and was soon operating near capacity, with its 350 employees being trained as quickly as possible to handle the necessary jobs. Plans to expand the facility were announced in October. By that time, the company employed almost 5,000 workers in the southwestern part of Alabama, and was establishing a trend of building or enlarging a factory every year.[14]

In October 1964, Vanity Fair launched a $1 million program to expand the warehouse, sewing, dyehouse and finishing operations in the

Monroeville area. The expanded facilities would employ 500 additional people. Monroeville residents responded eagerly to a request from Vanity Fair President M.O. Lee to raise about $250,000 through the sale of bonds, and to improve the appearance of the town.

"If we are going to settle upon Monroeville as virtually the Southern headquarters of our company, we are vitally interested in seeing the city have a planned program of progress, cleanliness and beautification," Lee said during a Monroeville community meeting. "We want our business visitors and executive personnel as well, to be impressed by our choice."[15]

Vanity Fair staged something of a coup in 1966 when it hired Henry C. Poe away from a 26-year career as director of golf at the Reading Country Club to serve as director of the company's nine-hole golf courses in three of the Alabama towns where it had factories. Some Reading Country Club members resented Whitey Lee for luring Poe to Alabama.

The golf professional was popular not only at the country club, but in regional and national golf associations, and had been an integral part of the Reading community. In addition to being responsible for the community membership golf courses in the Alabama towns of Monroeville, Jackson and Atmore, Poe oversaw operation of a guest house in Monroeville that was used by visiting company personnel and guests. His wife, Lillian, an accomplished hostess, presided with him at guest house functions.[16]

Expansion on Other Fronts

While new factories were being built in the South, the company's international presence also expanded. On July 5, 1962, Vanity Fair Mills formed an International Division to develop new foreign markets and expand those already in place. Robert G. Derx was put in charge.[17]

Changes were also taking place in the North. In May 1963, directors agreed to sell the building on Gordon Street in Reading, which the company had occupied since 1913. Except for Vanity Fair's offices, most of the large factory building had been vacant since the company's migration south in the 1940s. The offices were moved to a new executive

It was a pivotal moment when Vanity Fair was listed on the New York Stock Exchange in 1966. Its symbol on the Big Board: VFM.

Inset: M.O. Lee, center, bought the first 100 shares issued on the New York Stock Exchange. They sold for $37 each.

office building in Wyomissing, a suburb of Reading, in early 1964. The Gordon Street building was sold for $150,000 to the Reading-based Ace Carton Company, Inc., and was later demolished.[18] On the national front, the sales office in New York City was nearly doubled in size and a new sales office was opened in San Francisco.[19]

Fashions were changing quickly during this period, and Vanity Fair added new items to adapt to current trends. Miniskirts, which became popular around 1963, called for slips that were shorter than any on the market. Culottes, otherwise known as split skirts, called for slips that would accommodate this new design.[20]

The company continued its record-breaking streak in 1964, with sales of $48.2 million, a 14 percent increase from the previous year. Net profits of $3.9 million had grown by more than 25 percent in a single year.[21] Perhaps more impressive was the way the company had grown in the previous decade. A financial overview revealed that sales had more than doubled since 1955, and net profits had tripled.[22]

In September 1965, Harold Miller retired as chairman of the board, but retained a seat on the board. His stepping down was accepted with regret, with the meeting minutes noting Miller's long and outstanding service. Miller, a 1917 graduate of the College of Civil Engineering of Cornell University, had worked for Vanity Fair since 1919. Two years later, when Miller ultimately retired as director, he was cited for 48 years of service to the company.

"His wealth of experience has been vast, and his devotion to the Company incomparable. It is

with sincere and deep regret that his associates view his retirement from the Company's Board of Directors, and thereby from his active association with them and with the Company. Their affection, respect, and best wishes go with him always."[23]

M.O. Lee was elected to replace Miller as chairman.[24] Under Lee's leadership, the company would embark on a series of acquisitions that would change both the direction and dimension of Vanity Fair. Lee revealed his intentions to shareholders later in the year, when he noted that the company was "looking into the possibility of acquisitions in suitable circumstances."[25]

The Big Board and Bigger Profits

In February 1966, the trustees of the J.E. Barbey Estate and Trusts announced they would offer 405,806 shares of common stock from Barbey's estate to the public. This was slightly less than half of the stock owned by the trustees, who owned approximately 50 percent of all outstanding shares. Officials hoped that selling the stock would qualify the company for listing on the New York Stock Exchange.[26] Lee submitted an application in May, and on July 25, 1966, Vanity Fair Mills was listed on the Big Board under the symbol VFM.[27]

Inclusion on the New York Stock Exchange placed Vanity Fair among the elite of the corporate community. "The listing will not only broaden the financial base of the company and facilitate expansion, but it also will increase exposure of the firm's name to consumers," Lee told *Women's Wear Daily.*[28]

In May 1966, the company updated its price structure, adding between $1 to $5 to the retail cost of more than 60 items. Some competitors were angered at the way the increase was implemented. Normally, a price increase by an industry leader like Vanity Fair would be a green light for other companies to raise their prices as well.

Adhering to its image of simple elegance, VF launched its Grecian gown design in the mid-1960s. Made of trademark nylon tricot, the nightgown sold for $8.95.

Vanity Fair officials, however, had released word of the increase only after its competitors had completed their catalogs, price lists and sales promotion materials for the coming season.[29]

"They have so much going for them as it is. Did they have to have this too?" one competitor asked in *Women's Wear Daily.*[30] In a subsequent article, Lee noted that the increase was necessary to maintain quality, and was not intended to cause problems for competitors. "You cannot maintain quality in the face of rising costs without raising prices," he said. "We're dedicated to maintaining quality, not price points."[31]

Bayou La Batre

Expansion in Alabama continued in 1966. The chosen community that year was Bayou La Batre, a small town in Mobile County, in the southernmost part of the state. Vanity Fair's announcement was made in conjunction with

the annual blessing of the shrimp fleet, a reenactment of an ancient rite in which fishermen and shrimpers seek divine guidance for the coming season.

Governor George C. Wallace was on hand to announce the planned $1 million factory. In a ceremony at the parking lot of the Bayou Ice Company, Wallace said that the Vanity Fair plants already located in Alabama were "outstanding additions to the community," and that Bayou La Batre was lucky to be considered as a site. Again, residents and businesses were asked to sell bonds to finance construction.[32]

While Vanity Fair was enjoying its many successes in Alabama, the state itself was wracked with difficulties as it clung to its old ways. When Wallace faced down the National Guard in an attempt to keep public schools from becoming integrated, he may have been a hero within the state, but much of the rest of the nation considered him a symbol of a segregated, racist past.

Local newspapers still had a separate "colored" section for people admitted to and discharged from hospitals, and hiring practices were blatantly discriminatory. Blacks were prohibited from holding certain jobs, including ones in law enforcement. In 1965, Dr. Martin Luther King called upon blacks to boycott all Easter merchandise produced in Alabama to protest these practices. Several large unions joined the boycott.[33]

M.O. Lee appears to have been sympathetic to what he called the "colored problem," and Vanity Fair routinely hired blacks. William Foulke, a Vanity Fair director from 1957 to 1983, recalled Lee expressing his views on discrimination to townspeople in Alabama.

"He was masterful. He said: 'Now we love you here. We love your town. You've been good to us, and we're going to stay if you let us obey the law but we're not going to break the law, and if you want us to break the law, just forget it. We'll close the plant.' And it worked!"[34]

In notes Lee made some years earlier, he wrote that during a trip to Florida he visited a Mr. Holland to "see what can be done for the Negroes." Because blacks were not permitted on public beaches or at public pools, there was talk of making a "Negro beach," a move Lee supported as a means of improving conditions for blacks.[35]

Loungewear and Hostess Gowns

By the second half of the decade, fashion had become truly outlandish. Just as the old rules of society seemed to be breaking down, the rules of fashion seemed to follow. Tie-dyed shirts, bare feet and faded jeans were the uniform for a generation of rebellious youngsters. Hemlines could be found at every length, from long sweeping prairie skirts to tiny mini skirts that were considered barely decent. Space exploration inspired outlandish space-age looks, complete with silver boots and helmets. Some dresses were even made of paper.[36]

Vanity Fair's designers and promotion staff worked closely with the fashion coordination department. Fashion experts in the coordination department spent much of their time traveling the country, attending designer fashion shows, shopping in popular stores and keeping track of what American women were wearing. Fashion was changing quickly, and these experts helped the company keep track of trends as they developed in different locations.[37]

The Famous Traveler line was targeted to "globetrotters and homelovers alike" and was offered in aquarelle, pink fire and honeysuckle beige, new colors VF introduced.

Much emphasis was placed on leisure time during this period, and Vanity Fair envisioned the perfect clothes to enhance it. The company in 1966 announced plans to add women's robes and loungewear to its product line, another decision that would provide long-term benefits. Long and short robes, both simple and elaborate, were touted as fashionable stay-at-home wear.

The first robes and loungewear were introduced to a receptive market in the fall of 1967. This new line showcased the company's ability to strike a balance between staple business and innovation. The robes and lingerie — representing innovation — would establish Vanity Fair as a fashion leader. The staple business stock of foundation garments and lingerie would insulate the company against drastic swings in the fashion market. Some underwear styles had remained virtually unchanged since 1941 and still were selling in volume.[38]

As the company worked to promote its garments to retailers and the public, advertising remained fundamental. The company began using a "theme concept," offering foundations, lingerie and loungewear each season in coordinated styles and colors. Vanity Fair designers were convinced that women would respond favorably to this color coordination. "It's habit-forming," Janet Chatfield-Taylor, fashion and promotion director, told *Women's Wear Daily.* "A woman who has enjoyed the sense of good grooming that color coordination from the skin out gives her will never go back only to neutrals in intimate apparel."[39]

Themes in 1968, for example, included "a Moon Flight" in spring and "The Collectables" in fall.[40] The Collectables package featured 27 colors with such ethereal names as Blue Chips, Fuji Drama, Hush Honey, Cafe Society and Rhapsody-in-Bloom. Most of the colors were carried through the entire product line of bras, girdles, panties, pettiskirts, chemises, pettilegs, slips, nightgowns in three lengths, matching robes, pajamas, bedjackets, scuffs and at home wear, and a line of loungewear popularly known as hostess gowns.

Getting the Fashions to the Customers

Vanity Fair in 1967 expanded its research and development efforts to make sure it offered top quality and value to customers. The research

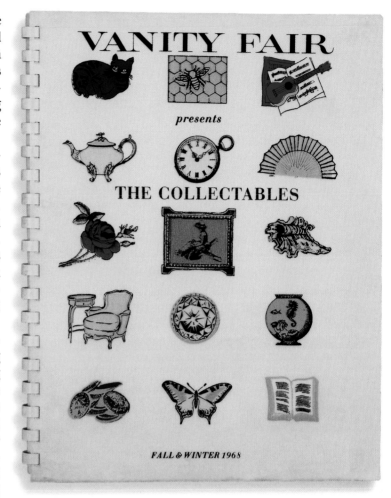

The Collectables line catalog for the late 1960s featured 27 colors carried through an entire lingerie line.

staff that year was credited with developing a completely automated machine that produced adjustable bra and slip straps in various lengths. It was also praised for inaugurating the novel practice of packing robes inside cartons on hangers, so they would be ready for display when they arrived in stores.[41]

The company also had a custom-designed warehousing system that reduced the time needed to assemble and ship orders and it offered retailers innovative options in receiving and paying for merchandise.[42]

Acutely aware that timely replenishment of goods was an integral part of giving the best possible service to the stores that sold its products, Vanity Fair developed an automatic, computer-controlled stock-replenishment program in 1968. Designed to enhance service — and sales — the program was based on the "Kimball ticket," the industry's standardized vendor-source marking system, but took the system several steps further. The Kimball ticket was a manual system used to track which styles were selling.

Using available information, Vanity Fair developed a procedure that permitted it to predict future sales based on past history and the current rate of sales. Not only did the basic stock replenishment system mean that retailers would no longer sit with empty shelves, but it gave Vanity Fair knowledge of how much of each product it would need to manufacture.[43]

John Jackson, who joined Vanity Fair in 1958 and retired in 1993 as vice president of operations of VF's Factory Outlet Division, helped create the system using an IBM computer that operated with punch cards. "It wasn't a fast process, but we figured it was a start and we knew eventually it would be a bar code or something else," he said. "We felt it was a good way to get started. We created an automatic reorder system for our key customers. ... The scary part was going into the holiday season on a smaller inventory amount, but it worked out pretty well."[44]

Larry Weidenheimer, who joined Vanity Fair in 1947 and retired as vice president for VF International Operations 40 years later, was also instrumental in the project. "We worked out the codes for the industry, and then we, as a manufacturer, put tickets on that retailers could use, and we got other companies in the lingerie business to use these tickets. So now a retailer could get information on a complete department from tickets that were supplied by a vendor."[45]

From this beginning, Vanity Fair devoted itself to using technology to meet the needs of its customers faster and more efficiently than its competitors. The system was the precursor to the sophisticated Market Response System the corporation employs today.

By 1968, Vanity Fair Mills operated nine plants in Alabama and Florida. All manufacturing processes — from knitting, dyeing and finishing cloth, to sewing, warehousing and shipping — were performed at the company's plants. The 60,000-square-foot facility in Milton, Florida, had come on line that year, and a pilot operation was established in Graceville, Florida. Even with the new facilities, all the mills remained within a 125-mile radius of Monroeville, where the company manufactured finished cloth and warehoused finished garments. The proximity of these facilities allowed finished cloth to be shipped quickly to cut-and-sew plants and finished garments to be easily transported to the central warehouse facilities.[46]

Acquiring Berkshire International

Vanity Fair's first acquisition was a major one. In January 1969, the company purchased the Reading-based Berkshire International Corporation, which at the time was the fifth-largest producer of hosiery in the nation, and at one time the largest hosiery manufac-

Retailers could choose from hundreds of swatches in dozens of patterns, most of them new to the market.

turer in the world. Vanity Fair paid $13.2 million for the company.[47] "I think it was probably one of the most significant moves we made because it showed the world that Vanity Fair had the financial ability to acquire other companies," said Peter Velardi, national sales manager for Vanity Fair Mills at the time.

"At the time, the urge to merge wasn't so prevalent. ... If you were a conglomerate, you had to be a real wheeler-dealer and that wasn't the reputation of Vanity Fair Mills ... It gave us two things. It gave us the basis to go out as a larger company and make further acquisitions. I don't think we could have purchased the Lee Company if we were just Vanity Fair alone. And the real estate that we acquired was tremendous because hosiery requires a lot of physical space to manufacture. The knitting machines are so large."[48]

That space later became the home of Vanity Fair's famous outlet facility in Wyomissing, Pennsylvania. Berkshire had a strong international operation, with 11 plants on five continents. Three plants were in the United States, two in Northern Ireland, and one each in Greece, South Africa, Colombia, Rhodesia, Japan and Spain.[49] With some of the Berkshire plants located only about a mile from the Vanity Fair executive offices in Reading, the companies teamed up to gain a major position in the hosiery industry, which at that time was growing more than 7 percent each year. Company officials expected that the ongoing development of new synthetic yarns,

Jeans represented everything American, from hard work to leisure. The H.D. Lee Company, which VF acquired at the end of the 1960s, dominated the jeans market.

the advent of pantyhose, and an increasing interest in hosiery as a fashion accessory would propel its new Berkshire division to even greater sales and profit in the coming years.[50]

The hosiery industry in general had enjoyed a renaissance during the 1960s when the first stretch nylon fibers had appeared. Stockings had until that point been manufactured in many different sizes and lengths because they did not have much capacity to stretch. Stretch nylon, however, made it possible to manufacture stockings in just three sizes that would fit 90 percent of the women who wore them.[51]

In the late 1960s, women discovered pantyhose and began purchasing them in earnest. Even though pantyhose cost twice as much as stockings, women preferred pantyhose under the short skirts and tight slacks that were fashionable at this time.[52] Berkshire, which had exclusive rights to manufacture hosiery under the Christian Dior label, filled niche markets with its manufacture of Engagement, pantyhose with a built-in panty girdle, and Naked Persuasion, a support panty hose as sheer as regular hose.[53]

Paul E. Guenther, Berkshire's president at the time of acquisition and for several months after, was replaced in 1969 by Alfred G. Hemmerich, who had joined Berkshire as an accounting clerk in 1951. Hemmerich had been named treasurer in 1958 and became executive vice president in 1967.

Vanity Fair Mills officially changed its name to VF Corporation in April 1969 to reflect its larger status.

Blue Jeans

Blue jeans, popular for decades, had always been more than merely articles of clothing. They were potent symbols of everything American. Somehow, blue jeans represented both hard work and leisure, rebellion and conformity. Faded and flared at the bottoms, blue jeans were practically the uniform of the sixties. On August 7, 1969, VF Corporation became part of this growing obsession when it purchased The H.D. Lee Company of Shawnee Mission, Kansas. The acquisition boosted Vanity Fair's employee roster to 14,500, with workers in 14 different states.

The H.D. Lee Company included a 10-year-old international division, which had made major inroads in the previous five years. Lee's sales of Western and casual wear in Europe alone had increased 400 percent during that time. [54]

Leonard W. Staples, who had joined Lee in 1928 and had been president since 1956, remained at the helm of the company. Under his leadership, Lee became one of the world's largest manufacturers of leisurewear.

It is difficult to imagine a decade of more dramatic growth than the 1960s were for VF Corporation. Operations had increased dramatically, both at home and overseas.

Lee, a name synonymous with jeans throughout the world, has its roots in the American Midwest.

CHAPTER SIX

A HISTORY OF LEE JEANS

1889–1997

"I don't think the president of Lee, Leonard W. Staples, felt he had the managerial horsepower to go ahead and grow the company as well as Vanity Fair could grow it."

— Harold McKemy, 1997[1]

LEE JEANS, OVERALLS AND coveralls have a long and romantic history, closely associated with such icons of American industry as railroad workers, loggers, cowboys, farmers and seamen. The Lee story begins in Vermont in 1849 with the birth of Henry David Lee. It is a tale of pioneers, entrepreneurs and invention in the name of necessity.

When Lee was 13 years old, his family moved west to Galion, Ohio. The young man got a job at a local hotel and managed to save nearly $1,200 in three years.[2] One of his responsibilities was to drive the hotel's livery team, noted E.H. Merrill, who joined H.D. Lee in 1910 and wrote about his employer and friend in a 1936 unpublished memoir. In those days, dry-good and clothing peddlers traveled by train, hiring local teams to transport them once they reached their territories. Drivers who knew the territory and could lend a hand selling products were great assets to these salesmen, and Lee soon became known as the best driver in the area. His knowledge, experience and polite demeanor made him an ideal salesman, and he was soon earning commissions based on the merchandise he sold.[3]

Lee invested his earnings in real estate and livery, and before long he was able to buy Central Oil Company, a wholesale distributor of kerosene, the main lighting oil at the time.[4]

An astute businessman, Lee was not as fortunate in his personal life. While still living in Galion, he married Emma Colborn. The marriage was soon annulled, and Lee remained single for the rest of his life.[5]

Unlucky in love, Lee also suffered health problems. He contracted tuberculosis while in Ohio and was advised by his doctors to slow his pace. In 1886, he sold half his interest in the oil company to John Rockefeller's Standard Oil Company, but continued to manage the business until 1888, when his health deteriorated further.[6] Believing a drier climate would improve his health, Lee moved to Salina, Kansas, and in 1889 established a wholesale grocery business, H.D. Lee Mercantile Company. It cost $100,000 to start up the company, with $25,000 reportedly contributed by the city of Salina, which was happy to attract such a promising enterprise.[7]

The company — the only one of its kind between Kansas City and Denver — expanded rapidly, and Lee saw tremendous opportunity for other business ventures. He founded three other companies in Salina: the H.D. Lee Flour Mills

Henry David Lee founded the H.D. Lee Mercantile Company, the basis of the modern Lee Jeans Company, in 1889.

Company, the Lee Hardware Company and Kansas Ice and Storage.[8]

The mercantile businesses continued to grow, and before long Lee had established himself as the dominant grocer in the Midwest. He expanded the grocery line to include school supplies, stationary furnishings and notions. He sold Lee brand coffee, prunes, kerosene lanterns and lamps, peppermint lozenges, green tea, mandarin oranges, cheese, waffle irons, matches, chili powder, paprika, cashews and stabilized wheat germ, marketed as Vit-A-Min Food.

Prosperity was interrupted on December 4, 1903, when the Lee Mercantile building and its stock were destroyed by fire. The loss was estimated at $575,000, of which $450,000 was stock.[9] Lee quickly had two larger, fireproof buildings built on the site and continued business. An October 4, 1908, account in the *Topeka Daily Capital* raved about the new buildings:

"It was then that Mr. Lee and his associates did the magnificent thing, erecting in place of the old four-story buildings two mammoth 6-story structures. ... This new plant easily outclasses anything of the kind in the United States — and to be right out in the very heart of bleeding Kansas within a commercial stone's throw of wonderful, marvelous, world-beating Kansas City; what do you think of that?"[10]

Lee soon found that he had a hard time keeping items in stock. Deliveries from the East were unreliable, and goods often were not available when customers wanted them. H.D. Lee decided that if he could not get the items he wanted, specifically work clothing, he would make them himself.

Union-Alls

Lee's first apparel plant opened in 1912 to produce overalls, jackets and dungarees.[11] The clothes were so popular that demand quickly outstripped production capacity. Lee's product innovation accounted for much of his success, and nothing exemplified this more than the 1913 introduction of the one-piece denim coverall known as the Lee Union-All.

Legend has it that H.D. Lee himself came up with the concept. According to the story, he saw that his chauffeur needed something to wear over his uniform when he was changing tires or repairing Lee's automobile. A coverall

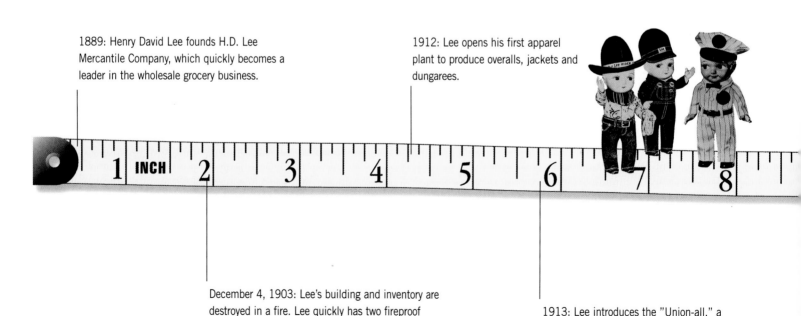

1889: Henry David Lee founds H.D. Lee Mercantile Company, which quickly becomes a leader in the wholesale grocery business.

1912: Lee opens his first apparel plant to produce overalls, jackets and dungarees.

December 4, 1903: Lee's building and inventory are destroyed in a fire. Lee quickly has two fireproof buildings constructed and continues business.

1913: Lee introduces the "Union-all," a coverall that united jacket with pants.

For good looks,
long wear,
real comfort, it's
Lee
Union-Alls

- BI-SWING BACK
- ZIPPER FRONT
- SAFETY POCKET
- EXCLUSIVE FABRICS
- PERFECT FIT FOR
  ANY BUILD
- SANFORIZED
  SIZES 00 TO 00
            $0.00

Mechanics, factory and farm workers adopted the Union-All, a one-piece denim coverup, as a convenient garment for work.

would protect the clothing of farmers and factory workers and prevent dirt and grime from lodging between clothing and skin. Lee asked employees to sew together a jacket and a pair of dungarees, creating the first Lee Union-All, so named because it was a union of jacket and trouser, much like the union suit underwear that was becoming popular at about the same time.[12] A one-piece suit cost about 20 percent less than trousers and jacket purchased separately.[13] Some believe, however, that Lee's chauffeur actually came up with the idea for the Union-Alls. If so, he never received credit for his invention. His only reward was the $5,000 Lee left him upon his death in 1928.[14]

Demand for Union-Alls became even greater during World War I, when the garment was adopted as the official doughboy fatigue. By the early 1920s, it was clear that the Lee Company was focusing on its growing garment business. Manufacturing plants were constructed in Minneapolis and Trenton, New Jersey, and warehouses were opened in San Francisco and Los Angeles.[15]

The Union Label

Between 1913 and 1916, factories were built in Kansas City, Kansas; Kansas City, Missouri; and South Bend, Indiana. The company unionized in 1916, when the Garment Workers of America asked it to manufacture goods under its union label. Since it already paid union-scale wages, the company was happy to have the label and began using its unionized status to appeal to consumers who were union members and wore Lee work clothing. The following year, the company's first national advertisement, in the *Saturday Evening Post*, promoted Lee as "the world's largest manufacturer of union-made workwear."[16] It later

1916: Lee plants are unionized.

1943: H.D. Lee Mercantile Company becomes the H.D. Lee Company, Inc.

March 15, 1928: H.D. Lee dies. His nephew, Leonard C. Staples, becomes president.

August 7, 1969: The VF Corporation acquires Lee.

used the slogan "every Lee garment union made ... union labeled."

In November 1949, the Lee Company was praised by *Business Week* magazine for its attitude toward labor unions and its unionized employees. The company provided pleasant working conditions and adequate pay and benefits. Retirement and pension plans were established in 1952, and picnics and Christmas parties were held every year. The Buddy Lee doll was a symbol of the good relations Lee enjoyed with union officials and members.[17]

First produced by Lee as a promotional gimmick in the 1920s, the doll became something of a union symbol, and was displayed at trade shows and union events. About 12 inches tall, the rosy-cheeked, chubby little doll first appeared in miniature Lee overalls. Soon, Buddy's popularity prompted the company to make Western and work clothing to fit the doll. By 1950, more than 700,000 Buddy Lee dolls had been produced, and today they are highly valued as collectors' items.[18]

The Depression and War Years

Product innovation continued. A long-wearing cowboy pant introduced in 1924 would eventually evolve into the famous Lee Rider. Pants were also designed especially for seamen and loggers. Other innovations intro-

Above: Every garment at Lee was "union made ... union labeled."

Left: Lee overalls promised perfect fit, even after 481 washes.

Right: The Buddy Lee doll symbolized the company's commitment to its workers.

duced during the twenties included jeans with zippers, work clothes with slide fasteners, the U-shaped saddle crotch, and "tailored sizing," which provided different lengths and rises for men of different proportions. In 1927, herringbone twills gave work clothing a new look.[19]

Despite his health problems, Lee lived to be 78 before dying of a heart attack on March 15, 1928. Leonard C. Staples, the husband of Lee's niece, became the company's second president.[20]

Production, sales and profits increased into the 1930s, when the Great Depression took its toll on the Lee Company. The setback was temporary, however, and growth resumed in 1936 when a Lee Riders plant opened in San Francisco. That year, the company developed Jelt denim, claiming it was the strongest denim ever produced. The material was so strong Lee used a "Ripley's Believe it or Not!" format for a 1930s ad campaign to stress the impressive durability of its denim.[21] When in 1939 the company celebrated its "Golden Jubi-Lee," it was the largest manufacturer of work clothes in the United States.[22]

Leonard C. Staples died in 1942 and was replaced by Roland B. Caywood. In 1943, the company's name was changed from the H.D. Lee Mercantile Company to the H.D. Lee Company, Inc.[23]

As it recovered from the Great Depression, America was again faced with war. Even before the United States joined World War II, factories were converted for wartime production, and women went to work in the factories. The whole country adjusted to the hardships of rationing and shortages.

Denim for civilian clothing was in short supply and the Lee company, which had converted its facilities to military production, was unable to meet civilian demand. In 1943, the company ran an advertisement in *Life* and other mag-

miles you drive, the very food on your table, the fuel to heat your home in winter. This is America at war!"[24]

The Western Market

When the war ended, Lee's growth accelerated again. Several workwear companies were acquired and, in 1949, Lady Lee Riders were introduced and promoted as the best fitting jeans on the market.[25] In 1950, the mercantile end of the Lee Company was sold for about $3 million to Chicago-based Consolidated Grocers, later Consolidated Foods. Throughout the fifties, Lee continued to acquire companies and build factories.[26] In 1952, Caywood died and Benjamin E. Kinney became Lee's fourth president. Together with Lee's chairman, C.A. Reynolds, who was founder of the Cowboy Hall of Fame and the Western Heritage Center, Kinney firmly established Lee's place in the western market.[27] Lee started producing leisure sportswear in 1954. The new line, called Leesures, was designed for weekend and casual wear and was advertised as "the new trim look for the Leesure hours." And, in 1957, Lee established itself as a player in the boyswear industry with its double knees jeans.[28]

The Lee Company introduced the Lee Westerner in 1959. It was a successful ploy to capitalize on Lee's western appeal and spread cowboy chic to mainstream America.[29]

The Lee Company advertised frequently in a great variety of publications. Westernwear was promoted in such magazines as *Hoof and Horns* and *Dude Rancher*, while Leesures and other men's clothing were advertised in

azines explaining that, due to military needs, civilian clothing was in short supply, but after that Great Day (of victory) Lee would resume civilian production at full tilt. Until that Great Day, consumers were encouraged to buy alternate Lee products if the ones they wanted were unavailable.

"You'll wake up one morning with the last belligerent Jap gone. The ghost of 'Heil Hitler' will no longer threaten slavery and death for free people. To hasten that day, you accepted rationing of the

Above left: Americans and American manufacturers rallied around the war effort.

Left: Lee used its Westernwear line to introduce the Western look to other regions.

Right: Expanding in the post-war boom, Lee introduced jeans for girls and women.

Playboy, Life and *Esquire.* Women's clothing was seen in *Ingenue, The New Yorker* and *Vogue,* while jeans for teenagers were advertised in *Boy's Life* and *Scholastic Roto.* Black consumers were targeted in *Ebony,* while work clothes appeared in *Farm Journal, American Farm Youth, Bricklayer, Mason and Plasterer,* and the *Coca-Cola Bottler.* Later ads would appear in *Professional Golfer, Seventeen, People* and many other publications.

Exports

As they have been since they were introduced, in the late 1950s blue jeans were popular throughout the world. Lee opened its International Division in New York in 1959 to handle a growing export business. The same year, the company was recognized with a Presidential citation for its outstanding export record. Five years later, its first overseas factory opened in Waas, Belgium, and the company received a second President's "E" Award for Excellence in Exporting.[30] By 1970, exports represented 12 percent of total sales, and the company was shipping to 81 foreign countries.[31]

In the 1960s, it seemed everyone was wearing denim. A postwar baby boom had created a notable increase in the teen population, and these youngsters had more disposable income than previous generations. Jeans were no longer just for work, but were worn by everybody from movie stars to housewives.

Lee struggled to keep up with demand. New plants were opened in Kansas, Louisiana, Missouri, Texas and Virginia. The company also kept up with

Above: Leesures and Lee Riders were targeted to young wearers.

Right: Leonard W. Staples accepted the President's "E" Award for Lee's outstanding export record.

changing fashions. In 1964, women's stretch denims and the Lee-Prest permanent press slack were introduced.

A few years later, the company introduced flared denim slacks, which proved immensely popular. The company's decision to produce more flares than straight-leg pants at this time was carefully thought out, based on careful study of the bell bottom trend. Lee officials would travel to cities throughout the nation and base their fashion predictions on personal observation of what people were wearing.[32]

Fashions of the Seventies

The stunning success of the Lee Company made it very attractive to corporate suitors during the late 1960s. Lee rejected a merger proposal from the Work Wear Corporation in 1967 and another from U.S. Industries in 1968.

At the end of the decade, however, the right match came along, and the VF Corporation acquired Lee on August 7, 1969. VF's additional capital allowed Lee to upgrade its manufacturing operations and expand its overseas production. Harold McKemy, who had been with Lee since 1957 and was treasurer at the time, said Lee's management and organization were not as sophisticated as VF's. "I don't think the president of Lee, Leonard W. Staples, felt he had the managerial horsepower to go ahead and grow the company as well as Vanity Fair could grow it," he said.[33]

Leonard W. Staples, president since 1956 and nephew of Leonard C. Staples, remained at the helm after the

merger and retired in 1971. Leonard C. Staples had been H.D. Lee's nephew by marriage. D.F. Hoopes, former executive vice president of the VF Corporation, took over. Hoopes was made president of the VF Corporation in 1974, at which time William McKenna became president of the Lee Company. The same year, it was announced that a new headquarters would be built in Merriam, Kansas, a suburb of Kansas City, Missouri.[34]

During the 1970s, the style revolution was in full swing, with adults as well as teens increasingly interested in wearing the latest fashions. The impact of changing styles was felt right in the Lee Company office, when women requested permission to wear pantsuits to work. A decision was finally made, and a memo addressed to "All Our Lovely Ladies" was issued November 3, 1970. The verdict: women could wear pantsuits, as long as they were neat, with tunic style jackets, vests or tops that coordinated with the slacks.

Slacks with blouses or sweaters were not permitted, and, while the jacket to a pantsuit could be removed while a woman was at her desk, it must be replaced before she left the desk to move about the office.[35] The following spring, women were told that culottes, shorts and hot pants were not considered appropriate work clothing and would not be tolerated in Lee offices.[36]

A 1974 advertisement in *Gentlemen's Quarterly* heralded the company's latest fashion statement, a lime green leisure suit made of 100 percent Dacron polyester double-knit. The outfit was advertised as western cut in every detail, "right down to the stylish flare." Lee's leisure suits, first introduced in 1972, were extremely popular for a short time, but disposing of excess invento-

ries became a major problem after fickle consumers tired of them.

Lee committed itself strongly to the women's market in 1973 when it launched the Ms. Lee label. The Youthwear division opened in 1979, giving the company the capacity to clothe every member of a family.[37]

The Eighties

The 1980s were extremely challenging years for the Lee Company. Total jeans sales peaked in the United States in 1981 at 502 million units, dropping to 417 million units by the end of 1987 and 385 million in 1990. Manufacturers, including Lee, felt the pinch. The company responded with characteristic aggressiveness, streamlining production, improving manufacturing and introducing new products such as stretch jeans, corduroy pants, big and tall menswear, clothing for infants and toddlers, and fuller-cut relaxed fit clothing for maturing baby boomers.[38] Lee also became a leader in the stonewashing phenomenon that swept the jeans industry, coming up with a great variety of finishes and looks for its products.[39] The problems persisted, and VF corporate officials undoubtedly had some sleepless nights trying to figure out how to fix what had broken at the Lee Company. During those years, the company saw several changes in leadership. Robert Gregory replaced McKenna as president in 1982, and Richard Redden took over a year later, when Gregory became corporate president. In 1984, Malcolm Winne was named president; William Crain took the job in 1986 when

Above left: D.F. Hoopes became president when Leonard W. Staples retired in 1971.

Above right: Lee Rider logo.

Center: Leisure suits, including this Western version, enjoyed a brief popularity in the early 1970s.

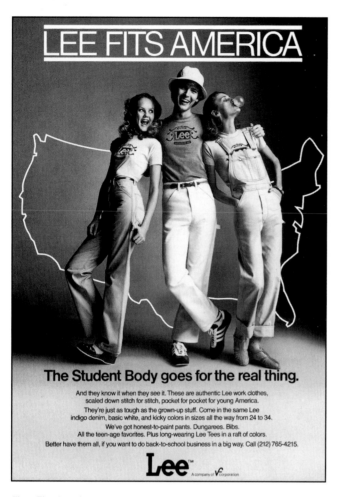

"Lee Fits America" campaign with styles of the 1980s.

Winne became chairman.[40] In 1988, Crain was replaced by a new chief operating officer, Richard C. Lamm.[41]

Company operations also were consolidated and five plants closed, but it was tighter fiscal controls that began to turn Lee around.

"The biggest problem was that they didn't understand costs," Lamm said later. "We had a standard cost system. They had a variable cost system and were very loose with their financial statements. I took my systems manager with me and we installed our system, and it made a world of difference. It really did."[42]

Despite the problems, VF was smart to buy Lee, Lamm said. "It was an excellent purchase. We went from number four in market share to number two while I was there."[43]

Lamm — who signed on as J.E. Barbey's station wagon driver and retired 45 years later as chairman of Lee — was a real-life Horatio Alger. He worked his way from driver, to office boy, to accountant and financial manager, earning a degree along the way from the prestigious Wharton School of Business. "It took me seven years to go through evening school, but I got my degree," he said later.[44]

Lamm retired in April 1990 after more than 45 years with the company. Frederick J. Rowan II was named president and chief executive officer.[45] Rowan soon was named a corporate group vice president, while retaining his duties at Lee. In March 1991, a reorganization of division responsibilities was announced at the corporate level, with Rowan to continue as president of Lee while assuming responsibility for several other divisions.[46]

Lee at this time was concentrating on its basic products, which were jeans and related items. It was, however, developing new finishes and styles, including the Baggy Rider and Easy Rider jeans for boys and the Elastic Rider and Relaxed Rider jeans for women.[47]

Rebounding in the Nineties

Lee's 1992 sales, spurred in part by a successful print and television advertising campaign aired for the first time during the Summer Olympics, increased 31 percent.[48] But Rowan had announced he would resign in May 1992 to take a job with the William Carter Company, a children's clothing manufacturer, and his resignation resulted in a reorganization of VF management.

Mackey McDonald, president of Wrangler and a group vice president, gave up the Wrangler presidency for expanded group vice president duties, including responsibility for Lee. Timothy A. Lambeth, president of Healthtex, who would eventually head VF's European and Asian division, was named president of Lee. Joseph Pacifico, vice president of Marketing at Lee, was named Lee's executive vice president.[49] Lambeth said in 1997:

"The biggest challenge we faced at Lee when I got there was that a fairly big chunk of

our sales (35 percent or so) were sold to discounters, Caldors, ShopCo, Venture, and so on. The only two discounters we didn't sell to were Kmart and Wal-Mart. Then we tried to sell to Sears, May, Federated and Penney's and frankly, it wasn't going very well. It doesn't work to have that many of your products at discounters and then try to sell them through the department store channel.[50]

VF executives decided to pull the Lee brand from discounters' shelves and replace it with Riders, a new brand.

Lambeth himself visited retailers to assure them the new product would be similar in quality to Lee jeans. "We may have lost some shelf space, but in the end we did sell every retailer that previously had Lee. We did put in Riders, and Riders was well on its way," he said. "The VF Corporation fared, I think, quite well with it."[51]

Lee's sales got an additional boost from the highly successful "The Brand that Fits" campaign, introduced during the 1993 Super Bowl. Lee, in fact, was named by *Advertising Age* magazine as one of American culture's top 200 super brands. The company again advertised during the Super Bowl in 1995, when it introduced its Authentic Clothing line.[52]

VF announced plans in 1994 for a joint venture with a Chinese company that would allow Lee jeans to be manufactured in China.[53] "We want to be ready for what we believe will be massive growth but it's probably five to seven years off," Lambeth said in a 1997 interview. "It's not going to happen as quickly as we had hoped."[54]

Lambeth became head of the VF Corporation's International Division on August 1, 1996, and Terry L. Lay, president of VF Jeanswear-Europe, took over as president of Lee. Early in 1997, Lee was made part of the corporation's new North and South American Jeanswear coalition, headed by John P. Schamberger. Lay remained president of Lee.

As part of a company-wide consolidation, VF Corporation officials announced in early 1997 they would eliminate more than 200 jobs — about half of the existing positions — at Lee's Merriam headquarters.

Lee employees — the company employs 10,400 worldwide and 8,600 in the United States — were saddened when the announcement was made, but not surprised. A woman who did not want to be identified but who said she has been a clerk in the company's financial department for 17 years, commented:

"All in all, this has been a very good company to work for. It's sad to see these jobs go, but I'd say overall they've been fair to us. This place is like a second home to me. I'm going to miss it here."[55]

Lee jeans — a fit for every body.

Vanity Fair lingerie sought to convey a look of simple elegance.

CHAPTER SEVEN

THE CORPORATE CONCEPT

1970–1979

"Our member companies are interrelated in the apparel field. They can, and do, contribute to and benefit from highly sophisticated management techniques and financial controls. As a result, we have been able to reduce costs, reduce inventories, increase our total corporate efficiency."

— M.O. Lee, 1971[1]

VF CORPORATION entered the seventies as three separate companies: Vanity Fair Mills, Inc., led by Charles Burg; Berkshire International Corporation, led by Alfred G. Hemmerich; and H.D. Lee Company, led by Leonard W. Staples. The challenge was to create an efficient corporation that still allowed the three organizations to operate autonomously.

VF embraced technology before many other companies, and a corporate-wide Management Information System (MIS) was installed in 1972. That improved inventory control and ordering. Advertising was coordinated in 1971, when VF hired Bozell & Jacobs, Inc., a New York City advertising agency, to direct advertising for the entire corporation. Until then, each division used its own agency. "While each company's advertising will have its individual personality, we want to project our overall VF philosophy of fashion and good taste," explained John R. Chalk, VF's director of Advertising.[2]

Specialized management activities — such as research and development, marketing, financial planning, international operations and management information techniques — were coordinated to benefit each company.[3]

The companies worked together, as with the 1970 introduction of Vanity Fair-brand hosiery.

The stockings were manufactured and marketed by Berkshire in colors that coordinated with Vanity Fair foundations and lingerie. Many stores that already carried Vanity Fair products accepted the stockings immediately.[4] The stockings were made from a new yarn called Curvare, developed by DuPont with assistance from Berkshire technicians. Curvare was more elastic than other yarns and retained its shape better. A new knitting technique called Double Graduation allowed the stockings to better follow the contours of the leg.[5]

Although there were some obvious synergies, the divisions still retained a great deal of autonomy, said Marilyn Bean, who joined VF in 1973.

"I looked at it as, we're the parent and they're the children. We just have to let them grow and do their things and make their mistakes and give them some guidance when they need it. When they need guidance we give it. I always keep in mind that if it weren't for the divisions, there wouldn't be a VF Corporation."[6]

The teen couple above were shown wearing Union-Alls, invented at the turn of the century but made "slimmer and trimmer" for the 1970s.

No Rules

It was a difficult period for the nation. U.S. troops had invaded Cambodia, and the fighting, viewed nightly in living rooms around the country, seriously divided the nation. Four student protesters were killed by National Guard troops at Kent State University in Ohio. Martin Luther King, Jr., and Robert F. Kennedy had been assassinated only two years earlier.

Fashion was in an uproar as well, leading *Vogue* to announce, "There are no rules in the fashion game now."[7] Hippies were still wearing headbands, beads and bell-bottoms. Short and tight, hot pants were in, sometimes paired with maxi coats for contrast. Feminists were turning their backs on traditional "feminine" fashions, while blacks and other minority groups celebrated their heritages by wearing ethnic clothing.[8]

At the same time, clothing was moving away from the exaggerated, flamboyant styles of the sixties. More women were working outside the home, and they needed working wardrobes of sensible business suits. The natural look was in, and models such as Cheryl Tiegs and Lauren Hutton radiated an athletic, clean-scrubbed quality. Concern about the environment led to a renewed interest in natural fibers.[9]

Vanity Fair, a VF division, continued to introduce new foundations to meet changing fashions. A line of shaping foundations, made of very lightweight fabric, was geared toward young buyers but became popular with women of all ages interested in the natural look. Slips were lengthened in anticipation of longer skirts, and new styles of panties, designed to be worn under pantsuits, were offered. The Tulip girdle collection, which had been available for several years, remained extremely popular.

After only three years in the loungewear business, Vanity Fair was already recognized as an industry leader. Tricopaque, an opaque nylon tricot suitable for wear at home or out in public, was introduced, and robes made from a light, velour-type material developed in Monroeville, remained extremely popular.[10]

Vanity Fair innovations for 1971 included bodysuits, "plus figure" foundations and Sunline swimwear, which featured bras and briefs sold separately. Women could buy the top and bottom in different sizes, assuring a better fit.[11] In 1973, the company introduced a slip that would not ride

1970: VF opens its first outlet store in space vacated by Berkshire International Corporation. The store was the first in a 50-outlet chain.

May 26, 1971: Rosalie Lee, wife of M.O. Lee, dies in plane crash.

May 1971: VF enters the knitwear arena by purchasing Kay Windsor, Inc.

1972: Ms. Lee Division is established to manufacture women's jeans and capitalize on the jeans craze.

up under the popular clingy knit fashions. Early in 1977, Vanity Fair Mills introduced a collection of terrycloth loungewear.[12]

Kay Windsor and the Promise of Knitwear

VF Corporation had targeted knitwear as a major growth area, and in May 1971, it invested in the future when it acquired Kay Windsor, Inc., manufacturer of five lines of women's sportswear and double-knit dresses.[13] Kay Windsor sold conservative clothes, believing that classic good taste would maximize profit potential while minimizing the hazard of fashion fads. It manufactured its own high-quality double-knit material.[14]

Explained M.O. Lee: "We see this growth in size and diversification as a stabilizing influence lessening vulnerability to change in an increasingly fashion-oriented world, as well as opening a diversity of new opportunities for growth and profit."[15] In the VF 1971 Annual Report, he noted that the companies could work together.

Shevelva was marketed as a low-maintenance alternative to velvet.

March 1972: VF builds central cutting facility in Monroeville to serve all its manufacturing plants.

October 25, 1976: Hoopes dies and Lee resumes duties as president.

February 19, 1974: M.O. Lee steps down as president and becomes chairman. Donald F. Hoopes is named to replace him.

April 1977: VF International Division established to centralize foreign operations.

"Our member companies are interrelated in the apparel field. They can, and do, contribute to and benefit from highly sophisticated management techniques and financial controls. As a result, we have been able to reduce costs, reduce inventories, increase our total corporate efficiency."[16]

In 1972, Kay Windsor opened two plants in Tennessee — a 55,000-square-foot cutting and sewing facility in Savannah, and a pilot plant in Hohenwald. Kay Windsor's sales increased 30 percent in 1973, with much of the success credited to the additional manufacturing capacity in Tennessee. In 1973, a 192,000-square-foot facility opened in North Dartmouth, Massachusetts, to house engineering and administrative departments as well as manufacturing facilities.[17]

Late in 1977, J.C. Penney Company agreed to sell clothing manufactured by Kay Windsor under the J.C. Penney name. Sales, however, were disappointing — the $317,000 profit realized in 1977 turned into a $195,000 loss in 1978.[18]

Strong Leadership

In October 1970, Lee accepted *Financial World*'s Bronze Oscar of Industry trophy in recognition of VF Corporation's annual report of the previous year, which was named the best in the industry. Lee attended the 26th Annual Report awards banquet in the ballroom of the New York Hilton & Towers and accepted the award before more than 1,200 business, industrial and financial leaders.[19]

This was the corporation's second major award of the year. It had also been honored on May 27 as a newcomer to *Fortune*'s list of the country's 500 largest industrial corporations. VF was ranked 431, a milestone celebrated during a dinner at the Four Seasons in New York City.[20]

The awards were a credit to M.O. Lee's leadership. "Everyone will tell you he has a very strong character," said Bill Pike, a former vice chairman of the Morgan Guaranty Trust Company of New York who was named a VF director in 1972.

"He was decisive and really a dominating kind of person. He dominated the company in every respect ... I would call him an intuitive manager. He didn't have the formal background one expects in a CEO today but he could talk to the people running the machines and they all thought that he could sit down at the machine and run it better than they could."[21]

William Foulke, who sat on the board of directors from 1957 until 1983, described Lee as a genius, but added that he had a "terrific temper." He credited Lee with keeping inventories low.[22]

Lee's secretary, Scotta Miller, said if Lee was not happy with an executive, he would call him into his office. "He wanted everybody to hear him give that person a good going-over," she said. "He'd leave the door open so everybody coming up and down the hall could hear everything he said."[23]

Vanessa Price, who joined VF's insurance area in 1977, described Lee as "very tall, very impressive, very gruff," and recalled that she found him more than a little intimidating.[24]

Personal Tragedy

While 1971 was a good year for VF Corporation, it was a disastrous one for M.O. Lee. Lee was an avid pilot and wanted his wife Rosalie to know how to fly in case he ever needed her assistance when they were in the air. At Lee's urging, Rosalie, his wife of more

Kay Windsor fashions — like this "dress of total charm" — targeted an upscale customer who had quiet, classic tastes.

than 40 years, took flying lessons. On May 26, she was practicing landings in a single-engine Piper Cherokee. At about 11:25 a.m., on her third solo flight of the morning, she crashed into an embankment at the Reading Municipal Airport. Rosalie was taken by ambulance to the Reading Hospital, where she was pronounced dead. Lee was summoned from his office and taken to the hospital to identify his wife's body.[25]

Lee continued on as normally as possible, but those who knew him well say he changed after the accident.

"As big a guy as he was to be chairman, he was an introvert," Miller said.[26]

VF's Reading outlet was its "flagship" and in 1997 was America's oldest outlet store still in operation. It was expanded and upgraded in 1993.

"His wife was his right arm. ... He used to depend on her. They would walk into a room and Mrs. Lee was the most wonderful woman. She was very outgoing and everybody loved her. She would be the one to make small talk so he didn't have to. He was never the same. He sort of blamed himself for insisting she learn how to fly."[27]

VF Outlet Philosophy

Lee's grief did not stop his train of ideas. In the early seventies, Berkshire's domestic operations decreased, leaving parts of the large factory buildings vacant. Some of this space was leased to industrial and commercial tenants, resulting in an early version of the current Wyomissing factory outlet complex, a major tourist attraction boasting such shops as Mikasa, Reebok, Tommy Hilfiger, Liz Claiborne, Godiva, American Tourister, Donna Karan and Panasonic.

VF's network of 50 outlet stores — which generate more than $400 million each year and give VF control over discontinued merchandise — grew from Lee's sudden inspiration. The resourceful leader decided to set up tables in some vacant factory space to sell off excess merchandise. With only word-of-mouth advertising, the sale was a tremendous success and the VF Factory Outlet was born.[28]

Expanding the Outlet Concept

In 1980, M.O. Lee's son, Frank, vice president of Public Relations for Vanity Fair Mills in Monroeville, Alabama, decided to open the corporation's second outlet store in some of the company's unused factory space in Monroeville. "They had been operating with merchandise thrown on tables and with pipe racks and a dropcloth," said Brad Bean, VF Factory Outlet vice president of Operations.[29]

"In 1980 they brought me in from Manufacturing to open the second outlet," said Bean, "We were going through some major changes, developed a new concept and opened several stores."[30] A third and fourth, in North Dartmouth, Massachusetts, and Boaz, Alabama, soon followed. The early bare bones look was much differ-

DARN YOU, KID ... THINK BIG!

WITH 50 MODERN stores located from Alabama to the State of Washington, VF factory outlets have come a long way from the original outlet sale in 1970.

It was M.O. Lee — then president of VF Corporation — who suggested holding a public sale one Saturday morning to clear out excess inventory of Berkshire International. That day, the merchandise completely sold out, even though the only advertising had been word of mouth. The store was so busy that even Lee bagged merchandise and manned the cash register. "You could see his mind working," said John Jackson, merchandise manager of Intimate Apparel at the time. "He was thinking he could make the store bigger. We just had a drop cloth on the back wall, and we kept moving it back."[1]

Pleased and surprised at the success of the sale, Lee scheduled a bigger one for two weeks later, with merchandise brought in from other VF sources. That sale was even more successful, and the VF outlet business was launched. Richard C. Lamm, who joined VF as a driver in 1944 and retired in 1990 as president and chief operating officer of Lee Jeans, recalled M.O. Lee's enthusiasm for the project.

"I'll never forget it. One day, M.O. Lee came over and said, 'We're going to start an outlet complex and I want you to tell me where we will put it, how much it will cost to get it started, and what kind of volume you'll do in the first year. I'm coming back at 3 o'clock and you better be ready.' So we crunched the numbers. ... He came over and we quoted him some conservative figures. He grabbed my shoulder and said, 'Darn you, young kid! I'm going to teach you to think big!' He took me to the building — the shop for all the full-fashion machines. Grease pits, lays, metal saws, just a greasy mess. He counted seven posts back and said, 'That's where we're going to put it. You've got three weeks to get it ready, because I have merchandise on the way in.' Man, did we scramble!"[2]

Selling Berkshire and Vanity Fair surplus products, the factory store was 5,000 square feet, with only a drop cloth separating it from the manufacturing facility.[3] VF Corporation — which opened the store in 1970 — was an early outlet operator, but not the first. Learbury Clothes is credited with opening the first outlet store in 1822, with Bates Mill Store following in 1950. About another 25 outlets had opened by the time VF hung out its 50-percent-off sign.[4] However, VF's Wyomissing outlet center is the nation's oldest still in operation.[5]

ent from today's well organized stores. Shoppers didn't seem to mind. A bargain was a bargain.

These first outlets, restricted to unused VF factory space, put the extra space to productive use by bringing in revenue. VF had previously sold overstocks to early discounters like Filene's Basement for pennies on the dollar whereas VF outlets recovered manufacturing costs. The outlets also allowed VF to retain control over its brand names, said Steve Lehmann, vice president of Administration. "The liquidators are going to do whatever they want with the merchandise. If they put big ads in the paper selling Lee jeans for four bucks, what does that do to your regular retail trade? It's better to keep it in-house."[31]

The outlets were placed under central management in 1983, and the next phase of VF's outlet development began. No longer restricting

![VF FACTORY OUTLET logo]

the outlets to unused factory space, the corporation started building factory outlets. A certain formula had to be followed, Bean said. The centers, which almost always included VF, Bannister shoes, Van Heusen and Prestige Fragrance and Cosmetics, could be located no closer than one hour from major markets. It wouldn't have been wise to compete with the retailers stocking VF-brand clothing in their stores. They also had to be near major highways, and easily accessible to shoppers. The formula worked, and by 1992 VF had 23 outlet store sites. When corporate officials took a hard look at its outlet business, however, they decided some changes were necessary.

"We had become developers," Bean said. "We were leasing space and doing too many extra things that required a lot of time and energy. That wasn't the business the corporation needed us to be in."[32]

The real estate interests in 21 of the 23 outlet centers were sold, but VF continued to operate

Above: The eye-catching outlet logo, as well as the bargains, attract about 10 million shoppers each year.

Below: VF opened its third outlet in North Dartmouth, Massachusetts, in what had been a Kay Windsor plant. The company sold its Kay Windsor Division in 1982.

its stores under lease agreements with the new owners.[33] Today, VF has 50 outlet stores in centers around the country, including the massive Sawgrass Mills in Florida, which offered generous incentives to lure VF. "We are rather unique because we're typically one of the largest footprints you'll find in any of these outlet malls," said Steve Fritz, who joined VF as a general auditor in 1984 and rose to VF Factory Outlet chief financial officer by 1996. "We have a wide variety of products and our prices are very aggressive."[34]

The Wyomissing outlet — still VF's largest — attracts about 10 million visitors a year, generating revenues in excess of $75 million, said Roger Eichlin, who retired in 1997 as assistant vice president for Risk and Real Estate Management. "This has been a gold mine," he said. "It has always been a great outlet center."[35]

The Wyomissing-based VF Factory Outlet was expanded and upgraded in 1993.[36] With tenants including Etienne Aigner, Perry Ellis, Eileen West, Jones New York and Finale, a new center, called Designers Place, was geared toward more

affluent shoppers than those previously profiled as outlet goers. Extensive studies showed that 51 percent of outlet shoppers were in the moderate income range, earning $35,000 or less, but that shoppers with higher incomes would patronize the outlets if the right mix of stores was there.[37]

The expansion project cost $4.4 million, converting the 73-year-old former Berkshire Knitting Mills factory into an upscale retail center. A central glass atrium was added, along with elevators and a central escalator. Display windows gave the outlet a retail feel, and skylights, recessed lighting and oak hardwood floors created a luxurious atmosphere.[38]

Valuable as the outlets are, VF never planned to make them a prime distribution channel. "If you look at companies like Phillips-Van Heusen,

---

While the outlet shops specialize in VF products, they also offer merchandise from Tommy Hilfiger, Reebok, American Tourister and other manufacturers.

The outlet stores, including VF's Tupelo, Mississippi, store, face stiff competition from discounters, but they continue to be a money-maker for the company.

they decided, 'Damn the torpedoes, full speed ahead, open up outlets'...what they quickly found is that if you have no retail distribution, your merchandise has little value at outlet prices," Bean said. "You have to have retail to establish the price/value equation."[39]

The outlet business has changed over the years, noted Fritz. "As the business has grown, nobody makes that much bad stuff. And the customer has changed. When these things started, they were dump-ins and whatever was there, people were willing to buy it, both blemished garments and things that were obviously three or four years out of date. Today, people want to find their size and color. So today, about half of what we sell are mistakes and half are goods that are planned."[40]

Five years after selling the outlet center real estate, VF officials are reassessing the situation. The outlet business has matured quickly, Bean explained, and the feeling is that customers are tiring of the fancy storefronts and not-so-discounted prices.

"The biggest challenge today is certainly the public. The outlets have gone through a metamorphosis — you can't differentiate between regular retail and outlet stores in terms of their look, presentation, fixtures or the type of mall they're in ... very upscale. Unfortunately, their prices are increasing. At the same time, retail is doing everything it can to be more competitive and is driving prices down. The customer isn't fooled. The problem is customers have a tendency to lump all outlet stores in a pack, so right now we're trying to differentiate ourselves, pull away from the pack, so the consumer will have a good reason to come back."[41]

VF Outlet officials are proposing to lease large buildings, such as vacant discount stores, and bring in about four other tenants to sell quality clothing at legitimate outlet retail prices. Such an outlet opened in 1997 in East Haven, Connecticut, in a former Kmart store. "If you think it sounds like what we used to do, you're right," Bean said. "We may have come full circle."[42]

The Corporate Concept in Alabama

To continue cost reductions through shared operations, VF announced in March 1972 that it would build a central cutting facility in Monroeville, Alabama, to serve all VF plants. The same year, the Jackson plant was expanded to hold 100 additional knitting machines, on which outerwear fabrics for Lee and Kay Windsor and double-knit fabrics for Vanity Fair's loungewear

would be produced.[43] That August, M.O. Lee and Alabama Governor George Wallace announced that the Lee Company would build three new plants in the northern Alabama communities of Huntsville, Russellville and Stevenson.

The announcement took place in the Spain Rehabilitation Center in Birmingham, where Wallace was recovering from the assassination attempt made while he was campaigning in Laurel, Maryland, on May 15. The news, along with pictures of Wallace and Lee, appeared in newspapers across the state. "VF Corporation has long been one of our finest corporate citizens," said Wallace. "With almost 9,000 employees, it is one of the state's top four industrial employers. The development of these three new locations could easily make VF the state's largest employer."[44]

VF had 22 plants scattered throughout Alabama, Georgia, Tennessee and Florida.

Left: George Wallace, seated, joined M.O. Lee and VF Mills Vice President Jake Neihuss, center, to announce the company's expansion plans. The man at right is not identified.

Below: The Monroeville central cutting facility served all VF plants.

Though labor costs were lower in the South than in the North, M.O. Lee was concerned that imports made it difficult for United States manufacturers to compete. The previous year, VF Corporation had started a "Buy American" campaign. Bumper stickers reading "Does the Label Say Made in USA?" were distributed to all of VF's employees in an effort to raise public awareness about foreign competition.[45]

As the company continued to build and expand in the South, M.O. Lee continued his "Buy American" effort. He explained his concern during the announcement with Wallace.

"I would be less than honest if I did not tell you that the odds are increasing daily against new plant locations in the United States. Manufacturers in Taiwan, Formosa, Indonesia and other offshore locations are sending 747s loaded with duty-free merchandise produced by labor at 10 or 15 cents per hour. The time is not around the corner. The time is already here that companies such as ours must face the necessity of building or buying plants offshore in order to compete. When that happens, happy events like this gathering will be a thing of the past."[46]

As the decade progressed, Vanity Fair foundations, lingerie and loungewear remained in high demand. Expansion plans announced in 1976 included a 60,000-square-foot sewing plant in Luverne, Alabama, a 30,000-square-foot sewing plant in Niceville, Florida, and an 80,000-square-foot addition for the central cutting plant in Monroeville.[47]

Trouble at Berkshire

At the start of the decade of the seventies, Berkshire International found itself struggling to compensate for industry-wide problems affecting hosiery manufacturers. Low-priced imports created new competition, and fluctuating skirt lengths made it difficult to predict which stockings would be in demand.[48] The popularity of pantyhose, which combined stockings and panties in one garment, also undermined stocking sales. Women who had started wearing pantyhose to accommodate their miniskirts found that they loved the comfort and practicality, and continued to wear pantyhose even with longer skirts. Then, because the fashion industry couldn't agree on skirt lengths, many women took the safe route and wore pants instead. One advantage of pantsuits

was that comfortable pantyhose could be worn beneath and didn't have to be replaced after a single rip or run. As long as the damage was not at the ankle or foot, who was to know? This was an economic advantage for women but not, unfortunately, for hosiery manufacturers.[49]

Berkshire was able to reduce prices by closing its Lebanon, Pennsylvania, plant and moving all production to Reading.[50] The introduction of knee-high stockings, which were popular with pantsuits wearers, and new patterns such as the tuxedo stripe, also helped to promote new business. It was at this time that Berkshire's employee store was expanded and opened to the public as Vanity Fair's first factory outlet.

To offset slumping hosiery sales, Berkshire teamed up with Vanity Fair Mills to produce bodysuits and the tights and pantyhose to match them.[51] The company also underwent extensive machine conversions, and in 1972 introduced a new type of pantyhose called Toe-to-Toe, which eliminated seams because the hose were knitted continuously. This innovative and popular concept was quickly copied by other manufacturers.[52]

By 1973, however, cotton and nylon were in short supply, and the cost of both was at record levels. Lee and Berkshire suffered most from the raw material shortages. Lee was forced to curtail some of its production of work and western wear, while Berkshire cut inventories by 35 percent.

Berkshire, buffeted by severe price competition and overcapacity, was in difficult straits. Because so much of its factory space was idle or vacant, the company formed the Berkshire Industrial Park and leased space to industrial and commercial tenants, joining the Vanity Fair/Berkshire outlet already in place. The company also divested its share of an unprofitable joint venture in Japan.

But Berkshire, which had been in business since 1906, refused to succumb. In 1973, it introduced a budget line of pantyhose called Eyecatchers. Although Eyecatchers competed for market share with pantyhose sold in supermarkets, Berkshire distributed its line of budget hose to specialty stores, where they were displayed on special modular display racks.[53]

Berkshire International's two Northern Ireland plants, which together employed about 1,000, remained profitable despite an influx of cheap imports from the Far East. New machinery was installed in the Irish plants in anticipation of increased demand and expanded opportunity within the enlarged European Economic Community.[54] Taking advantage of the corporate concept, the Berkshire Division in 1975 was pressed into service to produce men's shirt and stonewashed jeans for the Lee company. For the first time in five years, Berkshire turned a small profit.[55] However, in December 1976, VF sold its domestic Berkshire operation to the New York City-based Mayer-Beaton Corporation. The following year, the company sold its interest in Berkshire-Hellas to its Greek partner, and its interest in Berkshire de Colombia to its Colombian partner.[56]

During the 1970s, VF Vice Chairman Leonard W. Staples, right, and 23 other American manufacturers staged a trade mission to Japan. With him, from left, are Jack Peltier, vice president, International Division; Armin Meyer, U.S. ambassador to Japan, and Stanley Nehmer, deputy assistant secretary of Commerce.

The Blue Jean Revolution

Meanwhile, the Lee Company was performing better than ever. Once available only in blue denim, jeans were offered in stripes, patterns and a variety of contemporary colors. Lee made them with straight legs, flared legs and patch pockets. Practically the whole world by this time had embraced the jean look, including Eastern Europe and the Soviet Union. Anyone not wearing jeans was wearing double-knit slacks, also produced by Lee. In 1972, a Women's Leisure Division was established, marketing a line of clothing called Ms. Lee.[57] Terry Lay, president of Lee Apparel, would say in 1997:

"In the early seventies, Lee was pretty balanced across three categories: jeans, authentic work wear and sportswear. Plaids were all the rage at the time — I remember a lot of big, bold plaid slacks!"[58]

Jeans were no longer only for leisure hours or manual labor. The company began offering slacks, jackets and shirts suitable for business wear. Some major banks and other businesses had even commissioned Lee to make distinctive clothing for their white collar employees.[59] The growing popularity of Lee clothing called for expansion of facilities. Under the leadership of Donald Hoopes, who was promoted from executive vice president to president in 1971, plants were constructed in Florence, Alabama, and Trenton, Georgia. In 1971, Lee also established a new joint venture in Spain.[60]

In 1974, Lee began construction of a 152,000-square-foot plant and warehouse complex in North Bay, Ontario, and a headquarters building in Merriam, Kansas, a suburb of Kansas City.[61]

Three more plants were also constructed in Alabama: in Huntsville, Stevenson and Russellville. The Lee plants were located in the same state as other VF facilities to make it easy to share equipment and materials.[62]

Left: Lee overalls were among the products that made VF's Outlet Division so popular and profitable.

Below: Lee business clothes were designed to fit in at the office.

Prakash Bhatt, an engineer at Lee who rose to become vice president of manufacturing at Lee and is currently president of the VF Factory Outlet Division, recalled that the emphasis on manufacturing represented a real shift in philosophy. "From the mid-seventies to the mid-eighties, there was a lot of focus on making the process more efficient and cost-effective," he said. "Manufacturing was no longer just a cost of doing business. It was used as a competitive weapon."[63]

The Alabama towns in which VF Corporation plants were located were grateful for the financial boon provided by the factories. "Whitey" Lee, as he was affectionately known in Alabama, was honored October 25, 1973 by the Monroeville Chamber of Commerce. A banquet, attended by Governor Wallace, was given in Lee's honor, and the date proclaimed as Whitey Lee Day. Lee was praised for his efforts in locating factories in Monroeville, as well as his role in the Vanity Fair Foundation, which funded the park, community center, golf course, pool and other facilities.

"Though Mr. Lee is now a resident of Reading, and the plants which he heads are scattered throughout the world, we in Monroe County know that he continues to maintain a keen interest in our welfare," the banquet program read. "He remains one of us though his residence may have moved."[64]

While the Lee Company was providing jobs in Alabama, it was also expanding abroad. The company already had plants in Canada, Scotland and Belgium that produced goods for overseas distribution, as well as joint ventures and licensing agreements in 13 countries.[65] In 1974, joint ventures were established in Hong Kong and Brazil, and the following year manufacturing capacity in Spain was increased. The company also established licensing operations for the Caribbean Free Trade Area and Chile and became a direct sales force in major Common Market countries.

"When I came to Lee in 1971, it wasn't by any means a certainty that jeans were going to be the core product, but in the late 1970s, VF and Lee made a real investment in the jeanswear business," Terry Lay said. "That positioned us to really grow the category significantly."[66]

By 1979, Lee reported sales of $382.3 million, up $62 million from the previous year. Earnings

M.O. Lee became president and chairman of the board in late 1976. (Photo courtesy of Fabian Bachrach)

increased more than $8 million, to $30 million. The company's earnings had more than doubled since 1976, when they were reported at $14.9 million.[67] While noting how far the Lee Company had come, M.O. Lee said the credit must be given to VF Corporation. "They were a third-rate basement resource at the time," he said in a typically blunt statement. "We put them into Macy's."[68]

Lee was fond of art and eager to help local artists. It was his practice to buy the works of those artists and display them in corporate headquarters. Price tags would be left on the paintings so that employees and visitors could buy the works at the same price the corporation had paid.[69] In 1976, John Chalk, the corporation's advertising director and a former professional artist, had sculpted a life-sized rodeo cowboy, with detailed features that included spinning spurs. M.O. Lee reportedly was thrilled with the bronze sculpture. After it was displayed for a time at corporate headquarters in

Wyomissing, it was shipped to the new Lee head-quarters, where it has remained.[70]

The Corporate Concept Pays Off

On February 19, 1974, M.O. Lee left the presidency of VF Corporation to become chairman of the board. Lee recommended that Donald F. Hoopes, president of the Lee Company, be named to replace him. Hoopes, who had been with VF Corporation for more than 27 years, was elected president, and William J. McKenna became president of Lee. Lori M. Tarnoski became the first female corporate officer when she was named assistant corporate secretary in 1973. Tarnoski rose to corporate secretary in 1974 and was named vice president and corporate secretary in 1979.[71]

Despite the recession, VF sales increased nearly 13 percent in 1974.[72] Lee credited the corporate concept for the outstanding results, saying the strategy of diversifying product lines while maintaining high quality and increased efficiency had paid off. "We are gratified that it was possible to achieve these gains in spite of a very difficult business climate, particularly in the apparel industry," he said.[73]

Sales and profits again hit record levels in 1975, with sales of $396 million and net profits of $26.5 million. The feat was even more impressive considering unemployment had risen to 8.9 percent nationwide.[74]

On October 25, 1976, Hoopes, who effectively had retired in July due to ill health, died. M.O. Lee assumed the duties of president in addition to those of chairman of the board. The same year, the corporation's record-setting streak was broken, following its first downturn in profits. VF officials attributed the decline to several factors, including an oversupply of leisure suits manufactured by the Lee Company. Despite the demise of the leisure suit, the demand for Lee-manufactured clothing, particularly corduroy and denim-based designs, remained strong.

However, VF's foreign subsidiaries experienced their best year ever, contributing nearly 25 percent of total corporate sales. Demand for exports from the United States was also on the rise, and VF was enjoying increased sales volume from its unconsolidated joint venture operations in Greece, Spain, South Africa, Columbia, Brazil, Hong Kong and Australia.[75]

In April 1977, the VF Corporation International Division was established. The division, headed by Jack G. Peltier, a native of France who had joined the Lee Company as export manager in 1959, was designated to centralize the foreign operations of Lee, Vanity Fair and Kay Windsor.[76] A new distribution center and manufacturing facility was established in the United Kingdom.[77]

By 1977, the downward trend was reversed, with revenues increasing by $2 million to $470 million and profits jumping almost $7 million to $28 million.[78] That year, Gordon W. Heaton was named president and principal operating officer. Lee became chairman and chief executive officer. Robert H. Andrews, executive vice president, was elected vice chairman of the board.

Janet J. Peters and Gordon X. Reed were named vice presidents. Peters, who had joined the

Fantasy in Sapphire and Jade. Brilliant contrasts of color and texture, gorgeously entertaining anywhere. The quilt-jacket and skirt are velvety Dacron® polyester. The camisole, pure Glisanda® satin. Have it all in sizes 6 to 14, for about $125. Vanity Fair Mills, Inc., 640 Fifth Ave., New York

VANITY FAIR A company of VF corporation

Vanity Fair encouraged women to color-coordinate from the skin out.

company in 1951 as a fit model and had been vice president of Vanity Fair Mills, became the first female vice president of VF Corporation. She was commended for her work as director of Vanity Fair's private label business, which had seen significant gains in the past several years.

Once VF made the decision to create private labels, they launched "quite a number," Peters said in a 1996 interview. The garments were also targeted to different consumer groups. "For instance, Vanity Fair private label works differently from Vassarette," Peters explained. While Vassarette was channeled to discount stores like Kmart and Wal-Mart, VF private label goods were sold through department or specialty stores like Victoria's Secret and J.C. Penney.[79]

Technical improvements bolstered the new marketing strategy. By 1978, 90 percent of Vanity Fair's products were cut by computer-directed machines that increased productivity while decreasing fabric waste. The machines were so successful that the corporation ordered more for Lee's domestic and foreign plants and Kay Windsor factories.[80]

Late in 1978, M.O. Lee responded to a letter from President Jimmy Carter, asking the corporation to comply with his voluntary program of wage and price guidelines. The nation was still struggling to reduce inflation and unemployment, and the guidelines would limit price increases. Lee's response, which somehow made its way to *The New York Times*, called on government to reduce the level of federal deficit spending. "Government must do its part if it expects business to," Lee wrote. "Cut back, and bring your costs in line with your income."[81]

Just the thing for a brisk autumn day: casual corduroy.

The corporation's growth continued in 1979, despite the double-digit inflation that plagued the national economy. Record sales and earnings were accompanied by some major changes within the corporation. Heaton resigned as president and principal operating officer in October. He would be replaced the following February by Lawrence R. Pugh, a newcomer to VF Corporation. M.O. Lee filled in as interim president before Pugh came on board.

A graduate and trustee of Colby College in Waterville, Maine, Pugh had worked in the Milk and Ice Cream Division of dairy giant Borden and then served as a product manager in Hamilton Beach's small appliance business. He started as director of merchandising and planning for Samsonite, a subsidiary of Beatrice Foods, and served as president for six years. Pugh, who also filled Heaton's unexpired term on the VF board, moved with his family from Golden, Colorado, to Berks County.

It was almost a coincidence that Pugh came to VF Corporation at all. Then chief of Samsonite's luggage division, he was in New York City and, at his mother's suggestion, stopped to visit a cousin who was an executive recruiter.

"I hadn't seen Russell in a while," he said in a 1996 interview.[82] "We talked for a couple of hours about our families and so on, and then I went back to my hotel. There was a message to call Russell. He said, 'Larry, I know you're not looking for a job, but let me talk to you about this particular position.' It was to be president of VF Corporation in Wyomissing, Pennsylvania. I had never heard of Wyomissing and I had never heard of VF Corporation."[83]

Nevertheless, it was an excellent fit. "They weren't looking for someone from the apparel industry — they wanted someone who had general management experience and a background in marketing and sales," Pugh said.[84]

"My first impression, and it was confirmed, was that this is an exceptionally well-run company," Pugh said. "It has terrific brand names and a very strong balance sheet. When I came here, the CEO was a manufacturer himself, which was great from a quality standpoint. But times change, and we tried to balance the company to marketing, finance and manufacturing as opposed to just manufacturing."[85]

Lee and Pugh had different management styles, recalled Mike Martin, VF manager of Corporate Real Estate.

"M.O. Lee and Robert Andrews ran the company more as a family. It was not uncommon for people to get together on a Friday night and go out someplace, and for Mr. Lee to come by and drop $100 or $200 on the table and tell us all to have a good time. And that changed. Mr. Pugh was from a large corporation that was more in tune with the times, and he shaped the company into a more international and more businesslike climate. I think that probably took some of the fun away from the corporation's image, but it did make the company stronger."[86]

It might have also made corporate travel safer. When the company thought of itself as a family business, passengers were sometimes called on to help the pilot during the flight. "The corporation started out with one pilot and sometimes they would ask you to come up and fly co-pilot and check for other aircraft," Martin said in a 1997 interview.

"Once we were coming back from New York City in a sleet and rain storm and the pilot handed me a flashlight and asked me to check the wings for ice. Everybody was willing to help out and do whatever was necessary."[87]

Corporate flying became more sophisticated, if less exciting, as VF grew. "There are always two pilots now," Martin said. "The planes are more expensive and the technology is pretty good in those things."[88]

Robert L. Connors and Robert E. Gregory, Jr. joined the company as vice presidents, and John G. Johnson joined as executive vice president of the International Division. Connors, Gregory and Johnson were all newcomers to VF, a notable change for a corporation that traditionally had promoted from within to fill upper management positions. Lori M. Tarnoski, corporate secretary, was named vice president and secretary, joining Janet Peters as pioneering women executives at VF.[89]

Conditions at the end of the decade of the seventies were still difficult for American business and industry. The federal government had just promised to bail the Chrysler Corporation out with a $1.5 billion loan-guarantee plan, inflation was still high and spending was still low.

While VF officials were concerned about the nation's economy, they were confident the corporation was well prepared for continued growth in the 1980s.

Capital improvements, including high-tech Gerber cutting machines that wasted less fabric, powered VF through the 1980s.

CHAPTER EIGHT

CHANGING LEADERSHIP
1980–1988

"When Mr. Pugh came in and started running the business, things began to change for the better. Mr. Lee was mostly operations and Mr. Pugh was marketing. He started changing the way we do everything, the whole business. We started doing more advertising and promoting the brands."

– Marilyn Bean, 1996[1]

VF CORPORATION enjoyed record revenues in the early eighties, fueled by the extraordinary success of the Lee Division. Sales of the popular jeans accounted for 80 percent of VF's revenues in some years. The company's stringent inventory control and use of the most up-to-date technologies boosted earnings to new levels. In the first five years of the decade, VF acquired three additional clothing manufacturers. The first half of the decade was also marred by the death of long-time leader M.O. Lee. Lawrence R. Pugh, recruited from outside the company, would become VF's new leader.

As the "me" decade of the seventies turned into the "greed" decade of the eighties, flamboyant colors and styles settled into more restrained, muted fashions. The designer wardrobes of Ronald and Nancy Reagan caught the attention of the American public, especially as they contrasted with the more casual looks of Jimmy and Rosalyn Carter. Mrs. Reagan favored expensive couture clothes from old line designers such as Adolfo, Galanos and Bill Blass. Her style was especially popular with young urban professionals, known as Yuppies, who had money and were not afraid to show it by flaunting designer labels. The interlocking C's of the house of Chanel were often seen, as were Gucci's interlocking G's.

As the baby boomers aged and the teen population decreased, the youth culture no longer dictated fashion the way it had in the 1960s and 1970s. Another popular trend was the preppy look, consisting of clothing and accessories that were conformist yet unmistakably expensive. Vice President George Bush — a product of the country's prep schools and Yale University — was the administration's avatar of preppiness. He often was seen sporting preppy wardrobe staples: khakis, Izod shirts, Brooks Brothers suits and Bass Weejun shoes.

Increased Efficiency

M.O. Lee, who started the decade as chairman, chief executive officer and interim president, fought inefficiency with the same vigor he would fight cancer. A $50 million capital improvement program was launched to modernize plants worldwide; sophisticated, computerized equipment was brought on line and personnel honed their skills to better track and control all aspects of manufacturing.[2] High-precision cutting machines, known as the Gerber-Hughes

Despite a recession that clouded the early 1980s, VF retained its hold on the lingerie market by producing simple, classic styles.

system, were installed in VF plants worldwide, resulting in more accurately cut fabric with less waste. "[Chairman M.O. Lee] thought it would allow workers to cut faster and be less labor intensive," said Bill Pike, a member of the board of directors since 1972. "As it turned out, it was a brilliant decision because of something that nobody thought of — you got identical pieces, which made the sewing machine operators much more efficient."[3] Other machinery, such as automatic pocket setters and belt loopers, assured quality control.

Capital improvements were an important element of the strategy. In 1982, the corporation doubled its capital investments, spending $33.6 million on plants and equipment. The Lee Company alone added six plants in 1982 and early 1983.[4] A sewing plant was built in Boaz, Alabama, another sewing plant was acquired in Altoona, Alabama, and a facility was acquired in Fayetteville, Tennessee, to be used as a sewing and finishing plant and a distribution center.

Improvements in inventory control led to enhanced customer service and an improved bottom line. The importance of managing inventories

had been reinforced by the leisure suit overstock of the previous decade.

Losing a Legend

M.O. "Whitey" Lee lost his battle with cancer and died on March 5, 1982. His secretary, Scotta Miller, recalled how Lee refused to allow the disease to interfere with his leadership of VF. "He was the stubbornest man you'd ever want to see," she said. "He was taking chemotherapy and it would make him terribly sick, but he wouldn't stay home. He'd come to work and be sick in his office. In fact, he presided over a board meeting on February 16, a little more than two weeks before his death.[5]

"He went to Roosevelt Hospital in New York. He wouldn't go to Reading Hospital because he didn't want anybody to know he was having an operation. And he said to me, 'If you tell anybody where I am, I'll slit your throat.' He'd call me every day for the mail and to find out what was going on. I sent flowers, but I called one of his daughters in New York and had her send them. I wouldn't send them from here because the florist

1980: M.O. Lee embarks on a $50 million capital improvements program to modernize VF plants.

1982: VF spends $33.6 million to build new plants and continue modernization of existing facilities.

February 19, 1980: Lawrence Pugh joins VF as president and chief operating officer.

March 5, 1982: M.O. Lee dies of cancer. Pugh becomes chief executive officer in addition to president.

would know who they were for. Everybody in town knew Whitey Lee. Then he said, 'I'm laying in the hospital bed and not one single soul has sent me a card and the only flowers I got were from you and my daughters.' I said, 'What did you expect? You told me you'd slit my throat, so nobody knows you're there.'"[6]

A member of Sacred Heart Roman Catholic Church in West Reading, Lee was survived by four children: a son, William Frank, who worked for Vanity Fair in Monroeville, Alabama, and was later killed in a recreational vehicle accident; John Manford, who lived in Colorado; Regina Ann Lee, who lived in New York City; and Sylvia Parker, who lived in Baltimore, Maryland.

Marilyn Bean, a long-time employee, said everyone knew Lee was ill, but understood that he didn't want his illness to be an issue. "He'd lost a lot of weight, and you could see he had difficulty walking. He had a regular route he would take around the office, stopping to say hello to people and checking on things. He kept that up, but he lost the lively step he always had."[7]

That year, the annual report contained a special tribute to Lee, praising his strong leadership, compassion and warmth. It noted that Lee's business philosophy was to do every job right, on time, and to maintain hands-on control over every phase of operations.

"He was a man of strong character with an unparalleled reputation for honesty and integrity. 'Whitey,' as he was known to his friends, also had a great compassion for his people. He was, moreover, a fine teacher, not only of the business and its philosophy, but of every aspect of life."[8]

Since 1980, Lee had twice been recognized as one of three outstanding chief executive officers in the apparel industry. *Financial World*, one of the nation's leading investment publications, accorded him the honor in March 1980,[9] and the *Wall Street Transcript*, an investment publication, also honored him the following year, noting VF's outstanding return on investment.[10]

Lee never forgot that he had started as a factory supervisor and he maintained a great bond with the company's workers. Even late in his career, he was known to visit the factories, roll up his sleeves and help out on the floor. "He was very comfortable with the guys down at the outlet and the maintenance guys," Miller said. "He'd stop in every morning and have coffee with them."[11]

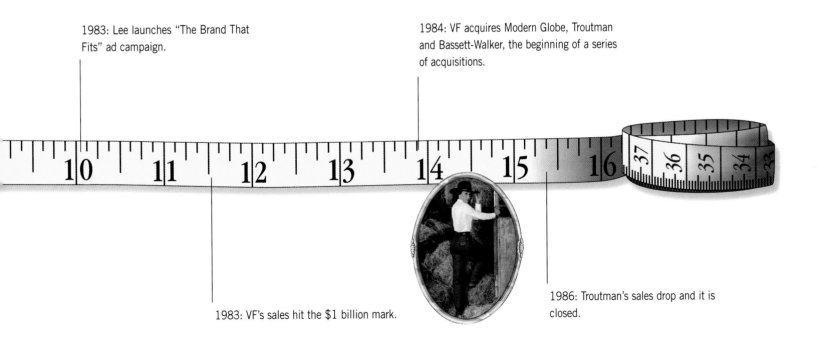

1983: Lee launches "The Brand That Fits" ad campaign.

1984: VF acquires Modern Globe, Troutman and Bassett-Walker, the beginning of a series of acquisitions.

1983: VF's sales hit the $1 billion mark.

1986: Troutman's sales drop and it is closed.

"On Saturdays I often go down to our factory and help out by driving a truck," Lee said in a 1972 interview. "I won't surround myself with a lot of front people. Most executives put themselves behind a big desk — a throne — and hide. They lose touch with reality, their own associates, the employees, the men who made them. I respect the right for a man to get in touch with me. I answer my own phone."[12]

Louis Fecile, who joined VF as assistant to the treasurer in 1980 and rose to become vice president of Employee Benefits, remembered Lee as "this huge bear of a man."

"He really wasn't that big, but he had a booming voice. He came across as being the toughest, hardest guy with the biggest heart, only his bark scared most people off. I must have been here only about three or four months when I walked

M.O. "Whitey" Lee, left, who began as a factory supervisor, was renowned for his hands-on management style. His death in 1982 was widely mourned.

down the hallway to get a cup of coffee. I walked by the executive area, and he was just hollering about inventories or something getting out of control. He cleared out every office and sent us all to the conference room, where he gave us a lecture. He was incredible."[13]

VF's directors held a special meeting at the corporation's New York headquarters four days after Lee's death. They observed a minute of silent prayer and then adopted a resolution honoring Lee. The resolution was to serve as "a lasting memorial to a great leader and a true friend."[14]

Lawrence Pugh

The board elected Robert H. Andrews chairman and Pugh president and chief executive officer.[15] At the end of 1982, when Andrews was 70, he resigned as an employee of the company and when his term as chairman expired in May 1983, Pugh filled the post. John Cline, executive vice president, was expected to assume the duties of president and Robert Gregory was slated to become executive vice president, while remaining president of the Lee Company.[16]

The thoughtfully planned transition of officers, however, was disrupted when Cline, 58, died of lung cancer April 8, 1983. Cline had joined VF in 1960 and served as assistant treasurer, assistant secretary, controller, vice president and a member of the board of directors. A North Carolina native, he was a graduate of the University of North Carolina and an Army Air Corps veteran of World War II. He was married, with two daughters and a son.[17] Those who worked with Cline said his death was a shock and came not long after Cline learned he was ill.

Instead of Cline, Gregory, who had been with VF since 1979, became VF Corporation president and principal operating officer. F. Richard Redden, formerly one of Lee's vice presidents, replaced Gregory as president of the Lee Company. In addition, Peter Velardi was named president of Vanity Fair Mills, a promotion from executive vice president, replacing Enoch Harding, Jr.

Velardi, who retired in 1994 after 44 years with VF, began as an office boy with Vanity Fair Mills' New York office. He applied "back in 1949, right out of high school," he said in a 1997 interview. "I was fortunate that my mother made me wear a tie that day, and I was lucky enough to get the $30 a week job."[18] He would eventually rise to chairman and chief executive office of Vanity Fair Mills, picking up a degree from New York University.

"Fortunately, NYU was a very good place for me to attend. Working for Vanity Fair afforded me the opportunity to argue with my professors. I was doing things during the day, and they were giving me theory at night that was sometimes outdated. So it was kind of fun, and a good experience to be working for Vanity Fair then."[19]

The transition from Lee to Pugh was one of the defining moments in VF history. Marilyn Bean, who worked as a secretary for John Cline, Robert Gregory and then for Pugh, said Pugh's management style was very different from Lee's. "When Mr. Pugh came in and started running the business, things began to change for the better," she said. "Mr. Lee was mostly operations and Mr. Pugh was marketing. He started changing the way we do everything, the whole business. We started doing more advertising and promoting. He told the divisions what he wanted and things happened."[20]

Pugh agreed that he emphasized marketing more than Lee did. "He had terrific intuitive strength, he was a superb manufacturing person, set very high standards, but in my judgment times had changed and we had to approach it in a different manner. We became active in the market and much more aggressive."[21]

Pugh also improved the value of VF stock by promoting the company to Wall Street, Velardi said.

"Mr. Lee was a doer and a genius, but frankly, he didn't give a damn what the brokers thought. He talked to them, but he could not articulate what they wanted to hear. The stock was always undervalued relative to the performance under Mr. Lee because he was not interested in the price of the stock. He was interested in building an empire. ... Mr. Pugh had a much greater ability to work with Wall Street analysts."[22]

Pugh saw that consumers did not connect the various VF brand names with the corporation behind them all because each division was responsible for its own advertising. He decided to change that.

"Fortunately, the financial institutions

Lawrence Pugh became president and CEO after Lee's death. Big changes were ahead.

know who VF is, and that is reflected in the performance of our stock, which we are very pleased with," Pugh told the *Reading Eagle* in 1986. "But a number of people do not know what VF is all about. So we started an advertising campaign in *The Wall Street Journal*, *Forbes* magazine and *Business Week* magazine."[23]

In 1984, Pugh was named top chief executive officer by *Wall Street Transcript*, which credited him with "enhancing the overall value of the enterprise for the benefit of the stockholders." The year before, he had been named outstanding chief executive officer of the apparel industry by *Financial World*, one of the nation's top investment publications, which wrote that Pugh had "an uncanny knack to call the trends and position VF at the forefront of its competitors."[24]

The Triumph of Lee Jeans

The VF Corporation again posted record gains in sales and earnings in 1981. Blue jeans remained tremendously popular, and Lee's sales of $545 million represented 73 percent of total sales. Vanity Fair accounted for 23 percent, and Kay Windsor delivered a mere 2 percent.[25]

Lee's success stemmed from its ability to meet customers' changing needs. The Ms. Lee brand, created in 1973 specifically for women, became the best-selling line of jeans in the country. Lee was also the first in the industry to intro-

duce stretch denim, and it was preparing to introduce budget-priced stretch fabric jeans and a new line of casual pants with jeans styling.[26]

"Our jeans line for women exploded in the early 1980s and caught fire," said Terry Lay, president of Lee Apparel, in a 1997 interview. "We found ourselves in every grade school, high school and college and on the backs of a lot of housewives, too. In that whole era when the Calvin Klein and the Gloria Vanderbilt jeans were launched, I think the Lee Company profited greatly. We had a great value and a great-looking product. We had spent a lot of time working on fit for the woman customer and really getting the product right. And it all came together."[27]

A series of 30-second television ads were tested in major selected markets in 1981, increasing consumer awareness of Lee and Vanity Fair products. Officials planned to run more ads the following year.[28]

"We exploded the business by marketing innovation and fashion innovation," Lay said. "We did some print ads that were very successful, where women would literally tear the ad out of the magazine, bring it to the store and say, 'I want this.' I was here, and I was glad to

Above: Vibrant colors in casual terrycloth made this "Terry Go Round" ensemble a hit at the beach and around the pool.

Right: Jeans remained a stronghold. The Lee division brought in the lion's share of revenues during most of the 1980s.

be here, when we really exploded the female side of the business."[29]

While Americans were "power dressing" for the work week, they were also more selective about their casual time and weekend wear. Black jeans, stonewashed jeans and overdyed denims gained favor among younger buyers, and Lee was a leader in the manufacture of these expressive denims. In 1982, Lee also introduced Ultracord, a cotton-polyester blend corduroy, and Dress Blues, denim garments that remained dark blue after continued washings.[30]

By 1983, Lee was responsible for nearly 80 percent of VF's total sales. By this time, the company's advertising campaign had established Lee as "The Brand That Fits." Television and print advertisements showcased Lee jeans and casual apparel for men, women, teenagers and children. The division offered a wide range of products, each size available in various styles that allowed buyers to choose either a tight or more relaxed fit. The company recognized that buyers' preferences were changing, and worked to meet their needs. "The silhouettes are changing, but denim is still very popular," Pugh said.[31]

The New Femininity

Demand for feminine underwear was increasing, perhaps to compensate for fashions that had become less feminine. Women in business recognized that suits were essential. Wide shouldered jackets that hung loosely over knee-length skirts disguised the waist and hips, creating a professional, but not overtly feminine, appearance.[32]

Business was so good that in 1981, Vanity Fair added a 60,000-square-foot building at the Monroeville distribution center. On-time delivery of merchandise continued to improve, leading to better sales.[33] The following year, the

division introduced Woolessence, a polyester-wool blend, and Snugallure, a brush-backed satin. Both were favorably received by retailers.[34]

Color-mixing, dyeing and finishing operations were improved in 1983, which made VF among the industry's most technologically advanced in these critical areas. Through new designs and marketing strategies, the company was reaching out to younger women, aged 25 to 35.[35] Sales for the Vanity Fair Division reached record levels of $199 million in 1983, but declined to $195 million the following year. Faced with strong competition from Victoria's Secret, which featured extremely feminine, sexy styles of underwear, Vanity Fair announced several new lines and entered a licensing agreement with well-known designer Fernando Sanchez to create a new line of upscale intimate and feminine apparel.[36] Sanchez was the owner of Fernando Sanchez, Ltd., New York City, and a three-time Coty Award winner. The lingerie he would design for Vanity Fair was to be very fashionable, but more reasonably priced than other brands for which Sanchez had created designs.

"I look forward to working with a company with a wonderful reputation as a leader in the industry," Sanchez said. "It is a company that will give me the opportunity to share my designs with a larger audience while still maintaining the utmost in quality."[37]

A full line of cotton panties was also introduced, and the division's large-size line was expanded to include fashionable full-figure bras. Vanity Fair also entered the petite market with an overhauled collection of sleepwear and loungewear.[38]

Overseas Difficulties

The International Division continued to suffer because of recessions in Europe and in Canada. It recorded

Perhaps because women were wearing more businesslike outerwear, they wanted filmy, feminine lingerie.

Above: Ricky Turbeville feeds fabric into a spinner that will remove excess dye.

Right: Giant bolts of newly dyed fabric are ready to be covered and shipped to cutting and sewing plants.

United Kingdom, Japan and the Scandinavian countries. Ironically, a major factor in the poor market conditions was the strength of the U.S. dollar in these countries, which boosted the cost of raw materials abroad.[41]

The division continued to improve the following year, after facilities in Belgium were consolidated and the Scandinavian marketing organization was restructured. Although the economies of some of the foreign markets had still not recovered from protracted recessions, earnings jumped to $7.3 million.[42]

VF Sells Kay Windsor

In 1982 VF officials finally dismantled the Kay Windsor division, which had been struggling for years. Its products were discontinued for sale in retail markets, and manufacturing operations were converted to contract manufacturing. "We knew nothing about the dress industry," said Lori Tarnoski, who worked in VF's corporate offices from 1961 until her 1997 retirement.

sales of $127 million in 1981, down from $146 million in 1980. Of even greater significance, the division reported a loss of $9 million for the year, compared to earnings of $7 million in 1980.[39]

In December 1981, directors voted to divest VF's unprofitable hosiery business in Northern Ireland. The sale would result in a $2.4 million loss for the corporation.[40] The following year, officials sold the hosiery and knitwear operations in the United Kingdom, leftovers from the days of the Berkshire Knitting Mills.

While the International Division returned to profitability in 1982 with earnings of $2.8 million, market conditions remained weak in Canada, the

"We tried to run KW as we did Vanity Fair, installing our cost and inventory control system. It just didn't work with a Seventh Avenue dress house."[45]

The $1 Billion Mark

In 1983, corporate sales exceeded $1 billion for the first time, and the company celebrated by posting its yearly results on the front cover of the 1983 Annual Report and throwing a party at corporate headquarters. CEO Larry Pugh called 1983 the "Billion Dollar Beginning," pledging that the corporation would continue to prosper.[46]

Brenda Gall, an apparel analyst for Merrill Lynch, praised the company in the *Reading Eagle.* "VF is an extremely well-run company," she said. "It has margins of better than 10 percent after taxes, which is extraordinary in the industry. It turns inventory better than anyone — which contributes to its profitability."[47]

Not content to rest on its laurels, VF continued its quest to increase efficiency, reduce costs and expand production capacity. To achieve this goal, the corporation in 1983 spent a record $59.8 million on capital improvements.[48]

The plant in Pulaski, Virginia, was operating at full capacity, so the company in 1983 acquired an additional sewing plant in El Paso, Texas. It also took over a former Kay Windsor facility in Savannah, Tennessee, and began expanding a sewing plant in Bayou La Batre, Alabama.[49]

Important Acquisitions

In 1984, VF Corporation acquired three new divisions: Modern Globe, Inc.; Troutman Industries, Inc.; and Bassett-Walker. Troutman and Modern Globe were acquired September 28, and Bassett-Walker was acquired November 1. It was also the most profitable year in the corporation's history, with sales of $1.17 billion and earnings of $125 million.[50]

From left, Ginny Gibbs, Bernice Rolin and Robbie Simpson inspect the quality of dyed fabric samples before the cloth is shipped.

'Cutting Edge' Technology Curbs Waste

THE GERBER-HUGHES high precision cutting machines are "really the stars of our machinery," said Dennis Zeigler, director of Equipment Engineering for the Lee Company. "They're some of the biggest, most expensive and fanciest machines we use in any of our operations." Lee has 18 of the machines, which carry a price tag of about $750,000 each. VF has 90 Gerber cutting machines throughout its operations, Zeigler said.

The sophisticated cutting machines, first introduced to VF factories in the early 1980s, have played an important role ever since. The great advantage of the computer-driven machines is the assurance of uniformity in the material they cut. "It gives you consistent parts that allow much greater efficiency in the sewing operation," Zeigler said.[1]

Specifications for hundreds of pattern pieces are placed into the memory of the machine's computer marking system, and the machine can be programmed to cut any combination of those pieces. The cutting machine, equipped with a knife that can rotate 360 degrees, can cut through 64 layers of denim at one time, producing parts for 32 pairs of jeans in about two hours. "Basically, the Gerber has a reciprocating knife," Zeigler said. "All you have to do is define the X-by-Y coordinates and this thing will run around the denim, cutting it all out."[2]

Despite machine-driven advantages, the cutting process is not completely automated. Workers, called

---

Above: The double stitch machine was one of the innovations VF introduced.

Opposite page: The automatic buttonholer also speeds production time and limits labor cost.

The new divisions each met three basic criteria Pugh set. Each was a member of the apparel industry; each had products that would allow VF to enter markets that were different, but compatible, with those it already served; and each had operating philosophies that were similar to VF's.[51] Harold McKemy, who became treasurer in 1971 and was vice president of Treasury and Financial Services from 1987 until his 1994 retirement, noted that when VF acquired a company, it looked for synergies that would increase the value of both organizations.

"If they're good companies — and we don't want them unless they are — there are other bidders out there. You can pay more if, when you combine it with your own company, you've got something that's better than that company standing alone."[52]

Modern Globe manufactured women's cotton panties and sleepwear and men's cotton undershirts and shorts. It had plants in Bakersville, Gastonia, and North Wilkesboro, North Carolina. The VF Corporation paid $37.4 million for the company, best known for its Lollipop brand of underwear.[53]

Troutman Industries, with five plants in North Carolina, manufactured men's and boy's casual slacks and shorts, mostly under private label agreements. VF acquired the outstanding common stock of Troutman Industries for $2.5 million.[54]

markers, are still needed to fit pattern pieces onto cloth to assure the least amount of waste. Denim is Lee's highest production cost, so limiting waste is crucial. "It's like a puzzle," Zeigler said. "You need to fit the pieces on the cloth so you use as much of it as possible."

Research is underway to have computers fit the pieces onto the cloth, he said, but human markers are still able to achieve better results. Right now, Zeigler said, markers can use 92 percent of the cloth, with only 8 percent waste. The best efficiency computers have been able to attain is 88 percent. "The day will come when computers will do that work, too," Zeigler said. "But not yet."

Gerber cutters have replaced nearly all of the older cutting machines, causing cutters to breathe a collective sigh of relief. The old machines were extremely difficult to use, Zeigler said, and were considered quite dangerous. Equipped with powerful motors, the machines were heavy and hard to push through the many layers of fabric that were to be cut.

The Gerber-Hughes cutters might be the stars of the VF factories, but they share the stage with many other important machines. Conventional machines, run by skilled operators, are used at Lee to sew together pieces of denim that form each pair of jeans. Some of the work, such as making pockets, flies and button holes, is automated. Much of it, though, still depends on machine operators. "We have a lot of automation, especially with the small-parts jobs," Zeigler said. "But, once you start putting the blue jeans together, it all depends on the skill and dexterity of the operators." About 24 different machines — including automatic belt loop tackers, safety stitch machines, double needle machines and sergers — are used in the production of jeans.

Today's advanced, sophisticated equipment has helped to change the perception of the garment industry, Zeigler said. "There used to be an image of the garment industry as a sweat shop industry, where you'd have old ladies bent over machines and working their fingers to the bone," Zeigler said. "I think that has changed drastically, and much of the change in perception is due to all this new, user-friendly, sophisticated machinery."[3]

Bassett-Walker

Bassett-Walker, a leading designer and manufacturer of knitted and fleece activewear, acquired for $293.3 million, was the most important of the three acquisitions because of the increasing popularity of fleeced sweatpants and sweatshirts. The trend was sparked partly by the off-the-shoulder sweatshirts worn by actress Jennifer Beal in the movie *Flashdance*.

Bassett-Walker's foundation goes back to 1928, when Samuel Walker founded the Virginia Underwear Company in Martinsville, Virginia, setting up shop with some used knitting machines.[55] Similarly, J.D. Bassett — who had bought the equipment of the defunct Bassett Mills, Inc., in Bassett, about 12 miles away — founded Bassett Knitting Corporation.[56] By 1940, company officials decided they needed someone with more experience to run the knitting company and recruited Walker. Bassett Knitting became the Bassett-Walker Knitting Company.[57]

Sales in 1941, the merged company's first year of operation, were $608,478 and profits were $47,291, a marked improvement from sales of $406,999 and profits of $2,157 in 1940.[58]

Under Walker's leadership both Bassett-Walker Knitting and the Virginia Underwear Company grew steadily throughout the 1940s and 1950s.[59] However, his leadership ended abruptly in 1960, when he suffered a heart attack while working in his office and died the same day.[60]

Walker's son, Dudley, assumed leadership of the company, and in 1964 merged the Virginia Underwear Company with the Bassett-Walker Knitting Company.[61] The combined company grew rapidly. Between 1965 and 1976, it established six divisions: the Stuart Division in 1965, the Fabrics Division in 1970, the Jacquard and Hillsville divisions in 1972, the Brookneal Division in 1974 and the Chatham Division in 1976.[62]

In 1979, the Bassett-Walker Knitting Company's main office was moved from Bassett, Virginia, to Martinsville, Virginia. In 1980, Bassett-Walker purchased the Johnston Mills Company, a knitting operation with three plants in North Carolina. The company became Bassett-Walker, Inc., in January 1980, with more divisions opening during the next several years.

When Bassett-Walker, Inc., was acquired by the VF Corporation in 1984, its headquarters remained in Martinsville, and operations continued at the company's 16 manufacturing sites in Virginia, North Carolina and Georgia.

The company operated 11 clothing plants that produced jogging suits, sweatshirts and similar items for men, women and children.[63] In 1985, Bassett-Walker replaced Vanity Fair as the second largest VF division, with revenue of $248 million representing nearly 17 percent of total VF sales. Profits were $18.5 million.[64]

Since the acquisition, Bassett-Walker has played an important role in VF's overall operation. Most Bassett-Walker products are produced under the Lee brand label, allowing VF to take advantage of the Lee brand's popularity.[65] The company became part of VF's newly formed Activewear sector in 1987 and expanded its product base in the early 1990s when it began producing T-shirts. By 1997 the company had

Samuel Walker guided the company that bore his name until he died suddenly in 1960. His son, Dudley, took the reins.

22 manufacturing facilities in Virginia, North Carolina, Georgia and Florida.[66]

As Bassett-Walker has grown and expanded, it has maintained a longstanding tradition of community service and adopted a slogan to reflect its citizenship: Bassett-Walker — The Fabric of Our Community.[67]

V-Backs and other Lingerie Innovations

The Lingerie Division in 1985 offered more petite and large-size selections and introduced the V-back bra, which was extremely well received by retailers and consumers.[68] In its first full year on the market, the V-back established itself as the most popular bra the company had ever introduced.

Fernando Sanchez's feminine designs, which used charmeuse, sheer moire and sculptured velvet, were very popular with Vanity Fair customers.[69] Charmeuse was used for nine items, including a bolero jacket, sleep shirt, tap pants and teddy. All the items were accented with lace appliques and available in blue forest, snow peach, black and cream. The showpiece of the charmeuse group was a long gown with crisscrossed spaghetti straps, a lace bodice and back, and a lace applique at the top of a side slit. A matching robe was also available. The sculptured velvet group, available in black, red and ivory, included a long, zip-front caftan, short zip-front shirt, fiber-filled jackets and trousers.[70]

Vanity Fair's product offering also included a white robe made of fake fur, described by the *Reading Eagle* as a "fashion must for women. ... The two-pocket white robe is so stunning that women will want to wear it to go out," wrote Dawn Maurer. "And they can."[71]

Vanity Fair Mills and Modern Globe, the companies in the intimate apparel group, increased sales and profits in 1989. Both companies conducted extensive consumer research programs, hoping to broaden their product lines to appeal to younger customers, while maintaining their traditional customer base.

Vanity Fair launched Softwear Essentials, a new line of bras aimed at younger, active women. It continued to promote My Favorite Fantasy and Bright Lines, two lines introduced the previous year that also targeted younger buyers. Modern Globe experienced dramatic increases in the T-shirt segment of its business.[72]

Two corporate vice presidents were added in 1985: Prakash C. Bhatt was named vice president of Manufacturing while Ardys A. Kussman was vice president of Operations and Planning. Bhatt had been vice president of Engineering at the Lee

The V-back bra was an important innovation and helped VF capture even more of the market share in intimate apparel.

Company, where he had worked since 1972. Kussman had been with Lee since 1971, most recently as vice president of Operations. The addition of Bhatt and Kussman brought the number of vice presidents to 12.

Late in 1985, VF acquired Willis & Geiger for $500,000. The small company manufactured high quality expedition-type clothing and boasted President Theodore Roosevelt, Charles Lindbergh and General Douglas MacArthur among its past patrons.[73] Two years later, the division was sold so VF could concentrate on brand names that better suited its overall strategy.

In a May 1985 interview, Robert Gregory, then president and chief operating officer, discussed how the acquisitions helped the company provide value for consumers.

"Our company is a little different. We try to concentrate on value. As opposed to being the fanciest designer in the industry, we try to give the consumer what they need over a long-term basis. We provide styling, fabrics and color innovations. But we believe people buy our product because of its basic inherent value."[74]

Merging Troutman into Lee

With the corporation involved with more important brands, the decision was made to dissolve the financially troubled Troutman Division in 1986. Lee picked up some of Troutman's production. "Troutman was the right idea with the wrong execution for VF," said Mackey McDonald, who was in charge of the company in 1985 and 1986.

"It was certainly the right idea to get into the casual pants business, and some of the marketing initiatives that we launched were the right initiatives for the marketplace. But the reason it was the wrong execution was that we bought a company that was primarily in the polyester pant business with the discounters, and there were so many problems with that business. We ended up spending a great deal of time wrestling with our problems in the business rather than focusing on the new initiatives that were beginning to emerge, which was the 100 percent cotton pant business

and strong marketing that was required to push across and brand that business."[75]

He noted that the tremendous opportunities offered by the Blue Bell companies, which VF acquired in 1986, overshadowed the potential of the Troutman organization and hastened the decision to close the division. "I had already identified the fact that Troutman could not and should not exist as a separate division of VF," he said.[76] The Blue Bell acquisition added the Wrangler brand, among others, to VF's holdings.

Pepsi Apparel America

In 1986, VF created Pepsi Apparel America, a corporate marketing group that would oversee the production of a sportswear line licensed under the Pepsi Cola label and designed to tie in with Pepsi's "new generation" advertising campaign.

Aimed primarily at 12- to 24-year-olds, the line included jeans, jackets, sweat suits, jogging suits and other sportswear produced by VF divisions, mostly made of denim and priced between $20 and $35.[77]

"We are delighted to join with Pepsi-Cola to market an exciting line of apparel products under one of the most well-known and admired consumer brands in the world," announced Robert Gregory at the time of the deal.

"Pepsi has captured the 'new generation' and we expect Pepsi Apparel America to follow suit. And we are delighted that the entire line is made in America."[78]

The line was launched in spectacular fashion with a showing at the American Museum of Natural History in New York City complete with hot air balloons, a laser show, and an appearance by Andy Warhol, the artist who most popularized commercial design.

The VF Corporation had initiated the Pepsi Apparel concept, but Pepsi President and Chief Executive Officer Roger A. Enrico was delighted with it.

"It gives us a chance to provide consumers with a quality product, increase Pepsi's visibility, and show support for the American textile and apparel industries."[79]

However, the Pepsi Apparel America line wasn't successful and was discontinued two years later.

Lee Stumbles

Lee's earnings decreased in 1986 for the first time in a decade. The division's troubles were blamed on bad timing. Researchers anticipated that consumers would begin demanding jeans made of different types of fabrics and in different colors and styles, but they had misjudged when the shift

The spring line in 1984 featured sophisticated yet simple designs in VF's trademark nylon.

would occur. As a result, Lee was unprepared when the demand came earlier than expected.[80]

In November 1986, Lee changed its advertising firm after being wooed by Minneapolis-based Fallon McElligott Rice. Hoping to attract the attention of Lee decision makers and playing off Lee's slogan "The Brand That Fits," Fallon McElligott had placed 14 half-page ads in the October 30 and 31 editions of the *Reading Eagle* and *Reading Times* featuring 70 employees dressed in Lee jeans. The ads read: "After 30 days of living, breathing and dreaming about Lee Jeans, one thing is clear: Lee Jeans fit Fallon McElligott."[81] Spending $15,000 on jeans and newspaper ads won Fallon McElligott Lee's $20 million jeans account.

Weak consumer spending in 1988 led to sluggish sales and profits. A 2 percent drop in overall volume was blamed on an industry-wide decline in demand for jeans. While VF's jeans sales overall increased 5 percent, the Lee Company actually lost ground. Sales of the company's other jeans lines were all up, driving VF Corporation's share of the total jeanswear market from 25 to 27 percent, despite Lee's disappointing performance.[82] Rustler, a basic, value-priced brand, was recognized as the fastest growing name in the jeanswear market.

Adding to Lee's problems was the rapidly growing popularity of a new line of casual slacks for men — Dockers, introduced by the Levi Strauss Company. Seen as an alternative to jeans, Dockers became a sort of uniform for many men. They were casual and comfortable and could be worn when jeans were not considered appropriate.

The Lee Company had been so busy trying to get its jeans business back on track that it had not paid sufficient attention to the competition. Now, it found that the sale of these new pants was cutting into sales of the old standby — blue jeans.[83] And to make matters even worse, compa-

ny officials were dealing with wildcat strikes at several of the Lee plants.[84]

To stoke sales and remedy some of its financial woes, the company decided to test the buying needs of women 25 to 44, Lee's largest market segment. Jamie Lockhard, named Director of Advertising and Public Relations in October 1997, said such testing was well worth the time it took. "We get consumers involved in three different kinds of product testing. So, when Lee brings a product to the market, the consumer has already said, 'Yes.'"[85]

In-store displays, intended to be viewed as "Lee shops" within the stores, promoted a broad mix of separate but coordinated Lee brand clothing, much of it manufactured by Bassett-Walker.

While Lee was struggling, Wrangler reported record growth. Wrangler western jeans were the largest-selling of their type, and the Wrangler American Hero line continued to flourish. In addition, Wrangler Rugged Wear, a line of outdoor clothing, was introduced in 1989. Rustler brand continued to do well as a basic, value-priced product, and Girbaud reported increased sales and profits.[86]

Improving Efficiency

VF Corporation, operating with 10 principal divisions, got back on track in 1987 with sales that increased 67 percent to $2.57 billion and earnings that jumped 32 percent to $179.7 million. On July 10, 1987, the VF Corporation was first listed on the Pacific Stock Exchange.[87]

By then, and reflecting the Blue Bell acquisition, VF was grouped into three major categories: Intimate Apparel, consisting of Vanity Fair and

In Wrangler jeans, a woman could look feminine even when pursuing a tough sport, as rodeo champion Marlene Eddleman illustrates.

Modern Globe; Jeanswear, consisting of Lee, Wrangler, Rustler and Girbaud; and Sportswear, made up of Bassett-Walker, Jantzen, JanSport and Pepsi Apparel America.

In a continuing quest to improve efficiency, the company began using bar-coded product identification tags on all its garments. The electronic system enabled retailers to quickly transmit sales information to VF, where it was used to determine inventory replenishment needs.[88]

Corporate management continued to improve synergy among all the divisions by coordinating manufacturing schedules. Jantzen manufactured robes

for Vanity Fair during its slow season, for instance, while Vanity Fair made swimsuits for Jantzen. Efforts also were made to better communicate and share among divisions expertise in marketing, operations, finance and other areas.[89] Directors sold a Lee joint venture operation in Brazil and the Canadian Wrangler operation and replaced them with licensing agreements, under which Lee and Wrangler clothing would be made to specification by a local manufacturer. A Lee facility in Belgium was no longer needed and was also closed.[90] The restructuring of the International division would pay dividends in the late 1980s. Wrangler had a strong showing in the United Kingdom, and a new Wrangler division was set up in West Germany. Officials were looking toward Eastern Europe and the Soviet Union as possible markets in light of dramatic political changes occurring there.[91]

Wall Street was hit by a tidal wave of selling on October 19, 1987. The Dow Jones Industrial Average plummeted 508 points, or 22.6 percent (by contrast, the average fell 12.8 percent in the 1929 crash). While few economists predicted a 1920s-style Depression, the spectre of a recession was very real.

Bob Cordero, who would rise to be president of VF's Asia Division by the late 1990s, recalled a crucial board meeting:

"The crash occurred on a Monday, and the board meeting on Tuesday. The look of shock and disbelief, not only on the faces of the VF officers but also on the faces of the board members, was certainly memorable. It was a time when everyone was looking for leadership. We had just purchased Blue Bell the year before. We had paid $750 million for it, and it was far and away the largest investment VF had ever made. We were all wondering if we should have passed on that acquisition, because now everything now was worth 30 percent less than it was a few days ago.

Girbaud, founded in France, embodied a Euro look, and its advertising campaigns were avant garde.

"But Larry Pugh assured us that the stock market was something beyond our control and that if we continued to do what we were employed to do things would work out. And they did."[92]

The corporation's strategy of providing good value through consolidation and efficiency would be recognized by the end of the eighties. VF Corporation was ranked 170 on *Fortune* magazine's Fortune 500 list and also was ranked as one of the magazine's 21 Superstars, a prestigious list that included such well-known companies as Kellogg, Maytag, Coca-Cola, *The Washington Post* and Anheuser Busch. Superstar list members averaged returns of at least 20 percent on year-end equity over the 1979-88 decade, without ever dropping below 15 percent. VF, ranked 17 out of the 21 companies listed, with an average equity return of 22.3 percent during the specified time period.[93]

The lessons learned during the difficult 1980s positioned the company for a strong future. "In retrospect, we can see the organization was too bureaucratic, that we didn't listen to the marketplace, and that when we did listen, we didn't respond well or quickly enough," Pugh said in April 1989.[94]

Company forecasters may have missed some vital clues, but they had the foresight to pursue the Blue Bell acquisition of 1986, which would bring VF Corporation the Wrangler brand and domination of the worldwide jeans market.

Katrina Nicholson operates a button machine at the Monroeville plant. The machine, which covers buttons with fabric to match the garment for a custom-made look, was installed as part of a capital improvements program.

Jeans, with Wrangler leading the pack, became the uniform of the young .

CHAPTER NINE

WRANGLER

1897–1997

"The World's Largest Producer of Work and Play Clothes."

—Wrangler slogan, 1947[1]

WORN BY COWBOYS and rodeo riders, country music stars and race car drivers, Wrangler jeans have a rich history stretching back to 1897, when Wrangler's parent company was founded by C.C. Hudson and his brother Homer. The brothers left their home on Spring Hill Farm in Williamson County, Tennessee, to seek their fortune in Greensboro, North Carolina.[2] C.C. got a job in an overall factory, sewing buttons on for 25 cents a day. When the plant closed, he purchased a few of the sewing machines. In 1904, he and his brother formed the Hudson Overall Company, operating from a loft over Coe Brothers Grocery on South Elm Street.[3]

The fledgling business soon outgrew the loft and the brothers moved it to an old church building on Arlington Street in Greensboro. To keep up with the orders that flowed in, the Hudsons hired farm women to work at home, sewing pieces of precut denim. In 1919, the brothers renamed their business the Blue Bell Overall Company, and moved manufacturing to their own factory on the corner of South Elm and Lee streets.[4]

Legend has it that Blue Bell was named after a bell given to C.C. Hudson by a group of railroad workers who bought overalls at Hudson's store whenever they passed through town. Hudson became friends with these men, who gave him a railroad bell as a token of their affection. After a time in the factory, the bell, like everything else, became covered with blue dust.[5]

Jellico Clothing

Meanwhile, the Jellico Clothing Manufacturing Company of Jellico, Tennessee emerged as one of Blue Bell's toughest competitors. Jellico, founded in 1907 by R.L. Raines and J.B. McKinley, grew from 12 sewing machines to 35 in eight years. Robert W. Baker came on board as secretary in 1915, and a year later became president and general manager. The company opened a large, modern plant in Middlesboro, Kentucky, in 1919 and changed its name to Big Ben Manufacturing. The Jellico plant closed two years later and its work was transferred to the newer Middlesboro factory.[6]

In 1923, Baker learned that his friend and competitor C.C. Hudson of Blue Bell was ill and wanted to sell his company. On January 1, 1926, Big Ben purchased Blue Bell for $585,000. Baker, president of the new company, moved its headquarters from Middlesboro to Greensboro and within two years doubled the

The Wrangler brand is tied into everything American.

size of Hudson's old plant.[7] Big Ben became the Blue Bell Overall Company in 1930.

The company used an interesting and successful marketing ploy in the late 1920s. It added a double suspender overall to its product line that, until then, had been only a single suspender-back garment. The new overall included a large bib pocket, which required more fabric and raised the manufacturing cost by 37.5 cents per dozen. Instead of increasing the cost of the overalls, the company surprised the industry by actually lowering the price by 50 cents per dozen.[8]

Globe Superior

In 1936, Blue Bell Overall and the Globe Superior Corporation of Abingdon, Illinois, were the two largest work clothes manufacturers in the world, each with yearly sales of more than $5 million. Blue Bell, with plants in Greensboro and Middlesboro, and Globe (which had factories in Abingdon and Canton, Illinois; Columbia City, Indiana; and Commerce, Georgia)[9] merged into the Blue Bell-Globe

Left: Wrangler got its start as part of the Blue Bell Overall Company of Greensboro, North Carolina.

Above right: They had been competitors, but in 1936, Blue Bell and Globe merged to effectively lock up the work-clothes market.

1904: Brothers C.C. and Homer Hudson found Hudson Overall Company.

1919: Hudson Overall Company renamed Blue Bell Company.

1907: Jellico Clothing Company, Hudson's chief competitor, founded.

1919: Jellico Clothing Company renamed Big Ben.

Manufacturing Company that year.[10]

Founded in 1889, the Globe Corporation was best known as the devel-

oper of sanforization, a process that shrinks cloth before it is cut. Sanforization was the brainchild of Jared C. Fox, a buyer for J.C. Penney Company who worked at his father's overall business in Atchison, Kansas, before he came to Globe.

Denim was particularly prone to shrinkage, losing up to 10 percent of its length when washed. Before sanforization, clothing manufacturers cut and sewed clothes much larger than the desired size, wasting yards of denim for each garment. Overalls, for example, were made up to seven inches longer than desired to allow for shrinkage.[11]

Fox looked to his friend, inventor Sanford L. Cluett, to help solve this problem. Cluett worked for the Cluett-Peabody firm of Troy, New York, the company that made Arrow collars. He was already experimenting with a process to stop shrinkage, and, at Fox's urging, concentrated his efforts on denim. Working together, the men were finally able to reduce shrinkage in denim to less than 1 percent.[12] Once the process was available, however, the men found that none of the textile mills they approached were willing to try it. For years, san-

Above: With the merger, Blue Bell was able to incorporate sanforizing, which reduced shrinkage and waste, into its clothing.

Right: Workers, using treadle-powered "stitching" machines, turn out overalls at a 1920s Blue Bell plant.

1936: Blue Bell merges with competitor Globe Superior Corporation.

1947: Wrangler Westernwear was born.

1943: Blue Bell acquires Casey Jones, and with it the Wrangler label.

1986: VF acquires Blue Bell.

forization went unused while manufacturers continued to waste cloth.

Eventually, Fox persuaded Erwin Mills, a large denim producer, to buy a sanforizing machine and produce sanforized denim cloth. The mill, in turn, sold the denim to Globe's Abingdon plant, which produced the first pairs of sanforized overalls, marketed under J.C. Penney's Big Mac label. Sanforized cloth caught on quickly, setting a new standard for the industry. Fox, who by then had resigned as a work clothes buyer and worked for Globe Superior, helped to put the Globe-Blue Bell merger together. He was named president and directing head of operations for the merged companies, while R.W. Baker became chairman of the board.[13] Fox and Edward A. Morris, an engineer who later became president of Blue Bell, took on the difficult project of combining the best features of both companies.

One of their earliest successes was the "proportioned fit" concept. Until the late 1930s, all overalls of one size had the same rise, which is the distance between the crotch and the top of the bib, even though the inseams were of different lengths. This, of course, made the overalls fit poorly, since a man with a 36-inch inseam would have a longer trunk than a man with a 30-inch inseam. Blue Bell-Globe began manufacturing overalls with a graduated rise, depending on the length of the inseam, and captured even more of the work clothes market it already dominated.[14]

The new design was a major innovation and established a new standard for the work clothes industry.

In 1940, Blue Bell-Globe acquired the assets of the H.D. Bob Company from Sears, Roebuck and Company, and converted its dress shirt plant in Natchez, Mississippi, to a work clothes manufacturing plant.[15] Three years later, it acquired the Casey Jones Company of Baltimore, Maryland, which also had five plants in Virginia.[16] With the Casey Jones acquisition came the rights to the company's rarely used brand name, Wrangler.[17]

Blue Bell-Globe became simply Blue Bell, Inc., at that time, and the firm opened a 50,000-square-foot plant in Lenoir, North Carolina, one year later.[18] By then, Blue Bell was immersed in war production. Denim was in short supply and demand for military clothing was great. Remarkably, Blue Bell turned out more than 24 million military garments during World War II, the equivalent of two pieces of clothing for each American serviceman.[19]

When the war ended in 1945, Blue Bell returned to civilian manufacture, only to discover consumer preferences had changed. Returning soldiers had become accustomed to the khaki pants and shirts they had worn overseas, and preferred them to the overalls worn by older men. Blue Bell adapted

Above: Blue Bell acquired the Casey Jones label in 1943 and, with it, the little-used Wrangler name.

Center: Wrangler developed a new overall design to accommodate men of different heights and physiques.

quickly, adding casual clothing to its traditional work wear line.

Westernwear Born

The company's 1947 entry into Westernwear prompted it to change its slogan from "The World's Larger Producer of Work Clothes" to "The World's Largest Producer of Work and Play Clothes."[20] That year Blue Bell acquired the Mid-South Garment Company, with five plants in Mississippi, boosting its shirt manufacturing capacity. A new division opened in Oneonta, Alabama, which grew eventually into three plants.[21] Edward Morris succeeded J.C. Fox as president of Blue Bell in 1948, and — perhaps most significantly — Wrangler Westernwear was born.

Blue Bell had been trying to sell jeans in the West without much success, said Bill Hervey, who came to Blue Bell as a salesman in 1957 and eventually rose to president of Wrangler Menswear. "Wrangler was just an unknown entity out there," Hervey said in a 1997 interview. Blue Bell had only Hervey and one other salesman for the entire southwestern U.S. "They didn't have more than five salesmen covering the entire United States."

The channel of distribution left much to be desired, also. "They sold to dry goods distributors, who handled everything from hairpins and notions to apparel. Just everything under the sun. The distributors had their own salesmen, who would take samples of what they had bought from Blue Bell and go out and take orders against the merchandise."

"Rodeo Ben," a famous designer of Westernwear, was called in to design the classic Wrangler jean.

"Pretty soon, it became obvious that the dry goods type of distribution was really on the wane because a store that amounted to anything wasn't going to pay what was virtually a middle man, so we began to seek out some of the better customers.

"We finally got to where we tried to set up in a hotel and get the word out — the Wrangler man is in town. But I would be up there for a week and not write an order for a single pair of jeans."[22]

Blue Bell hired "Rodeo Ben" of Philadelphia, a well-known rodeo clothing designer, to oversee creation of its Western jeans. Working with real cowboys, he tailored every feature of the jeans to their specification. The Wrangler label, for example, was made from pressed cord, rather than leather, because these jeans were made for cowboys who rode horses, and a leather label would stick to a leather saddle.[23] With the help of these cowboys, Rodeo Ben developed the 13MWZ jean, which featured deep front pockets, high back pockets and the "Rodeo Ben watch pocket."[24]

"Our keystone product was the 13MWZ jean," said Donald Laws, president of Wrangler Westernwear. "It is the brand of choice for about 98 percent of rodeo performers and working cowboys." The brand, which celebrated its 50th anniversary in 1997, was the result of many design attempts. It is named for its prototype number (13), the word "men's," the name Wrangler and the word "zipper," which differentiates it from button-fly jeans. "Our Western heritage is very important to us," Laws said.[25]

Until the 13MWZ, cowboy jeans had been cut square, with little thought given to proportion. The legs were wide all the way down, and cut much longer than normal to accommodate the

"riding up" that would occur when the cowboy mounted his horse. A buckle in the back cinched in the waist to hold the pants up.[26] Cowboys such as Harry Tompkins, Bill Linderman, Jim Shoulders, Gerald Roberts and Todd Whatley endorsed the better fitting Wrangler Westernwear, which became immensely popular.[27]

"Wrangler's success boils back down to the fact that people were smart enough to tie in with the rodeo world," Hervey said. "We developed a loyalty on both sides of the fence, us to them and them to us."[28]

Bob Coppage, who joined Wrangler in 1976 and rose to become president of Wrangler Europe, recalled the rodeo days.

Above left: The Wrangler tag was made from pressed cord so that it wouldn't stick to a leather saddle.

Below: Young Japanese eagerly embraced anything American, including Wrangler jeans.

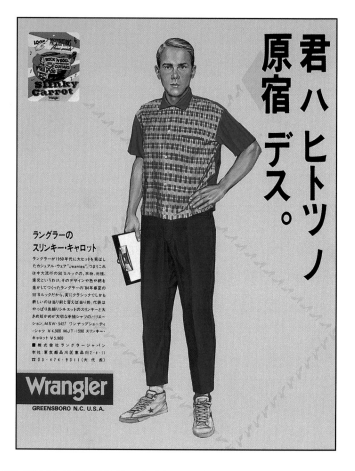

"I was fortunate in that one of the things I had a chance to do was to work in the Westernwear business and go to rodeos.

"That was always a thrill because you'd really feel the heart and soul of what Wrangler was all about. It would make you feel good to go out to that part of the country.

"We'd go out there to support our brand, to support the people involved in the Western lifestyle. We used to bring a tractor-trailer truck full of jeans — jeans and jackets and stuff like that — and we'd have all the rodeo cowboys come in and we'd fit them for the upcoming rodeo season. They enjoyed it and we got a big kick out of it."[29]

Retailing was different out West, said Mark Clift, who worked in the Westernwear Division before becoming president of DJ Industries. "You usually go out and call on stores like Macy's or Sears or Penney, and it's all cut and dried. Do this, make the money, ship it on time."

"But the Westernwear business is dominated by mom and pop stores, you know, Fred and Ethel really own the business. On one of my first trips, we went to talk to this retailer about the

business and they had baked us a cake, and told us, 'It's to welcome Wrangler Westernwear into our store.'

"And the next day, we're traveling to another store and they tell us, 'We've got to meet with you, and it's really important we meet with you at 7:30 in the morning, because we've got to work on the floor when the doors open at 9 a.m.' So we go to that store and every little lady who works there has made her favorite breakfast casserole. They served us breakfast and fixed us coffee. That's just one of the things about the Wrangler brand, which is such a big part of VF. It's that mutual respect and love."[30]

Above left: Wrangler and the Professional Rodeo Cowboys Association have enjoyed a long and colorful association.

Above right: Wrangler Rugged Wear was popular weekend attire.

Left: The SilverLake line was targeted to female rodeo fans.

Jeanies Introduced

Demand for leisure clothing continued to increase among men, women and children. Women's "jeanies" with a side zipper were introduced in 1949, ranging in price from $1.98 to $2.98. Wrangler marketed the first women's jeans with a front zipper in the early 1950s. Women's jeans were sized much differently than they are today. The waist was proportionately smaller, with more room in the hip, thigh and legs. A pair of size 12 jeans made in 1952, for example, would never fit today's size 12 woman, but might be comparable to a size six or eight.[31]

In the late 1940s and 1950s, a series of small books called *Great Moments in Rodeo* was included with each pair of jeans. The booklets included

Opposite page: Wrangler advertising was geared to capitalize on its strong Western roots.

Below: Wrangler built an impressive, modern headquarters building in 1994.

a "Qualitag," giving the buyer care instructions and a money back guarantee.[32]

In 1955, Blue Bell produced a Davy Crockett washable set for little boys, with denim pants and a fringed denim jacket complete with a frontier marshal's badge. The company's share of the Western market was significant, and Wrangler made sure America knew it, through magazine advertisements, Wrangler-sponsored rodeos, and its affiliation with the Professional Rodeo Cowboys Association.[33]

Expansion Abroad and at Home

With a firm hold on the Western and casual wear markets, Morris and Vice President Rodger LeMatty decided to expand overseas, opening a plant in Genk, Belgium, in 1962. The factory made jeans for the European market, where they proved extremely popular. Additional manufacturing plants were established in England, Malta and Canada during the decade.[34]

The company needed more manufacturing space to accommodate the growing Wrangler line, which then included Maverick, a brand

A BULL MARKET

AS IF PROOF THAT all things Texan loom large in the American psyche, a film about a lonely Texas oil worker had an extraordinary and immediate effect, a Wrangler old-timer said. The late-1970s *Urban Cowboy* spawned millions of wannabe Westerners, according to Bill Hervey, former president of Wrangler Menswear.

"When John Travolta got on that mechanical bull, he gave the jeans industry the biggest shot it's ever had," Hervey said. "At the time, the domestic market was going up and down the ladder between 300 and 400 million pairs. After that movie came out, everybody got the Western craze and we went to 510 million pairs a year. The whole country, a pair of jeans a piece!

"The whole industry — I'm talking boots and belts and hats and bandannas and jeans and whatever else you can think of — exploded. Retail stores opened up, a dozen a day, all across the country," Hervey said.[1]

"We hired everybody that walked down the street. We bought every building we could buy. We bought every sewing machine we could buy. The textile companies did the same thing. They geared up as if this thing was going to last forever," he said.

It didn't. "We should have known better," Hervey said. "Before we knew it, we were back to 400 million pairs." The jeans market has grown steadily since the early 1980s, he said, but no single event has captured the public's imagination in quite the same way Travolta did when he mounted the famous mechanical bull.[2]

made exclusively for wholesalers.[35] In 1966, Blue Bell acquired the Beaver Shirt Company, with four manufacturing facilities in North and South Carolina, and the Hackleburg Shirt Company of Hackleburg, Alabama. It also purchased the Coral Manufacturing Company in Mayaguez, Puerto Rico. Blue Bell of Puerto Rico, with three manufacturing plants, was established soon thereafter.[36]

Wrangler acquired the J.W. Carter Shoe Company of Nashville, Tennessee, in 1967 and converted its factory to make Western boots. The Hicks-Ponder Company, a slacks and jeans manufacturer based in El Paso, Texas, with three plants in Texas and New Mexico, was merged into Blue Bell in 1969.[37]

In 1972, Wrangler Japan, Inc., was formed to serve the growing Japanese market. Young people in Japan were fascinated with anything American, and nothing was more American than blue jeans. Ten million pairs of jeans were sold in Japan in 1972, most with the broken-in look favored in that country.[38]

LeMatty succeeded Morris as president of Blue Bell in 1966. Morris became chief executive officer.[39] By the early 1970s, Blue Bell was recognized as a major international apparel manufacturer. Sales of $231.7 million in 1970 exceeded the previous year by 18 percent, producing a seventh straight record year. Profit for the year was reported at $13.3 million, an increase of more than 21 percent.[40]

Changing and Growing

To accommodate the rapid growth, the company split into two divisions, Lady Wrangler and Mr. Wrangler. The first Wrangler Wranch, a franchise store, was opened in 1971 to carry the entire Wrangler line, as opposed to department or discount stores that offered limited Wrangler merchandise along with a variety of other clothing lines.[41]

The reorganization continued when L. Kimsey Mann became president in 1973 and chief executive officer in 1974. Mann worked to decentralize the rapidly growing company, paving the way for divisions.[42] He oversaw the formation of Sedgefield Sportswear, a line of upscale men's and boy's clothing. In 1975, the company launched Wrangler Kids while Mr. Wrangler was divided into sportswear and jeanswear groups. Two years later, Mr. Wrangler reorganized to form Wrangler menswear and Wrangler boyswear.[43]

Wrangler introduced the Long Time Friend line in 1978 to cater to mature women who wanted different types of jeans and casual clothing from those worn by younger women and teens.[44] Also that year, a new division of Blue Bell — "BBL Apparel" — was created to market work and utility clothes directly to retailers, and Maverick jeans and sportswear directly to wholesalers.[45]

Acquisition continued in the late 1970s and early 1980s. In 1979, Blue Bell purchased Sydney-based AMCO Holdings Limited, the top jeans producer in Australia. The manufacturer employed more than 1,000 at two plants in Australia and another in the Philippines.

The Rustler brand was added in 1979, giving Blue Bell a basic jean to be marketed through the mass merchandising channel, in addition to its Wrangler and Maverick lines. Rustler was immediately successful and has continued to hold a significant market share in its category.[46] The Wrangler America Brand was successfully introduced in 1984, marketed as "the most comfortable jeans known to man." It secured a stronghold on the market and began to diversify its offerings.

Celebrities Wear Wranglers

A peculiar mix of celebrities has endorsed Wrangler products. Already a leader in the jeans market, Wrangler garnered even greater recognition by sponsoring the Winston Cup Auto Racing and Dale Earnhardt's Wrangler Jeans Machine. Jackie Stewart, a world champion Grand Prix

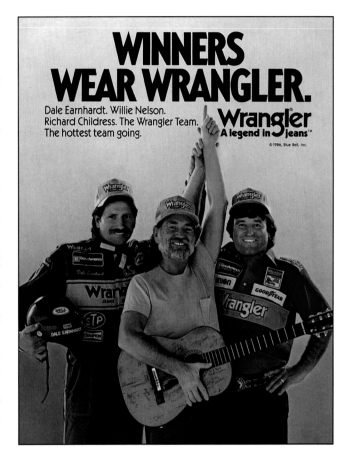

From left, Dale Earnhardt, Willie Nelson and Richard Childress are among the celebrities who have endorsed Wrangler.

race car driver, was a spokesman in the early 1970s, and golfer Lee Trevino served as a style consultant for Wrangler's Lee Trevino Sportswear Collection. Cowboys and rodeo stars, rodeo bullfighters and country music artists including Garth Brooks and Willie Nelson have all spoken, or sung, the praises of Wrangler.[47] But the company doesn't intend to rest on its laurels.

"We've got to maintain our hold on the Western lifestyle in America," said Bill Hervey, who became a Wrangler spokesperson after he retired as Wrangler Menswear president. "We've got to nourish and treasure and cherish our heritage there. We simply must do that."[48]

Freedom, comfort and chic — Girbaud jeans had it all buttoned up when VF acquired the company in 1986.

CHAPTER TEN

THE BLUE BELL BRANDS

1986–1989

"It was one of those situations where you knew immediately it was the right thing for the company."

— Lawrence Pugh, 1996[1]

WORK AND PLAY CLOTHES

IN 1986, VF Corporation nearly doubled its size with a single acquisition. The purchase of Blue Bell, Inc., was VF's most significant event since its founding, and furthered its goal of providing the best value for consumers by offering the staples of everyday wear. The $762 million acquisition created the world's largest publicly held apparel company, and added Wrangler and Rustler brand jeans along with Jantzen swimwear, JanSport casual wear and Red Kap workwear to VF's offerings.[2]

The merger made VF one of the two largest jeans makers in the world and captured more than 25 percent of the $6 billion worldwide jeans market. The acquisition arrived at the right time for both organizations. Blue Bell had fought off several takeover attempts before it approached VF. The first such attempt was by the Allegheny Corporation, said David Reklau, a financial controller of VF.[3]

"As the story goes, Ed Morris, who was chairman of Blue Bell, had been approached with — from Morris' perspective — a favorable solicitation of interest from Allegheny. They came forward with a proposal to acquire all of Blue Bell for a consideration that worked out to be $40 a share. At the time, Blue Bell was trading in the upper $20 range, so it was a significant premium over market. However, it was not a cash offer — it would have been debentures and other non-cash instruments."[4]

Kimsey Mann, Blue Bell president and CEO, opposed the deal, Reklau said, "because of the terms and losing Blue Bell's independence, becoming part of Allegheny," and the board was violently divided. "They ended up supporting Mann and not supporting their chairman, not supporting their vice chairman, so ultimately six corporate executive officers ended up resigning from Blue Bell."[5]

The flap attracted the attention of the Bass brothers, who were gaining renown for their ability to buy companies, streamline them and sell them at tremendous profit.[6] "With at least there being an indication that some of the management at Blue Bell were interested in selling out, the Bass brothers recognized that here was a company that had some hidden value," Reklau said.[7]

Blue Bell was the most significant acquisition in the company's history. With the stroke of a pen, VF captured 25 percent of the worldwide jeans market.

The brothers began buying Blue Bell stock, eventually acquiring 23 percent. Their plan, Reklau said, was to take control of the company, shut down European operations and focus on the more profitable domestic side. To prevent a Bass takeover, Blue Bell bought its own shares back at $50 in November 1983, when the company's common stock was trading in the $35 range.[8]

Within a month, another takeover attempt loomed. The Belzberg family of Canada, in Reklau's words, "came a-knocking. They had acquired something like 5 percent of the shares." Blue Bell managers became concerned when the family had acquired 10 percent of the stock. Already working on a leveraged buyout that would put stock into a trust for employees and allow them to maintain control of the company, they redoubled their efforts. When the buyout was finalized in November 1984, the Belzbergs walked away with a substantial return on their investment.[9]

Rank-and-file management "had very little to do with it," said Bill Hervey, who was president of the Wrangler Menswear Division, the largest Wrangler division. "In fact, the truth is we didn't even know it was going on until it was almost a *fait accompli.*"

Managers and officers "had to chip in and buy a certain amount of corporate stock, which we all did," Hervey said. "It worked wonderfully for the 25 owners and for the employees of Blue Bell. If we had let the company go, it would have been chopped up and sold away."[10]

Blue Bell had taken on considerable debt to finance the buyout, during a time when the apparel industry was lagging. "The debt was being worked down, and we were making all the required payments, but something more dramatic had to happen," Reklau said. Blue Bell looked at the field of suitors and decided to approach VF. "If you have to get into bed with somebody, you at least want to know who," Reklau said.[11]

"We were at least taken over by an apparel company," said Mark Clift, president of DJ Industries, which marketed the Girbaud line. "Anyway, it was a merger. VF bought the Blue Bell stock but it was definitely a merger. When VF came in, we'd have meetings which would sometimes get very heated because we'd been through a couple of bad years and we were battle tested."[12]

It was a good fit for both parties. The acquisition boosted VF's international exposure, noted John Johnson, who worked in the International

1980: Blue Bell buys Jantzen, a major swimwear manufacturer.

1982: Girbaud opens first American showroom.

Early 1980s: Blue Bell fends off several hostile takeover attempts.

Division from 1979 until his 1996 retirement as president of VF International Operations. "Obviously, the major thrust of the acquisition was here in the United States, but we also picked up a lot of business interests in Europe and other parts of the world," he said.[13]

When Ed Bauman became Blue Bell president in 1983, the company had more than 100 plants and warehouses in 17 states, Puerto Rico and foreign countries, with more than 30,000 workers worldwide.[14] Sales for the year were $1.2 billion, with earnings of $47.6 million, making it an attractive target.[15] VF, meanwhile, wanted to expand and diversify.

Blue Bell executives felt their company had much to offer.[16] "I'm convinced that the purchase of Blue Bell was the best move VF ever made," Hervey said. "Subsequent events proved that Blue Bell outperformed the companies they had acquired prior to that time."[17]

The previous year, Lee, with sales of $942 million (up from $884 million in 1984), accounted for 64 percent of VF's revenues.[18] Girl's and women's jeans were the most popular on the market and new products were continually introduced. That year, Lee introduced "Super Soft," a new kind of denim, and expanded its product lines for infants and toddlers. A new marketing program targeted the big and tall menswear market as Lee designers brought out new colors and fabrics.[19]

VF had also introduced its own brand of designer jeans. In the seventies and eighties, the designer jeans craze was in full swing, but VF was late entering the frenzied market. Its V.F. Jeans never caught on with consumers and were soon discontinued.

Girbaud Epitomized Euro Style

Girbaud's French founders Marithé Bachellerie and François Girbaud (pronounced "jer-bow") met in Paris, where she was an aspiring actress and he sold American jeans and T-shirts to rock performers at Western House, the city's first Westernwear boutique.[20] The couple, who became business partners but did not marry, teamed up to make a jean that was different.

They introduced their first collection in Europe in 1968 and immediately attracted a mixed group of buyers[21] and in 1982, the designers opened their first American showroom in New York City. Girbaud held licensing agreements with two American companies until Calvin Klein

1986: VF acquires the Blue Bell companies, adding Wrangler, Rustler, Red Kap, Jantzen, JanSport and Girbaud brands.

1984: Blue Bell buys JanSport, manufacturer of backpacks and daypacks.

1987: Wrangler and Lee work together to produce jeans under the VF umbrella.

Uniform Growth at Red Kap

Red Kap Industries, though also a member of the Blue Bell family, appealed to a far different market than did Girbaud. The company was founded in 1922, when William W. Harlin, Sr., and Claude H. Williams teamed up to sell and distribute bib overalls.[24] Both men were smokers, and they had admired a pouch of locally produced tobacco called Red Cap. They wanted to use the name for their company but the owner of the tobacco company told them the name was trademarked and could only be used if it was changed in some way. Determined to use the name, Harlin and Williams called their company Red Kap.[25]

The partnership took off and six years later Harlin and Williams opened their first manufacturing plant in Dickson, Tennessee, to produce chambray shirts, which sold at retail for 39 cents each. In 1933, they opened a factory in Clarksville, Tennessee, to make work pants. Like most businesses, the company's growth was interrupted by World War II, when Red Kap converted to wartime production, manufacturing gas mask carriers, combat fatigues and field jackets for its largest customer ever — the United States government.[26]

When the war ended, Red Kap contracted with a network of laundries to pick up, deliver and supply fresh uniforms — Red Kap brand, of course. By the early 1950s, these laundries were an important part of Red Kap's business and they remained so.[27] The company incorporated and went public in the 1960s, at the same time adding coveralls to its product line. Red Kap by that time had become a major player in the work clothes industry. Its success made it attractive to companies looking for acquisitions and in 1964 Red Kap was acquired by Blue Bell.

Expansion continued under Blue Bell, and by the end of the decade Red Kap boasted seven plants and a large regional warehouse.[28] In 1971 Red Kap built an impressive headquarters complex

bought Puritan, which had held one of the agreements. Girbaud, forced to look for another partner, found Blue Bell and a licensing agreement was struck.[22]

Girbaud remained part of VF for more than 20 years. In late 1997, VF announced that I.C. Isaacs would assume Girbaud's licensing agreement in the spring of 1998. "We had a fairly long, successful relationship, but the marketplace has changed and Girbaud sales have been soft for the last couple of years," said Mark Clift. "And it appeared that the best thing for VF, for the brand as a whole and even for François was to make a new move, go to somebody else and start all over again."[23]

Girbaud designers took their inspiration from the free-spirited 1960s. The brand enjoyed popularity in Europe as well as in the United States.

in Nashville, Tennessee, featuring an attached warehouse capable of storing three million garments.[29]

Wrangler, also a Blue Bell company, allowed Red Kap to use its name for brand recognition, and by the mid-1970s, Red Kap introduced Wrangler Uniforms. In 1982 it absorbed the operations of Big Ben, a retail work clothing business that was also owned by Blue Bell.

RED KAP INDUSTRIES

In the Swim with Jantzen

Today the largest swimwear manufacturer in America, Jantzen was founded in January 1910 by

Though the uniform industry is changing, workers still depend on sturdy, dependable Red Kap clothing. The company celebrated its 75th anniversary in 1997.

John A. Zehntbauer, his brother C. Roy Zehntbauer and Carl C. Jantzen — all in their twenties. The three young men pooled their savings and started a combination knitting operation and retail store in downtown Portland, Oregon. Portland Knitting Company, which had only a few hand-operated machines and a small showroom, specialized in heavy woolen sweaters, woolen hosiery, gloves and other knitted items — a far cry from today's swimwear.

A 1913 request from the Portland Rowing Club set the young company on the road to success. Club members needed clothing that would keep them warm during Portland's cold, rainy winters but would not restrict their movement when rowing. Carl Jantzen, the company's primary knitter, designed wool trunks and manufactured them on the machine used to make the sweaters cuffs. The rib-stitch trunks were immensely popular with club members, and Jantzen, after some testing in the local YMCA pool and the Willamette River, expanded the idea and made a suit to cover the whole body.[30]

The new swimwear was not ideal by any means, reportedly weighing eight pounds when wet. Still, it kept rowers warm, and soon the small company was turning out hundreds of the striped suits, each with its matching hat.[31] Soon both men and women were wearing the garment. There was little difference between the men's and women's styles, but women always donned long, black stockings to cover their legs.[32]

In June 1918 the company was renamed Jantzen Knitting Mills by agreement of the partners. Not only was Jantzen easier to pronounce than Zehntbauer, but the swimsuits had already become known as "Jantzen suits."[33] Early in the 1920s, Jantzen adopted the logo it still uses — the red silhouette of a woman diving. She appeared first in the company catalog, but soon the partners were sewing the cloth figure onto their swimwear. The popular figure became a fixture in Jantzen's advertising and promotions, and was sometimes called "America's first pinup girl."[34]

Before it could celebrate its 10th anniversary, the company outgrew its cramped quarters and moved to a larger Portland factory. As swimsuit sales soared, bathing suits became the company's principal product.[35] Jantzen closed its retail stores and concentrated exclusively on making swimsuits. Sales increased both in America and abroad and in 1925 a company in British Columbia was licensed to manufacture and sell Jantzen swimsuits. By the end of the Roaring Twenties, the company had manufacturing plants in Australia and England, and in 1930, Jantzen's sales hit $4.8 million. The partners had sold more than 1.5 million suits.

The Great Depression slowed Jantzen's rapid growth. New fabrics were developed to maintain consumers' interest, but swimsuits were not considered essential products and sales languished. Jantzen's goal at the time was simply to maintain its enviable position and await better times.[36] It is interesting, however, that even in the midst of the Great Depression, in 1934, Jantzen instituted a retirement plan for its employees, despite its own economic hardship.[37]

The country was still mired in the Depression, but Jantzen resumed production of sweaters in 1938. It also introduced foundations in 1939 and a line of casual sportswear called Sun Clothes in 1940, when the national economy started to improve.[38]

Jantzen, America's largest swimsuit company, got its start in damp Portland, Oregon, when its founders were asked to design uniforms for a rowing team.

World War II sidetracked Jantzen's expansion. Its factories converted to wartime production, and swimwear took a back seat as the company's machines turned out bomb parachutes, gas mask bags and sweaters for the troops fighting overseas.[39] Jantzen was well positioned when the war ended, the economy blossomed and Americans began to spend again. Jantzen expanded its product line and built a modern plant in Vancouver, Washington, in 1947.[40] In 1954 the company's name was changed to Jantzen, Inc., and more manufacturing facilities opened in South Carolina. The company bought out its Canadian licensee and made it a subsidiary.[41]

Nylon, first introduced during the 1940s, became immensely popular during the 1950s. Its fast drying properties made it extremely popular for swimsuits, and it also was used in sweaters and foundations.

Paul M. DeKoning replaced John Zehntbauer — one of the founders — as president in 1956. Changes continued and Jantzen split into four divisions (Misses, Mens, Intimate Apparel and International), in the 1960s. Each was responsible for its own planning, production, sales, finance and merchandising.[42] In 1966, Jantzen purchased Brenton Textiles, a North Carolina-based men's sweater contractor. When Robert W. Roth succeeded DeKoning as president in 1968, he guided the company toward production and sales of more sportswear.[43]

Jantzen was listed on the New York Stock Exchange in February 1970, and continued to expand that year by adding a men's clothing manufacturing plant in Eunice, Louisiana. Over the next several years Jantzen built factories in Hood River, Oregon, and Lincoln, Nebraska, but divested itself of the Australian subsidiary (in 1973) and the Intimate Apparel Division (in 1977).[44]

The company was growing by leaps and bounds and even considered buying Wrangler Jeans, said Dan MacFarlan, a Jantzen sales director who eventually became head of VF's coalition for intimate apparel, playwear and knitwear, but officials didn't foresee the merger with Blue Bell.

"Blue Bell made the offer while Roth was actually flying from Portland to New York. Not a whole lot

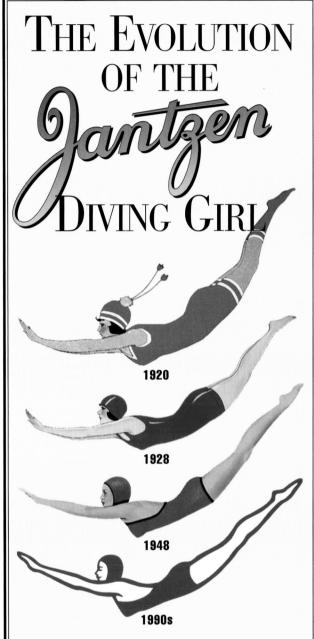

THE EVOLUTION OF THE *Jantzen* DIVING GIRL

1920

1928

1948

1990s

LIKE THE WOMEN who wear her namesake suits, the Jantzen girl has changed. Eager to shed anything that would slow her down, she left her hat and stockings on the shore sometime in the twenties. Her suit shorter and cap sleeker, she emerged from the tumultuous thirties and forties a new woman. For the 1990s and beyond, she's streamlined, athletic, fluid — and clearly in the swim of things.

of us really were close enough to the marketplace to realize we were vulnerable. So when Blue Bell bought us, everybody kind of grabbed books and said 'who the hell is Blue Bell?' — because there are Blue Bell potato chips and Blue Bell ice cream."

While most of Jantzen's managers had marketing backgrounds, "Blue Bell was an engineering-driven company," MacFarlan said. "So our first meetings were kind of like the Addams Family...it was pretty interesting." Blue Bell instituted psychological testing to determine if each manager's talents matched his job, but Jantzen had a simpler method, MacFarlan said. "They had a very unique pay system. You had a small monthly draw — the largest draw you could take was $2,000 a month — and you had to pay all your travel expenses and obviously live off that, which after taxes is not a lot of money. And then your commissions were settled once a year." This quickly winnowed out anyone who couldn't sell, couldn't plan ahead or couldn't manage money, he said.

After Blue Bell acquired Jantzen in 1980, fabric cutting operations for the Portland, Vancouver and Hood River factories were consolidated at the Portland plant, where an advanced Gerber-Hughes Scientific automatic cutting system was installed. Those weren't the only changes.

"In the early days an awful lot of people — a lot of senior management — opted to leave," MacFarlan said. "Blue Bell did re-engineer the company and take a harder look at the way we produced things because, as I said, they were engineers at heart. Not that they weren't gifted at doing their marketing pieces, but they really were efficient manufacturers. The first couple of years were pretty rocky but eventually it smoothed out."[45]

In 1983, Jerome M. Pool, who had been with the company 26 years, became Jantzen's fourth president. The following year, Blue Bell acquired JanSport, a backpack and outdoor/sports apparel manufacturer based in Appleton, Wisconsin.[46]

JanSport for the Sporting Life

In 1967, Murray Pletz, an industrial design student at the University of Washington, entered a contest sponsored by the Aluminum Company of America (Alcoa). The challenge was to create a product that best utilized the particular properties of aluminum.[47] In a room above his family's muffler shop, Pletz fashioned an aluminum frame for a backpack and Jan Lewis, his fiancée, sewed a bag to fit it. Hiking and backpacking were popular in Washington, and making a frame for a backpack seemed a logical use of strong, lightweight aluminum.

Pletz won the contest and decided to manufacture and sell the packs. His cousin, Skip Yowell, also a college student, was brought on board. The young entrepreneurs got a loan from their parents and JanSport was launched in the space above Pletz's father's muffler shop.[48]

Pletz named the company after his bride-to-be, but she said the name was not his first choice. "He thought it should be United Something-or-Other or Northwest Whatever. Then he thought it should have sport in the name. He considered JohnSport since John is his real first name. Then JanSport came up and it just fit."[49] The couple married but later divorced.

The company soon offered variations on its original backpack. A child-sized pack was developed for Eddie Bauer and the Recreational Equipment Co-op, outdoor products companies that were JanSport's first customers. Then a small day pack was created so skiers could carry their lunches. The pack was sold in the bookstore at the University of Washington in Seattle, and students soon began using it to carry books. "They needed something like that because Seattle is so rainy," Yowell said. "It was a good way to carry the books and keep them dry at the same time."[50] By 1972, annual sales were just under $500,000, and larger quarters were needed. The company moved to a 20,000-square-foot plant about 30 miles north of Seattle in Everett, Washington.[51]

The company, which had added domed, lightweight tents to its merchandise line, seemed poised to take off, but like many small companies, it had outgrown its start-up capital and was not able to keep up with the increasing costs associated with rapid growth. The company was sold to K2 Corporation, an alpine ski manufacturer based in Vashon Island, Washington.[52] Under K2, the company launched its first advertising campaign, added new products and sponsored its first Mount Rainier climb and seminar for dealers. Within two years,

Above: Cousins Murray Pletz, left, and Skip Yowell founded JanSport in a room over the family muffler shop. In this 1970s photo, they display an early daypack.

Right: Millions of students tote modern JanSport bookbags, backpacks and daypacks. Because kids' activities are many and varied, they use backpacks to organize their possessions for the day.

VF's Market Mastery

With four national brands of jeans instead of one, VF Corporation captured roughly one-fourth of the total jeans market — good news, because jeans were the largest of all apparel segments with worldwide revenues of about $6 billion a year. Acquiring Red Kap, Jantzen and JanSport further expanded and diversified its product line. "It was one of those situations where you knew immediately it was the right thing for the company," said Lawrence Pugh, CEO at the time.

"Not only did the numbers work, and they contributed significantly to our earnings per share right away, but it also gave us several more brands, and that was really the start of my strategy of trying to dominate a specific product category." [55]

The merger gave VF a significant lock on the jeans business, which might have been an obstacle had the Federal Trade Commission objected. "We went through an extensive investigation by the FTC, but it was approved," Pugh said. "We thought it would be, but naturally they looked at it."[56]

The move necessitated a change in marketing strategy for Lee. "What we wanted to do was sell jeans to all stores in the United States, and Lee was only

sales topped $1 million. By 1976 the company also made sleeping bags and some outerwear.[53]

JanSport was sold to Downers, which in turn sold the growing company to Jantzen in 1984. Jantzen was already owned by Blue Bell International, which would become part of VF Corporation just two years later.[54]

selling to certain levels of distribution. It was clear that department stores were not going to carry the products that discounters had, and vice versa. We needed to have multiple brands in a particular major category."[57]

Bringing Rivals Together

The corporation worked hard in 1987 to streamline Blue Bell and integrate its companies into VF operations. Blue Bell's Greensboro headquarters was closed and each division asked to assess its products and eliminate or modify lines that were unprofitable. Eight Wrangler sewing plants were phased out within three months, the company's separate marketing groups for its male and female jeans lines were consolidated, and other departments were combined.[58]

More than 1,600 workers were laid off in the months immediately following the merger, 900 as a result of closing the Wrangler sewing plants, and 200 from closing Blue Bell's headquarters.[59]

Lori Tarnoski, who rose to become VF vice president and corporate secretary, recalled that VF executives traveled to Blue Bell headquarters to analyze operations and determine appropriate strategies to streamline the business. Blue Bell executives dressed very casually, while VF executives wore suits, a practice that has since changed. "We at VF were very formal. They called us the blue suits," Tarnoski said.[60]

Lee and Wrangler had to put aside a fierce rivalry that had grown in the years prior to the acquisition.[61] A half-serious article in Blue Bell's company magazine, *The Bell Ringer*, compared the acquisition to news that the United States had been sold to the Soviet Union. "Wrangler, Lee and Levi were the three big names," noted Steve Lehmann, who joined Blue Bell in 1971 and rose to VF Factory Outlet vice president of administration.

"Lee bills itself as the brand that fits, and therefore does very well with female customers. Wrangler, on the other hand, targeted not only males, but Western males. ... To some extent, the actual targeted consumers were two different groups, but Lee was always trying to get some men's business and Wrangler was always trying to get some women's business. Levi, on the other hand, was known as a

Western brand because of its California origin, but they started to go after young, affluent urban customers. ... It was highly competitive, and it was a very odd feeling to be bought by VF Corporation and realize that it was Lee."[62]

Mackey McDonald, who became president of Wrangler in 1986 and VF president in 1993, recalled the challenge.

"There was a lot of suspicion and concern as you have with any acquisition, but particularly when two competitors try to pull something together. A lot of people were terminated as a result of the acquisition. ... It was clear to me what we needed was not new staffing but to make some decisions about our strategy and set a direction and use the people we had to execute it. We did that very effectively."[63]

Wrangler and Lee may have had their problems, but the partnership between Blue Bell and VF was mutually beneficial from the start. VF financial controller Reklau said the two organizations complemented each other. "Blue Bell had a reputation of being the best in the industry as far as manufacturing expertise, but wasn't real strong in the marketing areas. VF had a good reputation in marketing. So they thought there might be some situations where two plus two would equal four and a half — synergy or whatever you want to call it."[64]

Tim Lambeth, who had joined Blue Bell in 1968 and was vice president of Finance and Administration for Wrangler at the time, agreed. "One of the things VF brought to us was a very strong emphasis on operational and inventory controls," said Lambeth, who rose to become president of VF's European operations.[65]

Clift agreed. "VF brought some control onto the product line that Blue Bell never had. They really made us more product-focused."[66]

Bob Coppage, president of VF Europe Jeanswear, was working at Wrangler when the merger was announced. He remarked that VF officers brought with them values, ethics and discipline.

"I think it made us act like a much larger corporation. Literally, overnight we became a very large apparel corporation and a dominant force in the jeans business, in particular with the combination of

Wrangler and Lee under the same corporate parent. Among the many things that VF brought to Blue Bell were very good operating disciplines, very involved management at all levels, and a very professional group with very professional standards who were really dedicated to running the apparel business and moving the whole corporation forward."[67]

Despite some difficulties, officials looked back on the decade with great satisfaction. From two labels in 1980 — Vanity Fair and Lee — the corporation had expanded to 12 by 1989.[68] Sales and earnings more than quadrupled during the decade, and the 1989 value of a share of VF Corporation stock was more than 17 times its 1980 value.[69]

Putting aside their traditional rivalry, Wrangler and Lee united to manufacture and market their brands under the VF umbrella. VF now had a secure hold on the jeans market, and the future looked bright indeed.

The authentic "American Look," embodied in the Wrangler SilverLake Collection, goes international.

CHAPTER ELEVEN

BACK ON TRACK

1989–1992

"We make certain we have appropriate product value combined with honest brand names, and an emphasis on a flow-replenishment system which ensures that a product is on the shelf when the consumer needs it."

— Lawrence Pugh, 1993[1]

DESPITE WRANGLER'S success, the late 1980s got off to a financially precarious start for VF, in large part because Lee Jeans, faltering since the middle of the decade, had yet to recover. The decline in Lee's revenue was cause for concern, as Lee had accounted for 80 percent of VF's sales in 1983. By 1986, though Lee's sales grew, earnings had fallen 7.2 percent. "We just made some mistakes," Lawrence Pugh said in 1987. "We put out four product lines a year. In this business, if you miss two of them in a year, you can get into trouble," he said. "We missed two of them. We misread the market from a product standpoint. The color of denim was becoming lighter, the fit looser. We also got sloppy in some of our marketing programs. When I say sloppy, I mean the programs were not focused enough, and that includes advertising."[2]

Lee not only had to battle decreasing demand for its product, but its retailer response system suffered from a number of problems. As a result, five Lee plants closed that year. In addition, two distribution centers were slated to close in 1989, because a technically superior center would take their place.

Lee's product line was also streamlined and Richard C. Lamm was named new president and chief operating officer. Pugh hoped the changes would put Lee back on track. "About 50 percent of its troubles were due to a decline in the indus-

try, while the other 50 percent was due to our own mismanagement," he admitted.[3]

The Lee Company continued to post declines in sales and profits in 1989. Jeans sales remained flat throughout the industry, having fallen sharply since 1987. Sales in VF's Jeanswear group had decreased by 6 percent from 1988 and had fallen off by 11 percent since 1987. The problem, though, was primarily with Lee. Profits for Wrangler, Girbaud and Rustler had grown significantly in the previous two years, while Lee's continued to fall.[4]

Robert S. Stec, VF Corporation vice president of marketing, described 1989 as a "roller coaster" year for the jeans industry. Demand was heavy in the first part of the year, he said, and clothiers responded, flooding the market with dark denim jeans. But lighter shades, which jeansmakers had viewed as a fad, suddenly became the rage. Customers rejected the dark blue jeans and Lee — which had gone "back to basics" — was especially hard hit.[5]

The problems were so extreme that VF managers feared they wouldn't be able to save the company. They took steps in 1988 and 1989 to further streamline the organization, but those steps back-

---

Acquiring Healthtex gave VF a share of the thriving children's market.

fired. Lee had been experimenting with special cloth finishes for its jeans, but the plan was curtailed as part of the cutbacks. When in early 1989 there was a sudden spurt of demand for the special jeans, Lee couldn't meet it because its manufacturing capability had been hobbled.[6]

Lee's problems eroded the growth of its parent company. VF's 1990 sales increased 3 percent to $2.6 billion, but profits dropped nearly $95 million, from $176 million in 1989 to $81 million.[7] Part of the problem was that the corporation had spent $42.3 million to restructure the Lee and Jantzen divisions.[8] The Lee Company, which had seen domestic sales drop 14 percent since 1988, still required major changes. "We did not have a good 1990," Pugh explained. "Ninety percent of the reason was the mismanagement of The Lee Company."[9] When Richard C. Lamm, chairman, retired in April 1990 after more than 45 years with VF, Frederick J. Rowan II, who had served as president and chief operating officer, remained at Lee as president.[10]

Global Responsiveness

Regardless of its internal problems, VF Corporation in the nineties made progress on many fronts. The company implemented its unique Market Response System, continued its global growth and acquired a host of companies that expanded its product offerings.

The Market Response System was important for the corporation's long-term strategy in a highly competitive marketplace. All divisions were expected to take advantage of the detailed point-of-sale information it would provide. Corporate goals were to reduce cycle times 40 percent, total inventories 30 percent and costs 20 percent, all of which should be of benefit to the consumer as well, according to Lawrence Pugh.[11]

Mackey McDonald, then president of Wrangler, explained that an increase in the amount of retail space created more competition for consumers' dollars. The competition made it difficult to raise prices, so VF found ways to make both itself and the retailers it sold to more profitable. Its unique Market Response System strengthened VF's position as an industry innovator and leader.

Later that year, McDonald, was named one of the VF Corporation's four group vice presidents, joining Paul R. Charron, C. William Crain and Frederick J. Rowan II. McDonald, who replaced

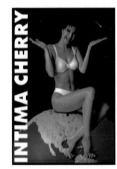

1986: Lee sales are up, but earnings drop.

1991: Wrangler makes uniforms for American soldiers fighting in the Persian Gulf.

1990: VF sales increase, but profits decline.

1991: VF acquires Healthtex, Barbizon and WorkWear.

H. Varnell Moore as vice president, also retained his leadership of Wrangler.[12]

Lee Bounces Back

The aggressive strategies paid off. VF Corporation's financial performance rebounded in 1991, with net income nearly doubling and sales climbing 13 percent to near the $3 billion mark.[13] Credit went to the Market Response System and to the Lee Company, which finally regained its footing and contributed to a 14 percent sales jump in the Jeanswear group. Lee introduced several new and successful styles, such as the Baggy Rider and Easy Rider jeans for boys, and Elastic Rider and Relaxed Rider jeans for women. These new lines were basically adaptations of existing styles but were very well received — the Relaxed and Easy Rider styles, in fact, were the best selling women's jeans in the industry.[14]

Lee also extended its product offering beyond jeans, selling fleece T-shirts, turtlenecks, polo shirts and other casual clothing manufactured by Bassett-Walker and marketed under the Lee label.[15] Sales of Lee-branded fleece clothing more than doubled in 1990, the corporation spent $5 million to add knitting equipment to increase production. Bassett-Walker retained a few private label accounts, but most of its output was earmarked for Lee.[16] In turn, Lee boosted its advertising for the fleece clothing line.[17]

Mackey McDonald became VF Group vice president of Jeanswear, which managed Lee and Wrangler. Tim Lambeth became president of Lee, and the company launched a successful print and television ad campaign during the Summer Olympics.[19] Lee's sales increased by an enviable 31 percent, boosting VF's share of the American jeanswear market from 27 percent to 30 percent.[20]

The division announced a marketing change late that year: all Lee brand jeans and casualwear would be sold only in department and specialty stores. A new Lee brand, Riders, would be sold to discount stores. Riders also would offer jeans and casualwear, much of which would be produced by Bassett-Walker.[21] Wrangler would still be sold at Wal-Mart and Kmart.

Analysts predicted that the change would further increase VF's market share. Lee's biggest competitor, the Levi Strauss Company, was opening its own stores, creating strategic new openings

December 1992: VF extends its European intimates business with the acquisitions of Vivesa and JBE.

May 1992: Mackey McDonald becomes president of Lee, replacing Frederick Rowan.

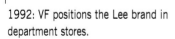

February 1992: VF sells off the real estate relating to 21 of its 23 factory outlet stores.

1992: VF positions the Lee brand in department stores.

on department store shelves. Lee was anxious to fill these openings with its jeans but had to remove its core brand from discount stores to do so.

"A lot of department stores won't buy [from the manufacturer] what's in Jamesway or Hills or Caldor," said Deborah Bronston, a New York analyst who profiled VF Corporation for Prudential Securities. But giving the discount stores another brand and moving Lee to department stores would solve the problem, she said.[22]

Tim Lambeth, who became Lee's president after McDonald, said the discounters' first reaction was negative but the company put diligent effort into changing their minds:

"I went around to every one of those retailers and told them what we were going to do. We had a phased-in approach. We told them we were going to take Lee away and make Riders their brand. They would have a period of time when we offered exactly the same product as Lee but it would have the Riders name on it."[23]

Wrangler Remains Strong

McDonald gave the business new focus, as he explained in 1996. "We got out of the women's business in the late 1980s because we were spending a lot of time in that area with little result. We intensified our focus on the Western business, which was the core business. We put together a group that would focus on the discount channel distribution because that was an important part of our business but it really didn't have a focus. They launched the [Wrangler] American Hero Program, which is now about a $600 million business."[24]

A line of outdoor clothing called Wrangler Rugged Wear was introduced in the late eighties, and the Timber Creek by Wrangler casual pant line was introduced in 1990.

With Westernwear sales booming, Wrangler dominated the marketplace in the nineties. But

the division also played an important role in one of the pivotal events of the decade.

On August 2, 1990, one hundred thousand Iraqi soldiers roared into Kuwait, quickly overwhelming the small country. The United States rushed troops to Saudi Arabia to forestall a possible attack against this poorly defended, vital oil-producing nation.

Reserves and national guardsmen were soon called up to face the Iraqi army, the fourth largest in the world. Wrangler was called upon in 1991 to produce one million pairs of combat fatigue trousers for the soldiers. The contract, valued at $17 million, required the desert-tan

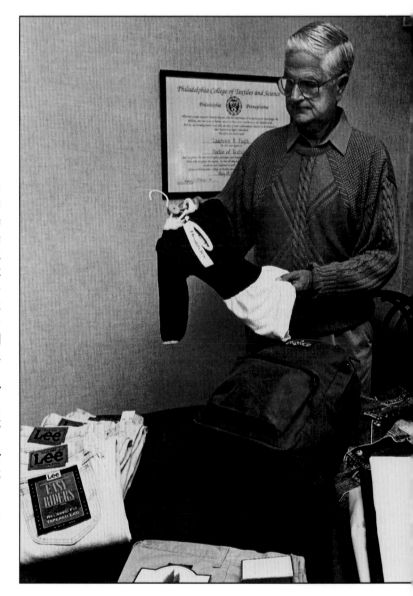

By the early 1990s, VF was producing everything from underwear to backpacks. Chairman Lawrence Pugh displays some of the company's many, and diversified, products.

fatigues to be lightweight and sturdy, to allow for freer movement as troops labored under the hot sun.[25]

Meanwhile, Wrangler dominated the market with its Westernwear jeans and shirts.[26] The division's success was due in part to the widespread popularity of country/western music. Once confined to a small group of fans, country/western has since become the most widely listened-to style of music in the United States. Garth Brooks' *No Fences* album, for example, sold more than 13 million copies in five years to become the top-selling country album of all time.[27] And it seemed that this new breed of listeners saw Western-style clothing as the perfect complement to the music. By 1992, Wrangler achieved record sales in all product lines.

Wrangler America, the line of basic fashion jeans sold through discount channels, became the leading brand in its category during 1992. Encouraged by this success, Wrangler launched a Wrangler America for Women line the following year. Wrangler Rugged Wear continued to expand its distribution throughout specialty and department stores.

John P. Schamberger became Wrangler president in 1992 when McDonald was named president of VF Corporation. In 1995, Schamberger became chairman of VF Corporation's Jeanswear Coalition, and Donald Laws became president of Wrangler.

The growth of market share made it necessary to expand Wrangler's production and distribution facilities. A capital improvement program was launched in 1992, to be continued the following year.[28]

International Expansion

The International Division, which focused primarily on expanding the overseas production and sales of the Lee and Wrangler brands, experienced record growth in the early nineties.[29] The worldwide jeans market had been growing rapid-

Mackey McDonald, who would become CEO and president of VF in 1996, had his hands full at Wrangler even before he became head of the parent company.

ly for several decades, and VF had established a network of wholly owned foreign subsidiaries, joint ventures and licensees. In 1990, VF Corporation brands were available in more than 150 countries around the world.[30]

In Western Europe, Lee and Wrangler brands were becoming increasingly popular. With that success in hand, VF officials were considering venture opportunities in Eastern Europe, particularly Hungary, Czechoslovakia and Poland.[31] "We've been shipping over the years into Eastern bloc countries," Pugh said. "Lee and Wrangler are the labels that are recognized and wanted. We think there are tremendous opportunities for our products in the Eastern countries."[32]

Cataclysmic changes were taking place in Eastern Europe. A cry for democracy was heard after Marxist economies failed in Hungary, East Germany, Czechoslovakia, Bulgaria and Romania. The Berlin Wall fell, officially reuniting East and West Germany for the first time in 40 years. Poland's first free election since the Communist takeover brought Lech Walesa's Solidarity party to power in 1989. The time was right for expansion into new markets.

Officials were also planning to introduce different products, such as T-shirts and fleece goods, to European markets. With trade initiatives among the United States, Canada and Mexico steadily improving, VF International was also poised for expansion in North America. Asian and Latin American markets were under consideration as well.[33]

Fashion was becoming more of an international phenomenon. The "American look," exemplified

VF demonstrated its global vision, expanding international operations and marketing products, including its Wrangler SilverLake line, extensively abroad.

by American jeans and by the fashions of such designers as Ralph Lauren, Calvin Klein, Bill Blass and Donna Karan, was extremely popular in many countries. In America, fashions reflecting the looks of other countries were popular. "The latest buzzword for fashion isn't mini or maxi or stretch. It's globalization," reported *The New York Times*.[34]

Mackey McDonald, who was president at the time and has since become chief executive officer, said making the company an international powerhouse has been challenging.

"You have to be able to take what you do well as a company and translate it into different global markets, while at the same time offering differences in your approach so you can offer the products that each market demands. You have to know what should remain the same and what strengths you can depend on and also understand what needs to be different in each market."[35]

He also noted that the export of Western fashions had provided tremendous opportunity for VF.

"Sports is one area that helps to drive what people want to wear, and a lot of that comes from the U.S. A lot of the entertainment, a lot of movies, TV shows that are seen worldwide come out of the U.S. A lot of the news and cable news is seen worldwide. So it helps to carry the message that what Americans wear is acceptable around the world, and there's nothing more American than jeans. ... So the demand for American jeans worldwide is very strong. Our brands are known in just about every country you go into. Jeans are acceptable everywhere, but the fit and styles are obviously different in

each market around the world. So you have to take what is known and consistent about jeans and adapt it to each market."[36]

Sportswear

Profits for the sportswear/activewear product group, which included Bassett-Walker, Jantzen and JanSport, declined in 1990. Problems at Jantzen were blamed for the drop, so to enhance relationships with retailers, the division divided products into four categories: women's casualwear, women's swimwear, men's sweaters and men's activewear. A marketing group was assigned to each category.[37]

Jantzen's performance rapidly improved, helping the casual/sportswear product group post profits of $38 million in 1991, up from $14.8 million. Sales rose from $487.6 million to $505.8 million.

JanSport, the little sister of the product group, continued to grow, producing JanSport Apparel, a line of outdoor clothing for men which was due to be introduced in stores early the following year.[38] JanSport was distinguished during 1992 by a 70 percent increase in operating profit, due primarily to record sales of day packs and backpacking gear.[39]

Intimate Apparel

In January 1990, the corporation purchased Vassarette and Form-O-Uth, the intimate apparel divisions of Munsingwear, Inc., for $11.5 million. The companies were integrated into the intimate apparel group but their products were marketed differently.

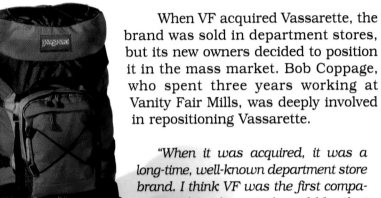

Above: For many outdoor sports enthusiasts, JanSport backpacks are essential gear.

Right: Award-winning Janet Peters, VF Corporation's first woman vice president, headed the profitable Private Label Division of Vanity Fair Mills.

When VF acquired Vassarette, the brand was sold in department stores, but its new owners decided to position it in the mass market. Bob Coppage, who spent three years working at Vanity Fair Mills, was deeply involved in repositioning Vassarette.

"When it was acquired, it was a long-time, well-known department store brand. I think VF was the first company to take a lingerie brand like that and re-position it for the mass merchandisers and the strategy was very smart in that Vanity Fair was uniquely positioned to leverage its credibility as a very well-known, fashionable, department store brand."[40]

After the repositioning, Form-O-Uth garments were manufactured through private labels. Vassarette was merchandised at first through Wal-Mart and later through Kmart and Target. Peter Velardi, who was national sales manager for Vanity Fair Mills, said the company's ability to penetrate new markets was critical to its success.

"Women are going to buy the same number of bras. The population has not risen dramatically. So to take a larger share of the market, you have to segment your market and go into new markets, which is why we acquired Vassarette and went into Wal-Mart. There was a customer there that we were missing because she could not afford the price points in the department store."[41]

The intimate apparel product group, made up of Vanity Fair, Modern Globe, Vassarette and Form-O-Uth, was the only group with overall increases in sales and

profits during 1990. Vanity Fair was the star of the group, with record gains in sales and profits.[42]

Vanity Fair's private label business — which produced lingerie for Victoria's Secret, J.C. Penney, Sears, Lane Bryant and others — represented an important part of the company's overall sales.[43] Vanity Fair's private label sales nearly doubled between 1990 and 1992.[44] The unit was headed by Janet Peters, VF Corporation's first woman vice president.

In November 1992, Peters won the apparel industry's prestigious Femmy Award by the Underfashion Club of New York. Peters, who had been employed by VF for 41 years, was described as an industry leader who had set an example for excellence.[45]

For Vanity Fair's own brand, the company formed a licensing agreement with Eileen West, a producer of all-natural fiber products for upscale department and specialty stores, to manufac-

ture daywear and foundations under the Eileen West label.[46]

Vanity Fair, the largest division within the intimate apparel group, experienced dramatic growth in sales and market share. It expanded its offerings of full-figure and cotton foundations and introduced the Slender Slip, a new line of shapewear that sold particularly well. Sleepwear sales also increased dramatically during the year.

Acquisitions

In 1991, VF Corporation acquired most of the operating assets of Healthtex, Inc., a leading manufacturer of children's clothing; Barbizon, a well-known manufacturer of sleepwear and loungewear; and WorkWear, a major occupational apparel brand. All three companies were in the midst of financial difficulties.

VF paid $29 million for Healthtex — which had been experiencing losses — and took over its factories in Warrenton, Georgia; Danville, Virginia; and Centreville, Alabama.[47] Healthtex, suffering growing pains during its first year as a VF company, posted a slight dip in profit despite increased sales. The company had neglected relationships with its customers, which the parent company rebuilt. Under the VF umbrella, Healthtex introduced new lines of bodysuits and mix-and-match separates for infants in 1992, along with an easy-to-use size chart that helped parents with purchases. More than one million charts were distributed.[48]

The purchase of Barbizon for slightly less than $20 million in July 1991 included Barbizon brand sleepwear and daywear and 43 Barbizon outlet stores, but no factories. Acquisition of the financially ailing company, based in Pine Brook, New Jersey, also gave VF two trademarked fabrics: Cuddleskin and Blendaire.[49] However, the acquisition did not work out as well as planned, admitted Controller Dave Reklau in 1997.

Raising consciousness and ringing up sales: Healthtex ads helped parents answer complicated questions.

"We had hoped to take the Barbizon brand name out of the department store channel of distribution and give it to discounters like Kmart. Wal-Mart had done pretty well with Vassarette, so hopefully Kmart or Sears would want the Barbizon name and we could do the same thing again. For whatever reasons, it didn't work. Some of the retailers liked the idea but they weren't willing to write the order. So we ended up trying to make a go of it with the Barbizon retail store concept. We expanded that to about 85 stores and finally figured out that we couldn't make that work either. So we are in the process of closing some of those stores."[50]

VF next acquired the WorkWear Corporation, Inc., which had filed for bankruptcy, for $11.5 million.[51] That sale included manufacturing plants in Erwin and Alexandria, Tennessee; Piedmont, Alabama; Vienna, Georgia; a central distribution center in Memphis, Tennessee; and three regional centers. VF also bought its inventories, machinery and equipment. WorkWear became a separate business within the Red Kap Division.[52]

In 1992, the Intimate Apparel product group was divided into the domestic and foreign categories. Vanity Fair had been sold through distributors in Europe for many years.

Modern Globe, formerly part of the domestic intimate apparel group, was reclassified as part of the casual/sportswear group and was manufacturing printable T-shirts instead of cotton underwear. The printable T-shirt business was booming, particularly those sold under the Lee brand, and provided a perfect partner to Bassett-Walker's fleece products.[53]

That left Vanity Fair, Vassarette and Barbizon in the domestic intimate apparel group, which posted a record increase of 26 percent in operating profit during 1992, despite a 7 percent drop in sales attributed to the loss of Modern Globe. Reduced overhead, improved manufacturing performance and tighter financial controls were credited with the profit increase.[54]

Going Green

VF purchased Los Angeles-based Green Cotton Environment early in 1992. The company produced items from 100 percent certified organic cotton, embellished with vegetable-based and water-based inks and dyes.[55] The new acquisition would serve as VF's connection to the "green" arena, which promised to be a major social, political and business force.

"Reduce, Reuse and Recycle" was the mantra of many environmentally conscious groups. School children and community groups organized projects to clean up, reduce waste and consume less. Furs and animal-tested cosmetics and shampoos were out, while natural, undyed, unbleached clothing was in. Eco-friendly stores were big news in United States and European cities, and saving rainforests became a mainstream topic of conversation.[56] Manufacturers of clothing, cosmetics and other products wanted to participate in this phenomenon.

Jantzen established Clean Water shops in some of the department stores that carried its merchandise. A cooperative effort between Jantzen, the retailer and local environmental groups, the campaign featured in-store displays of outdoorsy, environmentally minded clothing,

Jantzen became part of the "green" movement with its campaign for clean waterways.

while publicly reinforcing Jantzen's commitment to clean waterways.

The acquired Green Cotton became the O line marketed by Girbaud in September 1992, a collection of knit clothes for men and women that featured "green" materials and boasted environmentally sound manufacturing methods. Wrangler was also developing "Earth Wash," a new, environmentally friendly method of finishing jeans.[57]

International Growth and Acquisitions

On January 30, 1992, VF acquired the common stock of the Valero Group, a Paris-based manufacturer and marketer of women's intimate apparel, for $34.6 million.[58] Lawrence Pugh called the acquisition "the most important acquisition for VF since Blue Bell."

The Valero Group was made up of three companies under the name of DaMart, a publicly traded French company. The group produced and distributed intimate apparel under the Variance, Siltex, Bolero and Silhouette brand names.[59]

Michael Jonchére, who was general manager of Variance, recalled the transition. "Variance was really a $14 million business, which was a fairly large company in the French market. In the mass market, I think it was deemed the second player," he said in a 1997 interview.

"But when you run a small French company and you join a big company, you go to Reading and you can see the differences. They weren't all problems, but challenges. So our first challenge was to make them understand the fashion business in a small country as compared to the States. And the second was to send every week, every month all these figures dealing with the reporting sessions."[60]

The new financial discipline was healthy, Jonchére said.

"It really has been a great opportunity because a good system in terms of plans, forecast-

ing and process has allowed us to make huge progress. The business control has been built for an apparel company, not for a car company or a computer company."[61]

Jonchére rose to become president of VF Diffusion, which oversees European mass marketing of VF's intimate lines.

That year, VF also acquired the Spanish company Vivesa and its French affiliate Jean Bellanger Enterprises, for $116.3 million. These companies produced intimate apparel under the brand names of Intima Cherry, Lou, Carina, and Gemma. The acquisitions greatly increased VF's share of the European intimate apparel market.[62]

"Our company was a family business," said Pere Prat, Vivesa's executive vice president at the time of the acquisition.

"When we became part of VF, the company had an MRS system that was one of the most powerful in the trade. VF developed a system of Shared Services and Common Systems, supported by an efficient management team. To our surprise, its success went beyond our expectations. This has been the major impact of our careers. We have clear company goals. It is easy to reach the top managers. We work together and we fight difficulties as a team."[63]

Prat, who rose to VF International Intimates Coalition chairman in early 1998, had an early insight into the corporate culture.

"Mr. Larry Pugh, when he was negotiating the acquisition of our company, was interested in personally visiting the company, the manufacturing facilities, etc. He arrived very late at night in the company plane. The first word he said to me was that he had forgotten his passport. The Spanish immigration office accepted our proposal to guarantee Mr. Pugh's integrity, under promise of our presenting

INTIMA CHERRY

Above: In 1992, VF acquired Vivesa and Jean Bellanger, which produced lingerie under the Intima Cherry name.

Opposite page: Pere Prat, VF International Intimates Coalition chairman, got an insight into Lawrence Pugh's integrity when the latter left his passport home.

Mr. Pugh's passport at the official desk early the next morning.

"We contacted the U.S. consul in Barcelona. When Mr. Pugh arrived at the consulate with his photos, papers and so on, the employee at the desk asked him whether he had lost his passport or simply forgotten it. In the first case, the new passport would be for five years and free. In the second, it would be for 15 days and there would be a $100 fine.

"Mr. Pugh said, 'I've forgotten my passport at the office. I thought it was in my briefcase, but I've checked with my assistant and she says it's in my desk.' The employee smiled appreciatively and thanked Mr. Pugh. At that moment we were very relieved to see the ethics and integrity of the people we would work with in the future."[64]

With its newly acquired intimate apparel companies, VF International posted sales gains of 54 percent for 1992.[65] The division planned to continue its expansion in Europe with the establishment in 1992 of a centralized VF European organization in Brussels. Maverick jeanswear was introduced in France, Germany and Holland, and a new factory to manufacture Maverick, Lee and Wrangler brands was set to open in Poland in 1993.[66]

The division was also increasingly active in Mexico, having acquired three sewing plants there in 1990 when it purchased Vassarette and Form-O-Uth.[67]

A Scare and an Honor

On April 4, 1991, Chairman, Chief Executive Officer and President Lawrence Pugh underwent emergency coronary bypass surgery. He recovered quickly, was released from the hospital April 13, chaired the board of directors meeting April 15 and attended the annual shareholders' meeting April 16.[68]

Pugh was honored that September by the American Apparel Education Foundation during the American Apparel Manufacturers convention in Atlanta, Georgia. Past honorees included Sam W. Walton, chairman of Wal-Mart Stores, and Roger Milliken of Milliken & Company.[69]

By that time, VF offered 26 brands, and high demand prompted management to announce in February 1992 that it would hire 2,500 new employees nationwide during the year, bringing the total number of employees to about 51,500. The majority of new jobs would be in factories in North Carolina, Alabama, Virginia and Texas.[70]

The employment increase was good news to the Southern factory towns that would benefit. High unemployment had plagued the country for

RESPONDING TO A CHANGING MARKETPLACE

VF CORPORATION'S MARKET Response System keeps the garment conglomerate in front of its competition while providing a unique service for retailers and customers. The electronic inventory control system, first introduced in 1988, gives consumers the clothing they want and retailers the quick merchandise turnover so crucial to profitability.[1]

Traditionally, the ordering and replenishment process was based on projections rather than hard data. The apparel industry employed a lengthy procedure to get its products into stores. New jean styles were presented to retailers and orders taken to determine how many pairs of the jeans should be manufactured. Fabric would then be cut and sewn, and large quantities of the finished product would be stored while shipment was arranged to retailer warehouses. Finally, the product would arrive in the stores, sometimes as long as 18 months after the process began.[2]

This system had some obvious drawbacks. Consumers might lose interest in a product that had caught their collective fancy a year and a half before. This would result in excess inventory — and financial losses — for manufacturers. On the other hand, the product may catch on with the public, and leave the retailer with empty shelves.

VF's Market Response System was designed to eliminate those problems and make VF Corporation more flexible and competitive in all areas — from product design to retail sales.

"I think the most important part of it was that there was always a full inventory of sizes and colors and shapes at the retail outlet," said Bill Pike, a VF director. "A customer won't wait for his size to come in. He'll go across the street and buy from somebody else and you've lost that sale forever."[3]

The Market Response System unified inventory control at the point of sale, transferring all relevant information to the factory. For example, when a pair of Wranglers was purchased, the style, color, finish, size, and any other pertinent information would be transmitted electronically to the Wrangler Division. This allowed personnel to track trends so the division could manufacture enough of the items that were selling well, while reducing inventories of items that were less popular.[4]

Once the sale information was transmitted to Wrangler headquarters and to the retailer's

headquarters, the system would automatically issue a purchase order, a warehouse picking ticket and shipping instructions for an exact replacement pair of jeans, which could be sent directly to the store the very next day. The point-of-sale information also triggered the manufacturing cycle, keeping stock replenished within the division. And it gave retailers easy access to buying patterns, said Lawrence Pugh, VF chairman.

"We just knew that, long-term, we were going to have to understand and know how to service our retailers far better than we had in the past. Quick response was starting to be a buzz word within the industry. A lot of people were talking about it, but we were one of the first to really do something about it."[5]

The Market Response System, used by all divisions in 1991, allowed VF to replenish stock within a week, down from previous turnaround times as long as 90 days. The system also allowed more VF products to be on retailers' shelves at any given time. The rule of thumb in the apparel industry has been that 30 percent of a retailer's stock would be off the shelf at any given time, according to Gerald Johnson, VF's vice president for Finance and chief financial officer in 1996. However, the Market Response System's stock replenishment feature ensured the availability of the most popular items. "We've lowered that 30 percent number for missing stock to about 10 percent," Johnson said. "But the gain is much more than 20 percent. Considering these are the most popular lines where we've gained, the results show almost a doubling of sales."[6]

The company promoted the system with an ad campaign aimed at retailers. The ads, which first appeared in the June 3, 1991, issue of *Fortune*, described VF as a company that would work its hardest to give consumers what they wanted.[7]

"We identified the opportunity for increasing returns of inventory retail as being a growing opportunity to differentiate ourselves from other companies. ... We implemented a lot of technology for capturing sales data and we implemented ways to take that sales data and translate it into orders. Then we began to work on our manufacturing systems. We dramatically reduced the cycle time so we could respond very quickly to what is happening in retail. And we reduced our inventories throughout the process."[8]

"The secret of Vanity Fair and later VF was its controls — inventory control, manufacturing control," said Larry Weidenheimer, a VF employee since 1947. "It's what made the company. I've seen more than one drown in its own inventory."[9]

The Market Response System ensures that VF will maintain its competitive edge.

THE MALL

VF was the beneficiary when "business casual" caught on — and not just for Fridays.

the preceding several years, and remained at 7 percent in June 1991. "We are happy that VF Corporation is strong enough to help fuel the U.S. economy and provide much-needed employment opportunities," Pugh said.[71]

Directors voted in February 1992 to sell 21 of VF's 23 factory outlet store sites to Outlet Properties Corporation, a division of Carolina Pottery. VF would continue to operate the stores under a lease agreement. The corporation received approximately $67 million for the sites.[72]

The sale did not affect VF's original outlet in Wyomissing, Pennsylvania, or an outlet complex in North Dartmouth, Massachusetts. "It (the Wyomissing outlet) is the mothership for us, the home territory," said Harold McKemy, a retired VF vice president. "It is the largest one we have by far and one of the first in the country. We never considered selling it."[73]

Reflecting on 1992, Pugh said VF's success was due to a strict adherence to corporate strategy of giving consumers the products they want, when they want them and at a fair price. "We make certain we have appropriate product value combined with honest brand names, and an emphasis on a flow-replenishment system which ensures that a product is on the shelf when the consumer needs it," he said.[74]

"Another reason is the type of merchandise we sell: for the most part, casual wear, basics. Our products fit what the characteristics of lifestyle

were in 1992. We think we're a corporation for the 1990s. No question our lifestyle will become even more casual than it has been. Plus, people in the world in the 1990s are not going to have as much money to spend as they have previously, and that means they'll want products with value that they can believe in even more than in the past."[75]

Pugh was onto something. At VF and many other corporations across America, ties and jackets were no longer required. "Business casual" was catching on, and not just for Fridays. Khaki slacks or dress jeans were the order of the day for men, while women were free to wear slacks, jeans or more traditional businesswear. Melissa Sones, a contributing editor at the fashion magazine *Mirabella*, summed it up like this:

Chairman, President & CEO Pugh survived emergency coronary surgery in 1991 and continued to lead the company until he handed over the reins to Mackey McDonald later in the 1990s.

"Fashion used to filter down from the aristocracy to the average woman ... but today the so-called aristocracy has changed. While fashion still comes from the runways, we also have other influences: from the streets, from MTV, from rock and roll music, from films and from a multitude of things going on around us."[76]

Exercise clothing, once confined to gyms and tracks, had gone mainstream. "Exercise has been a big influence," Sones wrote. "Women began wearing their exercise clothing on the streets, so that it not only became acceptable to do so, but it bred a wide gamut of new leisure wear styles."[77]

VF, having survived several difficult years while maintaining its market edge, was ready to advance confidently through the 1990s.

VF Corporation grew and diversified in the 1990s, producing a wide variety of goods through a unique corporate structure.

CHAPTER TWELVE

LOOKING AHEAD:
A STRUCTURE FOR GROWTH

1993–1997

*"Innovation is a guidepost at VF. First there are the products. Second,
the innovations we make in our Market Response System, and third, the
way we manage our brands."*

—Mackey McDonald, 1993[1]

IN THE 1990s, executives began to rethink the way VF Corporation did business internally and externally. New manufacturing and inventory methods cut costs, and growth continued domestically and overseas.

But perhaps the biggest change occurred within the headquarters itself. Leadership changed as Lawrence Pugh gradually handed over the reins to Mackey McDonald, who would first become president, then CEO. And McDonald would institute a unique consumerization program that would better position VF for the nineties and beyond.

The New Guard

In September 1993, McDonald replaced Pugh as president. Paul R. Charron was appointed executive vice president, a newly created post, while Pugh remained chairman and CEO to concentrate on international expansion and future acquisitions.[2]

"We will be involved in developing a vision for the corporation, a vision of where we're going and a strategy on how we're going to get there," McDonald told the *Reading Eagle*. "Innovation is a guidepost at VF. First, there are the products. Second, the innovations we make in our Market Response System, and third, the way we manage our brands."[3]

McDonald had joined the corporation as the Lee Company's assistant vice president of Product and Technical Services. He rose through the corporate ranks, eventually becoming group vice president in charge of the Lee, Wrangler, JanSport and Healthtex divisions.[4]

In 1996, McDonald succeeded Pugh as CEO and joined the executive committee, though Pugh remained chairman of the board.[5] After having led the company as it grew from two brands and annual sales of $600 million to nearly two dozen brands and sales of more than $5 billion, Pugh was ready to pass the reins.

"Being CEO of this company has been one of the best jobs in corporate America. I look on it very positively. I've had my time and it's been terrific with no regrets. But we're going to move on, as I'm sure the company will too."[6]

McDonald, described by Pugh as "one of the most respected leaders in the apparel industry today," pledged to keep the company on the course Pugh established. Analysts approved: "This company is building for the future and Mackey is

---

The VF Corporation logo, much like the company itself, has been streamlined over time.

the guy," said Jay Meltzer, director of retail-industry watchdog Johnson Redbook Services in New York City. "He did the job in bringing them to the powerhouse position they are in now."[7] Richard C. Lamm, who was chief executive officer of Lee when McDonald worked there, described the new CEO as "a great talent."[8]

McDonald moved into his new responsibilities smoothly. "Obviously, the two personalities have their own thoughts and basic philosophies of what they'd like to see the company become," said Donald Laws, president of Wrangler Westernwear, "but the root of those philosophies is the same."[9]

"Larry was very driven, and he made his mark," said Steve Ludeman, Jantzen executive vice president. "He did a lot of great things for VF and really positioned where it was going to go. And when he named Mackey, he was very emphatic that this was Mackey's company to run,

that he would advise but he wouldn't get in the way."[10]

Paul Delorey, president of JanSport, said each man "is unique in a pretty interesting way."

"Larry is quick to decide. Mackey takes a little more time. Their styles are somewhat dissimilar but, I think, complementary. They do have one thing in common. Both men are extremely honest, extremely loyal."[11]

Consumerization

Consumerization is the key to successfully positioning VF for the future, McDonald said. "Consumerization, as we define it, is re-orienting

---

At JanSport, "we like to think we think young," said Paul Delorey, its president.

1991: Market Response System, used in all divisions, allows stock replenishment within one week's time.

January 1994: VF acquires Cutler and Nutmeg.

September 21, 1993: Mackey McDonald becomes president.

September 1993: VF acquires Central Corsetera of Spain.

everything we do — manufacturing, product development, systems — toward fulfilling the needs of specific consumers."

Consumers are searching for a greater variety of apparel solutions, McDonald explained. Instead of following one or two trends that steer the market, today's consumer wants to express individuality, and uses apparel to do that.

"It's a major change in the way people buy apparel," McDonald said. "Consumerization was designed to help us better understand these very specific needs and ensure we have the variety of products to meet them."

Because the previous corporate structure was too complicated to efficiently accomplish this, McDonald initiated the coalition concept, balanced manufacturing strategy, and a move to common systems and shared services. "It's an integrated business strategy with consumerization behind all of the major changes."[12]

The Coalition Structure

The VF empire had operated in business groups, and the corporation's earnings reflected its efficient organization. By the end of 1996,

VF's earnings had increased 90 percent to reach a record $299.5 million (up from $157 million the year before).[13] But McDonald focused on what would keep VF successful in the global economy. "We're proud of these results, but we're not going to spend much time looking back," he told analysts in February 1997.

He outlined a new organizational structure for the corporation. Under the plan, VF's 17 domestic and foreign divisions were consolidated into five working groups, called coalitions: Jeanswear, Intimate Apparel, Knitwear, Playwear and International.

The corporation had been operating under a coalition system for several years, but the new organization further consolidated the divisions into one company. "We've been moving toward coalition thinking for the past year and a half," McDonald said in 1997. "Now we're moving to coalition structure."[14]

For example, Lee and Wrangler could combine manufacturing operations, explained Prakash Bhatt, an engineer at Lee from 1972 to 1985 before moving to VF. "To the average customer, it would look like two different products — but as far as the sewing line is concerned, it would not," he said. "To

September 1994: Company announces plans for joint venture in China.

February 1997: VF creates coalition management structure to unite its 17 divisions.

1996: McDonald succeeds Lawrence Pugh as CEO. Pugh remains chairman.

October 1997: VF announces it will move headquarters from Wyomissing to Greensboro, North Carolina.

keep their brand identity, you want to have differentiation in terms of the label and some unique items. You want to maintain the brand identity in terms of how they fit."[15]

The restructuring cost about $150 million, but McDonald said VF should save at least that much each year as a result. The company also planned to streamline many functions. A new service center in Greensboro, North Carolina, was created to centralize information systems and transaction processing for all domestic operations. Vanity Fair brought all administrative operations for Intimate Apparel together under one roof in Atlanta in February 1997.

By late 1997, the new system was well established: the Jeanswear Coalition managed the Wrangler, Lee and Red Kap lines as well as DJ Industries, which oversaw Girbaud and Joe Boxer. The Intimate Apparel Coalition comprised Vanity Fair, Jantzen and JanSport while H.H. Cutler and Healthtex comprise the Playwear Coalition. The Knitwear Coalition consisted of Bassett-Walker and Nutmeg, while the International Coalition managed all overseas operations.

VF's Corporate Culture

The emerging coalition structure would, inevitably, have an effect on VF and on the way its employees viewed the company. "I would say that the corporate culture is changing," said Terry Lay, president of Lee Apparel, late in 1997.

"VF has always stood for honesty, integrity, high energy, very bright people. But because the divisions had their own cultures, we never really looked at it as one big culture. So, really, there's a lot of redefinition going on now."[16]

But honesty and integrity remain central themes throughout the divisions. "I can't overstress the honesty and integrity of this company," said Mark Clift, president of DJ Industries. "We don't bull our employees and we don't stretch things to our retailers."[17]

Frank Urban, vice president of Finance and Administration for the International Coalition, said VF's corporate culture encourages initiative

and responsibility, "but management still likes some control. They don't step back and throw you to the wolves."[18]

The Market Response System

VF continues to improve the way it keeps tabs on customer preferences through the company's proprietary Market Response System. Though all divisions continued to make good use of the system, the Nutmeg and Cutler divisions found it especially valuable for inventory control for dozens of sports teams, graphics and sizes in dozens of locations. Even increased demand for team clothing in a particular area before a big game had to be considered.

VF took the Market Response System a step further in January 1997 with MRS 2000. VF

Lee flares enjoyed a popular resurgence in the 1990s.

formed VF Services Company, a free-standing but wholly owned entity, which established shared computer, financial, inventory, human resources and sourcing systems for all VF divisions. The thinking is that with the "nuts and bolts" aspects of business handled, the divisions will be free to grow their market shares and profits, said Tom Payne, president of VF Services.

"It goes beyond inventory management — it's all of our processes, which include all supply chains, all sales chains, product development and finance. It's part of the movement to transform VF from more of a holding company to more of an operating company. The way Mackey has decided to do it is to organize and leverage the divisions around shared services. The goals are to cut costs and be more efficient, but we'll also generate some revenue growth if we do these processes right."[19]

VF has set a goal of $2 billion in revenue growth by the year 2000, and the MRS initiative is expected to save $150 million per year, he said.[20]

The Brand That Fits

After Lee launched its highly successful "The Brand That Fits" advertising campaign during the 1993 Super Bowl, *Advertising Age* magazine listed Lee as one of the top 200 American super brands. Product innovation continued in 1995, when the company introduced Lee Riveted jeans, produced from premium fabrics and finishes, and Lee Authentic casual clothing. The company also inaugurated Lee Fitfinder, an in-store kiosk system to help women determine what sizes and styles would best suit them.[21] Lee Sport Genuine Casualwear, introduced in department stores in 1996, was designed with business casual days in mind, featuring National Football League team logos in an understated style.[22]

The Brand That Fits ... Abroad

Lee was also expanding overseas. In February 1993, John G. Johnson, president of VF's International Division, announced that the company would begin manufacturing in a leased

Street athletes and skateboarders were the inspiration for Lee's wide leg jeans, which were soon worn by a diverse group of urban and suburban kids.

100,000-square-foot factory in Lodz, Poland. Even more exciting was the joint venture in Guangdong Province, China, under which jeans would be manufactured by a Chinese company to Lee specifications.[23]

Pugh had taken a 12-day journey to China, Hong Kong and Singapore in 1994 to finalize the deal. The new company, in which VF would hold 72 percent ownership, initially would market Lee jeans to department and specialty stores in the Southern Province of Guangdong, China's wealthiest province, he said.[24]

John Johnson, who retired in April 1996, said the Chinese venture gave the corporation a foothold in the Far East and Pacific Rim. "We are addressing the potential of businesses in Indonesia, Malaysia and India," he said.

"That's the area that's going to develop more rapidly in the near future. The European markets are more akin to being mature, as is the United States. South America is another area that will develop in the near future and VF is looking at how to structure its business there."[25]

VF identified Mexico as a natural market. In January 1995 the company paid $12.1 million for an 80 percent interest in Paragon, a company that manufactured and marketed Lee brand products there. "Mexico will have a population of over 100 million by the year 2000, and a large percentage of that will be young people who are heavily influenced by U.S. fashions and trends. That translates into a major marketing opportunity for the Lee brand," said Frank Pickard, VF vice president and treasurer.[26] In March 1995, VF Corporation announced it would launch its Lee jeans in India through a technical assistance agreement between Lee and an Indian company.[27]

Girbaud

Ellen L. Rohde, president of Healthtex, became president of Girbaud in 1993 and remained at the helm until 1995 when Mark Clift took her place.[28] Rohde would rise to president of Vanity Fair by late 1997. VF announced in 1997 that I.C. Isaacs would assume Girbaud's license in 1998. Management had been transferred to DJ Industries, a VF division that handled the Girbaud and Joe Boxer lines, and the decision was made to discontinue the Girbaud contract.

Jantzen and JanSport

McDonald's intention not to rest on VF's laurels clearly had filtered down to individual

Kids carry all manner of things in their backpacks, so JanSport markets packs with compartments for CD players, laptop computers and more.

companies like Jantzen and JanSport. Both had achieved much, and both looked to find ways to extend their respective market shares.[29] "Even though we have 18 to 20 percent of the swimwear market, we think we can get 30 to 35 percent of it," said Steve Ludeman, Jantzen executive vice president, in a 1997 interview.

"Our challenge is to be the complete swimwear company to our customers. We have room to grow, so we're going to keep pushing. We're spending money learning what the consumer wants and going to the retailer to package it for her. We're going to get much better at managing the floor space with our retail partners, so they can say, 'Let Jantzen run your swimwear business.' So we're concentrating our research on the consumer and bringing it back to the retailer."[30]

At JanSport, where the primary focus is the daypack, a smaller version of the backpack, consumer research is also underway. JanSport recently conducted a "deprivation study," in which it took away teenagers' daypacks for several weeks. Without the packs, teens could zero in on the features they missed most. Executives learned that teens use JanSport packs to carry tape and compact disc players, laptop computers, skateboards and in-line skates, in addition to books, lunches and school supplies.

"Kids use a pack as a way to organize their lives," Paul Delorey of JanSport said. "You'll find kids carry everything they need for the day in their bags — for example, we have one pack that is built to carry a CD player, one that's built to carry a laptop computer. You've got to test, you've got to talk to the consumer."[31] He said JanSport had to keep its customers in perspective, rather than "just sit back thousands of miles away from where your consumer is and dream things up." JanSport was founded by young entrepreneurs and "we like to think we think young," Delorey said.

"I kid about this, but we used to have a rule that anyone over 30 couldn't work here. Then we all passed 30, and we changed it to 40, and it's been bumped up several times since then."[32]

Red Kap

In 1991, VF acquired the WorkWear Corporation and absorbed it into Red Kap over a three-year period. In December 1992, Red Kap was incorporated as a separate legal entity operating as a wholly owned VF subsidiary.

Still strongly focused on the rental laundry industry, which picks up, washes and delivers uniforms to businesses, Red Kap in the late 1990s began to respond to retail apparel trends. Uniform wearers "are beginning to have more input into product designs in the uniform business," said Robert Matthews, president of Red Kap. "This industry's going through a lot of changes. The rental laundry industry has been our primary customer base. And because of that, we've been a couple of steps removed from the ultimate consumer of our product." But there are forces at work that will change that.

"Historically, in our business, you think of the old gas station attendant in a light blue shirt and navy blue pants. The impact of casual wear is beginning to have a pretty significant effect on the uniform market — nobody wants to be uniformed in that light blue shirt and navy pant anymore. Our challenge, frankly, is to get closer to the consumer, have the consumer more knowledgeable about our company and what value we bring to the apparel they're wearing."[33]

In 1997, Red Kap celebrated its 75th anniversary. "It's not a big marketplace splash, but we've done a video where we've interviewed all the surviving Red Kap presidents and key sales and manufacturing people throughout the company's history," Matthews said. "It's a great company, and it's great because of its people. What makes Red Kap what it is, is all the people that have

been involved with this company these 75 years regardless of corporate affiliation."[34]

European Intimates

In 1993, VF acquired Central Corsetera, an intimate apparel company in Spain, for $17.6 million. The acquisition, in addition to three other European intimate apparel companies purchased the previous year, gave VF a stronger foothold in the European market.[35] Central Corsetera sold intimate apparel under the Belcor brand name. "Belcor is well-known among consumers and sells well in department stores," said former Executive Vice President Paul Charron. "The reason we wanted the assets is because we wanted the brand name. It is very viable in the minds of the consumers."[36]

Nutmeg

In January 1994, VF acquired two licensed apparel companies: Nutmeg Industries (for $352.2 million) and the H.H. Cutler Company (for $154.7 million). These two brands helped catapult VF Corporation to become the second-largest maker of licensed sports apparel. The National Basketball Association, the National Hockey League and Major League Baseball awarded Nutmeg, a collegiate apparel manufacturer, valuable and prestigious licenses in 1987. A year later the National Football League followed. Working in such an environment has its own rewards, noted Ed Doran, president of VF's Licensed Knitwear Marketing Group. "We're a little unconventional in the way we do things here," he said. "Our operation is fairly informal and we all seem to work well that way. We work hard but we have some fun, too."[37]

Nutmeg had hit on the winning formula. Licensed clothing caught the fancy of urban teens in the late eighties and early nineties, setting the fashion tone for young people around the country, noted Rick Becker, vice president of sales. Within a few years, however, urban kids moved away from licensed apparel and towards designers like Polo, Nautica, Nike and Tommy Hilfiger, which caused Nutmeg's sales to dip in 1995. A baseball strike, a canceled World Series, and a National Hockey League strike complicated things further. The

sports apparel industry suffered its first decline since 1976.

Hoping to cash in on consumers' wide recognition of its Lee brand, VF started marketing most of Nutmeg's line under the Lee Sport label. Daniel G. MacFarlan was named president of Nutmeg late in 1994, and founders Mark and Dick Jacobsen left the business. Nutmeg became part of the VF Knitwear Coalition.

Cutler

The H.H. Cutler Company, founded by Henry Hubbard Cutler in 1950, began as a manufacturer of quality infant clothing and accessories. Business grew until the mid-1970s, when many consumers stopped buying baby items from department and specialty stores, preferring the less expensive national chains and discount stores. The Cutlers knew their company had to change.[38] Noting that jogging suits had quickly gained popularity among adults and pre-teens, Cutler began to manufacture similar garments for babies and toddlers. The suits were made of fleece fabric, which was comfortable, low maintenance, and warm.[39]

After the clothing lines were expanded to include garments for older children, the company grew quickly. It was divided into two primary groups: sleepwear and sports apparel. Sales increased by approximately 70 percent between 1989 and 1992, making the company attractive to corporate suitors.[40]

When VF acquired Cutler, it was headed by Hal C. Smith, the grandson of H.H. Cutler. It owned five manufacturing plants and was shipping more than 46,000 garments each week.[41] Lawrence Pugh said Cutler was a natural fit:

"Cutler is the premier company in the youthwear business in its channel of distribution, and has achieved its success as a result of superior product

Nutmeg, specializing in clothing bearing college and team logos, gave VF a foothold in the licensed apparel market.

and outstanding customer service. The fit with VF is terrific. We share similar business objectives as well as management philosophies."[42]

Unfortunately, Nutmeg and Cutler both experienced a profit drop in 1995 because the sports fashion trend had weakened, said Daniel MacFarlan, then president of Decorated Knitwear.[43] By the end of 1995, the Cutler Sports Apparel Division and Nutmeg were consolidated and the Cutler Sports Apparel factory in Grand Rapids, Michigan closed.[44] In 1997, the two separated.

Nutmeg became part of VF Knitwear and Cutler joined VF Playwear, along with Healthtex, in 1997.

Marketing Playwear and Nike

In late 1997, VF's Playwear Division joined Healthtex and Cutler groups and introduced Nike licensed apparel. "Our goals are three," said Gary Simmons, division president. "We first have to consolidate the two companies, keeping the marketing units separate and unique. Then we want to move forward with a series of initiatives for Healthtex and Nike and then, under Nike, expand the girls' implementation and get some wider distribution in sports specialty stores." The division planned to begin marketing infants' and childrens' clothing emblazoned with the Nike logo in early 1998.

The Playwear Division markets only infant, children and pre-teen clothing and has begun to focus on more sports-oriented apparel. Simmons said in 1997:

"Better makers like Nike, Reebok and Adidas weren't even in children's wear two or three years ago. There was some business but it was nothing like it is today. So the market has definitely changed."

Couples may be having fewer children, but America's population has grown significantly since the big-family 1950s, he said. "Immigration is very important to the mix. A lot of immigrants are younger and they are starting families. With that, obviously, comes children."[45]

Bassett-Walker markets licensed Nike apparel for adults as part of the VF Knitwear Coalition. "We are Nike's largest apparel provider," said George Derhofer, Bassett-Walker president, in 1997. "The name Bassett-Walker doesn't mean anything to anybody because we principally make things for other people." The company manufactures for J.C. Penney, Sears and Kohl's, for instance. "We make about 100 million garments a year, 82 million pounds of fabric," he said.[46]

Giving Back

The corporation maintained a tradition of giving back to the communities where it operated, supporting local chambers of commerce,

Above: Disney favorites and cartoon characters adorned Cutler's baby and kids' clothes.

Below: An old and respected name in children's wear, by 1963 Cutler had established an extensive line. Its founder, H.H. Cutler, had developed a boilable vinyl that made bibs and baby pants more durable.

Lions Clubs and charitable organizations. In Reading, the factory outlet sponsors jazz festivals and the corporation supports the local homeless shelter. In 1993, VF contributed $500,000 to help set up a "character education program" in 20 Alabama communities. The program, geared for children in kindergarten through grade six, enriched the schools' existing curriculum and provided extra learning aids and special programs that were not available.[47]

In 1996, VF Corporation sponsored a major national campaign to raise $1 million for breast cancer research, education, screening and treatment. On October 28, designated Lee National Denim Day, employers were asked to allow workers to wear denim in exchange for a $5 contribution per employee. The proceeds were donated to the nonprofit Susan G. Komen Breast Cancer Foundation.[48]

Producing More with Less

Sales had climbed to break the $5 billion mark in 1995, but that achievement was offset by a dramatic drop in net income, which had fallen from $274.5 million to little more than $157 million. The figures revealed fundamental changes within the industry: Baby boomers — the economic drivers in the United States — worried about saving enough for their children's education, and their own eventual retirement. They wanted more for less, without compromising quality.[49]

Maintaining low prices with high quality and wide selection meant VF had to cut elsewhere. VF slashed administrative expenses while funneling money into consumer research, product development and brand marketing. The corporate offices employed roughly 100 people in 1997, said Sandy McMullen, who began there in 1981. "That takes into consideration all the treasury people, the tax department, maintenance people, things like that. The corporate staff is extremely lean."[50]

Moving Offshore

Another way to cut costs is to reduce the cost of labor. The company in the mid-1990s made the difficult decision to move more of its manufacturing operations offshore. VF stepped up its manufacturing in Mexico, the Caribbean and other areas, creating skilled jobs and expanding the economy in those areas. Executives said they hoped to increase offshore manufacturing over the next two years to 35 percent, up from 20 percent in 1995.[51] "Most of our competitors went offshore before we did," said Cindy Knoebel, director of Investor Relations. "Most will continue to have more offshore manufacturing as a percentage of total manufacturing than VF will."[52]

By the end of 1995, VF officials announced they would close nine plants and lay off 3,800 workers in Southern mills. Lower operating expenses in Mexico, Central America and other countries spurred the move.[53]

"Over the last couple of years, ever since NAFTA was enacted, we've been shifting production out of the States. The reason, obviously, is the lower manufacturing cost," explained Mike Martin, director of Corporate Real Estate.

"My job has kept me busy, because so many companies are facing the same situation and there is an oversupply of buildings in the marketplace. ... Most of the buildings we will use will be built from scratch. Because of the quick move in certain areas where we're trying to get production up and running, we leased buildings."[54]

VF's Playwear Division announced in 1997 its intention to market Nike licensed clothes for kids.

The trend is widespread, Pugh said, but that doesn't make it any more palatable.

"What we decided was that we were going to have to change our ways from a manufacturing standpoint. The major move was the disruption of the people in the U.S. plants we had to close. Not pleasant. It's a tough, tough situation, and unfortunately, manufacturing in the apparel industry is leaving the United States as fast as it can. I don't know what the end is going to be."[55]

"We decided to move some commodity manufacturing offshore to compete with apparel companies that are 100 percent offshore now," McDonald said. "We will still invest in, and maintain, a highly responsive and flexible U.S. base."[56]

About 600 people in Monroeville lost their jobs between 1994 and 1997 as more than half of Vanity Fair's sewing facilities moved out of the United States, with the goal of eventually moving commodity manufacturing 85 percent abroad.

Planning for the Future

VF's strategy to maintain and grow its market share is "to do our best to understand what each of our brands stands for and what customers each serves," said Dan MacFarlan, head of the Intimate Apparel Coalition. "Understand what folks want — give them the right stuff, under a brand that they recognize, trust and actually feel better wearing. If we can do that, we're gonna win."[57]

Janet Peters, who began as a fit model in 1951 and became senior vice president for Intimate Apparel product design in 1995, said VF must stay flexible in a highly competitive marketplace.

"For instance, in the sixties, robes used to be so popular — we had a big business in robes. Now the robe business has slacked off because you have more sportswear. You have sweatsuits and jumpsuits, and people appear to be wearing those more than the robe. So lingerie changes as people's living habits change. ... The biggest challenge I see is always looking for new ideas, new fabrics, new ways of doing things to make the woman want to buy your product. Our challenge is keeping up with what's going on out there. We have to forsee the change."[58]

Fashions in jeans change, too, said Mark Clift. "Interestingly enough, we're back in a designer denim fad," he said in 1997. "People's closets are full of the big, national brands and there's an attitude that if you buy the designer brand today you buy that lifestyle. Physically, most jeans are similar — heavyweight denim, stitch it together and here you go. But you buy that Polo and you look like those people in the Polo ad."[59]

How to make the office staff happy while raising money for a good cause: companies who participated in "National Denim Day" allowed employees to dress in denim for a day if they contributed at least $5 for breast cancer research.

"I would say that consistently growing the business, especially the jeans business, is by far the greatest challenge," said Bob Cordero, president of VF's Asia-Pacific Division, late in 1997. "Per capita consumption of jeans in the U.S. has hit a plateau or perhaps even declined. Profitably growing sales is your number one challenge."[60]

Angelo LaGrega, president of VF Jeanswear-Mass Market, said VF's dominant position in fashion does not mean it can relax.

"We've had such dramatic success over the last 10 years and our brands represent such a force in the market that there's a lot of competition niche-ing around us. Our challenge is to keep on growing our share, because if somebody gets their foot in the door or if something changes, it tends to affect the people who have the lion's share of the business."[61]

Cordero agrees: "Anyone in the consumer products business knows that there's always someone waiting in the wings to take your market share away."[62]

VF's challenge is to address "attitude shifts" with the right product. And attitude is, of course, tough to track, commented Terry Lay, president of Lee Apparel. "For instance, we now have a product called Pipes, which really addresses the street athlete."

"It was originally founded around skateboarding — the pockets are deep, the fit is baggy. And, if you speak to that consumer, there's a reason for every feature on that jean. It's not something your mom or dad would wear, but don't tell kids that isn't the right product they need on their body. And it's a fashion statement. It's exciting, and it was born out of a lifestyle shift."[63]

Corporate Headquarters Relocates

Another shift occurred when VF announced plans to relocate its headquarters from Wyomissing to Greensboro, North Carolina. The move is scheduled to begin in early 1998 and be completed by June. The move affects 100 people who worked in the corporate headquarters. "This was a difficult decision to make, in view of the fact that Berks County has been a supportive home to VF for many years, but the move is a competitive necessity for us," McDonald said.[64]

"VF is undergoing enormous change, including the development of groundbreaking new systems and processes to support our 'consumerization' efforts, and much of this work is taking place in Greensboro. We must be closer to our key marketing units and support groups in order to speed decision making, share information better and, ultimately, benefit both customers and consumers."

McDonald said the company plans to transfer most corporate office positions to Greensboro and keep VF's factory outlet operation, which employs 450, in Wyomissing. "We will work with our people to ensure a smooth transition. Our goal is to take care of everyone affected and provide the relocation and career assistance they will need."[65] Martin said VF will lease space temporarily when it moves to Greensboro. "We might buy or we might want a long-term lease. The decision hasn't been made yet," he said in late 1997. "The majority of people who work in the corporate office now have been asked to relocate. Our aircraft will fly anyone who's interested down on one of three consecutive weekends."[66] This was just for the initial visit, said Cindy Knoebel, director of Investor Relations. Employees who decided to relocate were offered subsequent plane trips to house-hunt.

The moves appear to be paying off. In October 1997 — the day before it announced its corporate headquarters would move — VF announced record third-quarter and year-to-date profits, split its stock 2-for-1 and raised dividends. Net income in the third quarter was $108.7 million, up from 1996's third quarter $91 million. Sales were $1.41 billion for the quarter and $3.93 billion for the first nine months of 1997. "Results for the most recent period surpassed our expectations, particularly given the good third quarter we had last year," McDonald said.[67]

Although international sales of jeans and lingerie slipped 11 percent, McDonald said Vassarette, Red Kap, Healthtex, Wrangler Westernwear and Lee brands remain strong. And though jeans sales lag in Western Europe, they are on the upswing in Mexico, Canada and Eastern Europe, he said.[68]

VF is able to track its sales so clearly in part because it has in place a sophisticated consumer response system that serves as a link between its brand and consumers. The process, however, will be taken several steps further in a strategy designed to focus everything the corporation does toward the needs of those buying the products. Already in place at the corporate level is the VF Consumer Monitor, a method of measuring consumer response to various products. Consumer profiles are drawn up, studies are conducted and results are tabulated and put into use.

In addition, VF plans to spend $250 million to market its strongest product categories: jeanswear, intimate apparel, workwear and daypacks. The money will be used for new consumer research, product development, in-store marketing programs and advertising. McDonald said the corporation will invest $1.25 billion in its brands over the next four years. "Micromarketing" will be an area of concentration since it will allow VF to customize product mix and presentation in various stores. For example, products and advertising in a college town would be very different from that in a retirement community. "When you take a Wal-Mart with 2,500 stores, we can cluster these stores by consumer characteristics so the mix of products is right for each store," McDonald said. "This is one of the ways we can greatly increase the productivity of the products we have on retail shelves."[69]

Retail space management will be another primary focus and retail presentation will change dramatically, officials said. "We're looking at changes that will redefine the playing field in the apparel industry," McDonald said.

McDonald stressed that these new "consumerization initiatives" are not advertising tools but scientific methods of studying consumer needs. "We'll change

the definition of state-of-the-art in technology and consumer research," he said.[70]

With its consumerization strategy firmly in place, there's every reason to expect VF to continue to grow its market share. McDonald notes:

"VF is a company that has gone through a number of changes in size, in product scope, in brands, in channels of distribution and global markets, but it's always been able to maintain a very close relationship with consumers. It has done that by ensuring that the decision making is done close to the retailers and close to the customers. ... We will continue to go through a number of changes as we utilize more synergies within the company in order to reduce costs and put more money into marketing our brands and studying the consumer and deciding what products they need. But we'll do that in a way that will allow us to continue to have decentralized decision making. I think that's been one of the strengths of VF. It means you have to have strong management throughout the operating divisions. We've had that and we continue to have that. ... Throughout different changes in the company, that's been a constant." [71]

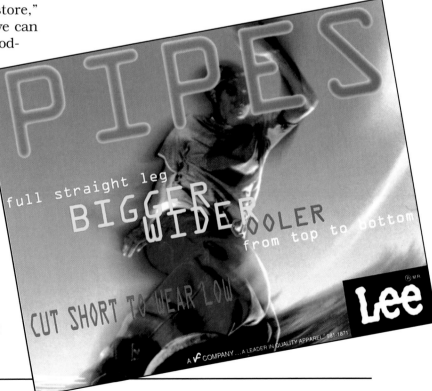

There's a reason for every design element in Pipes. The legs are baggy and pockets are deep because street athletes need these features.

NOTES TO SOURCES

Chapter One

1. *Reading Eagle,* Reading, Pennsylvania, March 12, 1911, p. 10.
2. Holton, James L., *Berks County – the Green Diamond of Pennsylvania,* Windsor Publications, Inc., Chatsworth, CA, 1993, p. 17.
3. Fox, Cyrus T., *Reading and Berks County, Pennsylvania – A History,* Lewis Historical Publishing Co., Inc., New York, New York, 1925, pp. 234-260.
4. Holton, *Berks County – the Green Diamond of Pennsylvania,* p. 17.
5. *Ibid,* p. 54.
6. *Ibid,* p. 30.
7. Berks County Historical Society, p. 56.
8. Holton, *Berks County,* p. 31.
9. *Ibid,* p. 33.
10. *Ibid,* p. 54.
11. Holton, James L. *Fifty Golden Years History of the Full-Fashioned Hosiery Industry in Berks County, Pennsylvania.* Schuylkill River Greenways Association, Wyomissing, PA, 1993, p. 13.
12. *Ibid.*
13. Montgomery, Morton L., *History of Berks County;* Everts, Peck & Richards, Philadelphia, PA, 1886, p. 89.
14. Hall, Lee, *Common Threads, A Parade of American Clothing,* Little, Brown and Company, Boston, Toronto, London, 1992, pp. 122-125.
15. Reading Glove and Mitten Manufacturing Company minutes, November 6, 1899, p. 1.
16. *Ibid.*
17. *Ibid.*
18. *Ibid,* p. 2.
19. Reading Glove and Mitten Manufacturing Company minutes, February 28, 1900, p. 4.
20. Boyd, W.H., *Boyd's City Directory,* Reading, Pennsylvania, W.G. Roland, 1900, p. 47.
21. Reading Glove and Mitten Manufacturing Company minutes, February 28, 1900, p. 5.
22. Holton, *Fifty Golden Years,* p. 54.
23. Reading Glove and Mitten Manufacturing Company minutes, August 10, 1900, p. 15.
24. Commonwealth of Pennsylvania Articles of Incorporation, Harrisburg, Pennsylvania, 1899, p. 1.
25. Reading Glove and Mitten Manufacturing Company minutes, November 9, 1900, p. 18.
26. Rodengen, Jeffrey, *The Legend of York,* Write Stuff Syndicate, Fort Lauderdale, Florida, 1997, p. 29.
27. Reading Glove and Mitten Manufacturing Company minutes, October 21, 1902, p. 52.
28. *Ibid,* pp. 76-77.
29. Reading Glove and Mitten Manufacturing Company minutes, December 5, 1904, p. 78.
30. Reading Glove and Mitten Manufacturing Company minutes, September 9, 1905, p. 86; October 24, 1905, p. 87; February 9, 1906, p. 89 and December 7, 1906, p. 98.
31. Reading Glove and Mitten Manufacturing Company minutes, June 10, 1910, p. 129.
32. Reading Glove and Mitten Manufacturing Company minutes, September 12, 1910, p. 132.
33. Reading Glove and Mitten Manufacturing Company minutes, October 21, 1910, p. 134.
34. Marquis, Albert Nelson, *Who's Who in Pennsylvania,* A.N. Marquis Company, Chicago, Illinois, 1939, Vol. 1, p. 41.
35. Reading Glove and Mitten Manufacturing Company minutes, March 3, 1911, pp. 136-137.
36. *Biographical Sketches of Leading Citizens of Berks County,* p. 17.
37. *Reading Eagle,* Reading, Pennsylvania, December 28, 1939, p. 16.
38. *Reading Eagle,* Reading, Pennsylvania, March 12, 1911, p. 10.
39. Reading Glove and Mitten Manufacturing Company minutes, December 31, 1912, p. 148.
40. Schuylkill Silk Mills minutes, April 7, 1913, p. 149.
41. Schuylkill Silk Mills minutes, November 19, 1913, December 3, 1913, pp. 153, 161.
42. Batterberry, Michael and Ariane, *Mirror, Mirror: A Social History of Fashion,* Holt, Rinehart & Winston, p. 266.
43. *History of Vanity Fair II,* unpublished manuscript, author unknown, Reading, Pennsylvania, p. 1.
44. Ewing, Elizabeth, *Underwear, A History,* Theatre Arts Books, New York, New York, 1972, pp. 83-85.
45. Ewing, *Underwear, A History,* pp. 83-85.
46. *History of Vanity Fair II,* p. 1.
47. Schuylkill Silk Mills minutes, January 20, 1917, p. 181.
48. *History of Vanity Fair I.*
49. Schuylkill Silk Mills minutes, September 1, 1917, p. 186.
50. *History of Vanity Fair III,* unpublished manuscript, author unknown, Reading, Pennsylvania, p. 2.
51. Marquis, p. 41.
52. *History of Vanity Fair I.*

Chapter Two

1. Ewing, Elizabeth, *Underwear, A History,* Theatre Arts Books, New York, New York, 1972, p. 90.
2. *Reading Eagle,* Reading, Pennsylvania, January 18, 1920, p. 18.
3. *Ibid.*
4. Vanity Fair Silk Mills minutes, June 30, 1920 and September 30, 1920, pp. 102, 104.
5. Ewing, p. 90.
6. *History of Vanity Fair III,* unpublished manuscript, author unknown, p. 2.
7. Holton, *Fifty Golden Years,* Schuylkill River Greenways Association, Wyomissing, PA, 1993, pp. 34, 59.
8. Vanity Fair Silk Mills minutes, May 25, 1923, p. 126.
9. *Reading Eagle,* June 3, 1925, p. 3.
10. *Reading Eagle,* June 4, 1925, pp. 1, 5, 24.
11. *Reading Eagle,* July 10, 1927.
12. *Top Drawer by Vanity Fair,* Vol. 1, No. 2, September 1953, pp. 8-9
13. Holton, *Fifty Golden Years,* p. 35.
14. Holton, *Berks County, The Green Diamond of Pennsylvania,* Windsor Publications, Inc., Chatsworth, CA, 1993, p. 69.
15. Vanity Fair Corporate History, unpublished manuscript, author unknown, Reading, Pennsylvania, p. 1.
16. Holton, *Fifty Golden Years,* p. 53.
17. *Ibid.*
18. Vanity Fair Silk Mills Financial Records, 1929-1931.
19. *Reading Eagle,* August 9, 1931.
20. *Reading Eagle,* September 27, 1931.
21. *"The Role of Advertising,"* unpublished manuscript, author unknown, Vanity Fair archives.
22. Edwin Barbey, interviewed by the author, October 8, 1997, transcript p. 1.
23. Edwin Barbey interview, transcript pp. 3-5.
24. Vanity Fair Silk Mills Financial Records, 1934.

25. *History of Vanity Fair III*, unpublished manuscript, author unknown, from Vanity Fair archives.
26. Ewing, p. 103.
27. Ewing, pp. 105-106.
28. Murray, Maggie Pexton, *Changing Styles in Fashion: Who, What, Why*, Fairchild Publications, Division of Capital Cities Media, Inc., New York, New York, 1989, pp. 106-107.
29, Nunn, Joan, *Fashion in Costume: 1200-1980*, p. 184.
30. Ewing, p. 106.
31. *The New York Times*, June 8, 1948.
32. Vanity Fair Silk Mills Financial Records, 1935.
33. Holton, *Fifty Golden Years*, p. 59.
34. Holton, *Berks County*, p. 76.
35. *Ibid.*
36. *Monroe Journal*, Monroeville, Alabama, June 11, 1987, Section 2, p. 1.
37. *Ibid.*
38. *Monroeville Journal*, June 11, 1987, Section 2, p. 8.
39. *Ibid*, p. 1.
40. *Ibid.*
41. *Ibid*
42. *Ibid.*
43. *Ibid*, p. 2.
44. *Ibid*, p. 3.
45. *Ibid*, p. 1.
46. *Ibid.*
47. Janet Peters, interviewed by the author, December 10, 1996, transcript pp. 11, 12.
48. *Reading Eagle*, December 2, 1938
49. *Reading Eagle*, December 28, 1939, p. 1.

Chapter Three

1. *His Life in Our Hands*, Vanity Fair Mills, Inc., Reading, Pennsylvania, 1944.
2. Holton, James L., *Berks County – the Green Diamond of Pennsylvania*, Windsor Publications, Inc., Chatsworth, CA, 1993, pp. 80-81.
3. Holton, James L., *Fifty Golden Years History of the Full-Fashioned Hosiery Industry in Berks County, Pennsylvania*, Schuylkill River Greenways Association, Wyomissing, Pennsylvania, 1993, p. 65
4. *Ibid.*
5. *Ibid.*
6. Baker, Patricia, *Fashions of A Decade – the 1940s*, Facts on File, New York, 1992, p. 5.
7. Holton, *Fifty Golden Years*, p. 65
8. *Ibid.*
9. *Ibid.*
10. *Ibid*, p. 67.
11. *Ibid*, p. 66.

12. *Monroe Journal*, June 11, 1987, Special Supplement, Section 2, p. 5.
13. *Ibid.*
14. *History of Vanity Fair*, unpublished manuscript, author unknown.
15. *His Life in Our Hands.*
16. Baker, p. 29.
17. Baker, p. 17.
18. Baker, p. 29.
19. Vanity Fair Silk Mills Minutes, June 28, 1940.
20. *Monroe Journal*, June 11, 1987, Special Supplement, Section 2, p. 7.
21. Vanity Fair Mills minutes, March 17, 1942.
22. Vanity Fair Mills minutes, March 27, 1942.
23. Vanity Fair Silk Mills minutes, June 27, 1941.
24. *Monroe Journal*, December 6, 1962, Special Supplement, Section C, p. 1.
25. Sunday Magazine of the Midlands, Supplement to the *Omaha World-Herald*, Omaha, Nebraska, March 12, 1972, p. 25.
26. Sunday Magazine of the Midlands, p. 24.
27. Baker, p. 29.
28. Vanity Fair Mills Minutes, June 22, 1943.
29. The *South Alabamian*, Jackson, Alabama, June 18, 1958, p. 4.
30. *Ibid*, p. 1.
31. Vanity Fair Mills Minutes, February 22, 1946.
32. Vanity Fair Minutes, December 18, 1947 and Edwin Barbey, interviewed by the author, October 8, 1997.
33. *Reading Eagle*, August 19, 1948, p. 1.
34. *Reading Eagle*, August 17, 1948, p. 1.
35. *Reading Eagle*, August 17, 1948, p. 3.
36. Grace Fidler, interviewed by Susan Shelly, October 12, 1996.
37. Gladys Knight, interviewed by Susan Shelly, October 12, 1996.
38. June Miller, interviewed by Susan Shelly, October 12, 1996.
39. *Monroe Journal*, June 11, 1987, Special Supplement, Section 6, p. 1.
40. *The New York Times*, June 8, 1948.
41. *Ibid.*
42. *Monroe Journal*, December 6, 1962, Special Supplement, Section C, p. 3.
43. *Ibid.*
44. *History of Vanity Fair.*
45. Peter Velardi, interviewed by the author, May 14, 1997. transcript p. 6.
46. Vanity Fair Mills Minutes, December 3, 1948.

Chapter Four

1. *Christian Science Monitor*, October 14, 1950.
2. Grun, Bernard, *The Timetables of History: A Horizontal Linkage of People and Events*, Simon & Schuster/Touchstone, New York, New York, 1963, p. 531.
3. Memorandum of agreement between Kayser and Vanity Fair Mills, December 7, 1949, p. 3, Contained in the minutes book (Volume 3) of Vanity Fair Mills.
4. Holton, James L. *Fifty Golden Years History of the Full-Fashioned Hosiery Industry in Berks County, Pennsylvania*, (Wyomissing, PA, Schuylkill River Greenways Association, 1993), pp. 73-75.
5. Reprint of article in *Demopolis Times*, Special Edition, October 14, 1967, p. 1.
6. *The South Alabamian*, Jackson, Alabama, June 18, 1959, p. 8.
7. *Ibid.*
8. Corporate History of Vanity Fair, unpublished manuscript, author unknown, p. 2.
9. Holton, *Fifty Golden Years*, pp. 72, 73.
10. Vanity Fair News, Number 11, October 1950, Inhouse newsletter, p. 1.
11. Murray, Maggie Pexton, *Changing Styles in Fashion: Who, What, Why*, Fairchild Publications, Division of Capital Cities Media, Inc., New York, New York, 1989, p. 175.
12. *The Christian Science Monitor*, October 14, 1950.
13. *Vanity Fair News*, Number 11, October 1950, Inhouse newsletter, p. 1.
14. Vanity Fair Mills Minutes, Volume 3, April 17, 1951.
15. Excerpt from a letter to stockholders from J.E. Barbey, March 5, 1951.
16. Vanity Fair Mills Minutes, Volume 3, April 17, 1951.
17. The *Monroe Journal*, December 6, 1962, Special Supplement, Section B, p. 1.
18. Vanity Fair Mills Minutes, Volume 3, February 5, 1952.
19. Edwin Barbey, interviewed by the author, October 8, 1997, transcript p. 9.
20. *Ibid*, p. 10.
21. *Ibid*, p. 14.
22. Vanity Fair Mills Minutes, Volume 3, April 21, 1953.
23. Vanity Fair Mills Inc. Annual Report, 1952, pp. 3-4.
24. *Top Drawer by Vanity Fair*, Volume 1, Number 2, September 1953.

25. Article reprinted from the *Christian Science Monitor,* 1960
26. *Growth and Volume; A History of Vanity Fair,* unpublished manuscript, author unknown.
27. Vanity Fair Mills advertising materials, 1952-54.
28. *Ibid.*
29. Edwin Barbey interview, transcript p. 5.
30. Vanity Fair Mills minutes, Volume 4, September 26, 1955.
31. Scotta Miller, interviewed by Susan Shelly, August 1996, transcript p. 4.
32. *Ibid.*
33. *Ibid.*
34. *Corporate History,* unpublished manuscript, author unknown, April 1964, p. 3.
35. Vanity Fair Mills Minutes, Volume 4, October 22, 1956.
36. Vanity Fair Mills Minutes, Volume 4, September 26, 1955.
37. Edwin Barbey interview, transcript p. 11.
38. Vanity Fair Mills Inc. Annual Report, 1956, p. 3.
39. The *Monroe Journal,* December 6, 1962, Special Supplement, Section B, p. 5.
40. Vanity Fair Mills Minutes, Volume 4, April 16, 1957.
41. Vanity Fair Annual Report, 1957, p. 3.
42. Peter Velardi, interviewed by the author, May 14, 1997, transcript pp. 9, 10.
43. Vanity Fair Mills Minutes, Volume 5, April 21, 1959.
44. *Monroe Journal,* December 6, 1962, p. 5-C.
45. Vanity Fair Annual Report, 1958, p. 3.
46. Vanity Fair Mills Minutes, Volume 5, April 21, 1959.
47. Richard C. Lamm, interviewed by the author, June 2, 1997, transcript p. 12.
48. Velardi interview, transcript p. 9.

Chapter Five

1. *Women's Wear Daily,* July 28, 1966, p. 1.
2. Connikie, Yvonne, *Fashions of a Decade: The 1960s,* New York, Facts on File, Inc., 1990, pp. 9-10.
3. Vanity Fair Mills, Inc. 1960 Annual Report, p. 3.
4. Vanity Fair promotional material as distributed to retailers, 1960.
5. Vanity Fair Mills, Inc. 1961 Annual Report, p. 3.
6. Advertisement in *The New York Times,* November 28, 1961.

7. Vanity Fair MIlls, Inc. 1961 Annual Report, p. 4.
8. Vanity Fair MIlls, Inc. 1962 Annual Report, p. 3.
9. *Ibid.*
10. *Monroe Journal,* Monroeville, Alabama, December 6, 1962, p. 1-A.
11. *Monroe Journal,* August 23, 1962.
12. *Mobile Press,* Mobile, Alabama, August 23, 1962.
13. The *Baldwin County Times,* Bay Minette, Alabama, September 20, 1962.
14. *Baldwin County Times,* October 31, 1963.
15. *Monroe Journal,* October 23, 1964.
16. *Reading Eagle,* June 23, 1966, p. 15.
17. Vanity Fair Mills, Inc. 1962 Annual Report, p. 3.
18. Vanity Fair Mills, Inc. Minutes, Volume V, May 21, 1963.
19. Vanity Fair MIlls, Inc. 1963 Annual Report, p. 3.
20. Connikie, *Fashions of a Decade,* p. 19.
21. Vanity Fair Mills, Inc. 1964 Annual Report, p. 4.
22. Vanity Fair Mills, Inc. 1964 Annual Report, pp. 10-11.
23. Vanity Fair Mills, Inc. Minutes, Volume VI, April 18, 1967.
24. Vanity Fair Mills, Inc. Minutes, Volume V, August 29, 1965, April 18, 1967.
25. Vanity Fair Mills, Inc. 1965 Annual Report, p. 4.
26. Vanity Fair Mills, Inc. press release from company archives, February 10, 1966.
27. *Reading Eagle,* Reading, Pennsylvania, July 26, 1966, p. 15.
28. *Women's Wear Daily,* New York, New York, July 28, 1966, p. 19.
29. *Women's Wear Daily,* June 2, 1966, p. 1.
30. *Women's Wear Daily,* May 26, 1966, p. 30.
31. *Women's Wear Daily,* July 28, 1966, p. 19.
32. The *Mobile Press,* May 19, 1966.
33. *Women's Wear Daily,* April 1, 1965, p. 19.
34. William Foulke, interviewed by the author, June 9, 1997, transcript p. 12.
35. Notes from M.O. Lee, contained in Vanity Fair archives.
36. Smith, Pamela, *Instant Expert: Vintage Fashions and Fabrics,* Alliance Publishing, Inc. Brooklyn, New York, 1995. pp. 82-84.
37. Vanity Fair Mills, Inc. 1968 Annual Report, p. 5.

38. Vanity Fair Mills, Inc. 1967 Annual Report, p. 2.
39. Statement from Vanity Fair to *Women's Wear Daily,* September 7, 1966, contained in Vanity Fair archives.
40. Vanity Fair Mills, Inc. 1967 Annual Report, p. 2.
41. Vanity Fair Mills, Inc. 1967 Annual Report, p. 3.
42. *Ibid.*
43. *Women's Wear Daily,* June 19, 1968, p. 12.
44. John Johnson, interviewed by the author, June 2, 1997, transcript pp. 3-5.
45. Larry Weidenheimer, interviewed by the author, June 3, 1997, transcript p. 9.
46. Vanity Fair Mills, Inc. 1968 Annual Report, p. 5.
47. Vanity Fair Mills, Inc. 1968 Annual Report, p. 2.
48. Peter Velardi, interviewed by the author, May 14, 1997, transcript p. 10.
49. VF Corporation 1969 Annual Report, pp. 14-15.
50. VF Corporation 1968 Annual Report, p. 3.
51. VF Corporation 1969 Annual Report, pp. 14-15.
52. *Ibid.*
53. VF Corporation 1969 Annual Report, p. 3
54. *Ibid.*

Chapter Six

1. Harold McKemy, interviewed by the author, June 3, 1997, transcript p. 2.
2. *One Hundred Years of Excellence,* published by The Lee Company, Merriam, Kansas, 1989.
3. *The History of the H.D. Lee Mercantile Company, the Origin of Union-Alls and the Development of the Work Garment Line,* unpublished manuscript by E.H. Merrill, 1936.
4. *One Hundred Years of Excellence.*
5. *Ibid.*
6. *Ibid.*
7. *Ibid.*
8. *Ibid.*
9. *Ibid.*
10. *Topeka Daily Capital,* October 4, 1908.
11. *One Hundred Years of Excellence.*
12. *Ibid.*
13. *The History of the H.D. Lee Mercantile Company.*
14. *One Hundred Years of Excellence.*
15. *Ibid.*
16. H.D. Lee Mercantile Company minutes, March 23, 1917.

17. *Business Week* magazine, November 5, 1949, p. 17.
18. *One Hundred Years of Excellence.*
19. *Ibid.*
20. *Ibid.*
21. "Lee Celebrates its 100th Year of Denim Fashions," Lee Press Release, The Lee Company, 1989.
22. *One Hundred Years of Excellence.*
23. *Ibid.*
24. *Ibid.*
25. *Ibid.*
26. *Ibid.*
27. *Ibid.*
28. Advertisement from *Playboy* magazine, October 1962, p. 41.
29. *One Hundred Years of Excellence.*
30. *Ibid.*
31. The *Kansas City Star*, May 17, 1970, p. 2E.
32. *Men's Wear* magazine, January 9, 1970, p. 9.
33. Harold McKemy, interviewed by the author, June 3, 1997, transcript p. 2.
34. *One Hundred Years of Excellence.*
35. Memo to Lee women employees from W.L. Nott, November 3, 1970.
36. The Lee Company inhouse memo, May 14, 1971.
37. *One Hundred Years of Excellence.*
38. *Ibid.*
39. *Ibid.*
40. *Ibid.*
41. VF Corporation 1988 Annual Report, p. 25.
42. Richard C. Lamm, interviewed by the author, June 2, 1997, transcript p. 8.
43. *Ibid.*, p. 7.
44. *Ibid.*, p. 3.
45. VF Corporation Minutes, Volume VII, April 17, 1990.
46. *Reading Times*, March 15, 1991, p. 23.
47. VF Corporation 1991 Annual Report, p. 8.
48. VF Corporation 1992 Annual Report, p. 7.
49. *Reading Eagle*, May 14, 1992, p. D9.
50. Timothy A. Lambeth, interviewed by the author, September 15, 1997, transcript p. 14.
51. *Ibid.*, p. 15.
52. *Reading Eagle*, March 27, 1995, p. A10.
53. VF Corporation Minutes, Volume VIII, July 8, 1994.
54. Lambeth interview, transcript p. 17.
55. Informal interview with Laurie, last name unknown. The Lee Company headquarters, Merriam, Kansas March 7, 1997.

Chapter Seven

1. VF Corporation 1971 Annual Report, p. 1.

2. *Reading Eagle*, April 1, 1971.
3. VF Corporation 1970 Annual Report, pp. 1, 3.
4. VF Corporation 1970 Annual Report, p. 10.
5. VF Corporation 1970 Annual Report, p. 6.
6. Marilyn Bean, interviewed by the author, December 12, 1996, transcript p. 6.
7. Herald, Jacqueline, *Fashions of a Decade: the 1970s*, Facts on File, New York, New York, 1992, p. 24.
8. *Ibid*, pp. 10, 17, 62.
9. Herald, p. 17.
10. VF Corporation 1970 Annual Report, p. 10.
11. VF Corporation 1971 Annual Report, p. 2.
12. VF Corporation 1977 Annual Report, p. 5.
13. VF Corporation 1971 Annual Report, p. 1.
14. VF Corporation 1972 Annual Report, p. 4.
15. *Reading Eagle*, October 8, 1970, p. 12.
16. VF Corporation 1971 Annual Report, p. 1.
17. VF Corporation 1973 Annual Report, p. 11.
18. VF Corporation 1978 Annual Report, p. 5.
19. *Reading Eagle*, October 8, 1970, p. 12.
20. *Reading Eagle*, May 28, 1970, p. 39.
21. Bill Pike, interviewed by the author, May 14, 1997, transcript p. 4.
22. William Foulke, interviewed by the author, June 9, 1997, transcript p. 10.
23. Scotta Miller, interviewed by the author, June 3, 1997, transcript p. 21.
24. Vanessa Price, interviewed by the author, December 10, 1996, transcript p. 9.
25. *Reading Eagle*, June 26, 1971, p. 1.
26. Scotta Miller, interviewed by the author, June 3, 1997, transcript pp. 13, 20.
27. Miller interview, transcript p. 13.
28. Brad Bean, interviewed by the author, October 10, 1997, transcript p. 7.
29. *Ibid.*
30. Brad Bean interview, transcript p. 3.
31. Steve Lehmann, interviewed by the author, December 10, 1996, transcript p. 28.
32. Brad Bean, interviewed by Susan Shelly, March 12, 1997.
33. VF Corporation minutes, Volume VII, February 18, 1992.
34. Steve Fritz, interviewed by the author, December 11, 1996, transcript p. 16.

35. Roger Eichlin, interviewed by the author, December 10, 1996, transcript p. 10.
36. *Reading Eagle*, March 12, 1994, p. D7.
37. *Reading Eagle*, March 21, 1993, p. B1.
38. *Reading Eagle*, March 17, 1993, p. A1.
39. Brad Bean, interviewed by the author, October 10, 1997, transcript p. 8.
40. Fritz interview, transcript p. 15.
41. Brad Bean interview, transcript p. 8.
42. Brad Bean, interviewed by Susan Shelly, March 12, 1997.
43. The *Monroe Journal*, Monroeville, Alabama, August 10, 1972, p. 1-A
44. *Ibid.*
45. *Reading Eagle*, October 9, 1971.
46. The *Monroe Journal,* August 10, 1972, p. 1-A.
47. VF Corporation 1976 Annual Report, pp. 4-5.
48. VF Corporation 1970 Annual Report, p. 6.
49. VF Corporation 1971 Annual Report, p. 4.
50. VF Corporation 1970 Annual Report, p. 6.
51. VF Corporation 1971 Annual Report, p. 4.
52. *Ibid*, pp. 4-5.
53. VF Corporation 1973 Annual Report, p. 6.
54. VF Corporation 1975 Annual Report, p. 3.
55. *Ibid*, p. 4.
56. VF Corporation Minutes, Volume II, May 3, 1977 and July 19, 1977.
57. VF Corporation 1972 Annual Report, p. 4.
58. Terry Lay, interviewed by Catherine Lackner, November 3, 1997, transcript p. 2.
59. VF Corporation 1973 Annual Report, p. 8.
60. VF Corporation 1971 Annual Report, p. 6.
61. VF Corporation 1974 Annual Report, pp. 2-3.
62. VF Corporation 1973 Annual Report, p. 8.
63. Prakash Bhatt, interviewed by the author, December 11, 1996, transcript p. 5.
64. Banquet program of the Monroeville Chamber of Commerce program, October 25, 1973.
65. VF Corporation 1973 Annual Report, p. 8.
66. Lay interview, transcript p. 3.
67. VF Corporation 1979 Annual Report, pp. 6-7.

68. *Reading Eagle*, May 2, 1979.
69. *Reading Eagle*, January 21, 1976.
70. *Ibid.*
71. VF Corporation 1974 Annual Report, p. 10.
72. *Ibid.*
73. VF Corporation 1973 Annual Report, p.8.
74. VF Corporation 1975, Annual Report, p. 2.
75. VF Corporation 1976 Annual Report, pp. 2-3.
76. VF Corporation 1973 Annual Report, p. 8.
77. VF Corporation 1977 Annual Report, p. 4.
78. *Ibid*, p. 1.
79. Janet Peters, interviewed by the author, December 10, 1996, transcript p. 4.
80. VF Corporation 1978 Annual Report, p. 5.
81. The *Reading Eagle*, December 17, 1978.
82. Lawrence Pugh, interviewed by the author, December 11, 1996, transcript p. 1.
83. *Ibid*, p. 1.
84. *Ibid*, p. 2.
85. *Ibid*, p. 2.
86. Mike Martin, interviewed by Catherine Lackner, November 10, 1997, transcript p. 9.
87. Martin interview, transcript p. 10.
88. *Ibid.*
89. VF Corporation 1979 Annual Report, pp. 4-5, 28.

Chapter Seven Sidebar

1. John Jackson, interviewed by the author, June 2, 1997, transcript pp. 9-10.
2. Richard Lamm, interviewed by the author June 2, 1997, transcript pp. 4, 5.
3. *Vanity Fair Factory Outlet History*, unpublished manuscript, author unknown, from VF archives.
4. *Value Retail News*, Largo, Florida, February 1997, p. 15.
5. *Ibid*, p. 22.

Chapter Eight

1. Marilyn Bean, interviewed by the author, December 10, 1996, transcript p. 10.
2. VF Corporation 1980 Annual Report, p. 2.
3. Bill Pike, interviewed by the author May 14, 1997, transcript p. 7.
4. VF Corporation Annual Report, pp. 2-3.

5. Scotta Miller, interviewed by Susan Shelly, August 19,1996.
6. *Ibid.*
7. Marilyn Bean interview, transcript p. 5.
8. VF Corporation 1981 Annual Report, p. 2.
9. *Reading Times*, March 16, 1980.
10. *Reading Eagle*, December 27, 1981.
11. Miller interview, transcript p. 20.
12. *Sunday World-Herald Magazine of the Midlands*, Supplement to the *Omaha World-Herald*, March 12, 1972, pp. 24-25.
13. Louis Fecile, interviewed by the author, December 10, 1996, transcript, p. 11.
14. VF Corporation Minutes, Volume III, March 9, 1982.
15. *Ibid.*
16. *Ibid.*
17. VF Corporation Minutes, Volume III, October 19, 1982.
18. *Reading Eagle*, April 8, 1983.
19. Peter Velardi, interviewed by the author, May 14, 1997, transcript p. 1.
20. *Ibid*, p. 3.
21. Marilyn Bean interview, transcript p. 10.
21. Lawrence Pugh, interviewed by the author, December 11, 1996, transcript p. 4.
22. Velardi interview, transcript p. 24.
23. *Reading Eagle*, February 16, 1986.
24. *Reading Eagle*, January 1, 1984.
25. VF Corporation 1981 Annual Report, pp. 16-17.
26. Schusteff, Sandy, *International Directory of Company Histories*, Volume V, Saint James Press, New York & London, 1992, p. 391.
27. Terry Lay, interviewed by Catherine Lackner, November 3, 1997, transcript pp. 4-5.
28. VF Corporation 1981 Annual Report, p. 6.
29. Lay interview, transcript pp. 4, 5.
30. VF Corporation 1982 Annual Report, p. 7.
31. *Reading Eagle*, February 26, 1984.
32. Carnegy, Vicky, F*ashions of a Decade: the 1980s*, Facts on File, New York, New York, 1990, pp. 32-33.
33. VF Corporation 1981 Annual Report, p. 4.
34. VF Corporation 1982 Annual Report, p. 5.
35. VF Corporation 1983 Annual Report, p. 5.
36. VF Corporation 1984 Annual Report, p. 6.
37. *Reading Eagle*, December 16, 1984.

38. VF Corporation 1984 Annual Report, p. 5.
39. VF Corporation 1981 Annual Report, pp. 8, 9, and VF Corporation 1982 Annual Report, pp. 3, 4.
40. VF Corporation Minutes, Volume III, December 8, 1981.
41. VF Corporation 1982 Annual Report, p. 9.
42. VF Corporation 1983 Annual Report, p. 9.
43. Brad Bean, interviewed by the author, October 10, 1997, transcript pp. 15-16.
44. Bean interview, transcript p.16.
45. Lori Tarnoski, interviewed by the author, June 3, 1997, transcript p. 11.
46. *Reading Eagle*, February 26, 1984.
47. *Ibid.*
48. VF Corporation 1983 Annual Report, p. 2.
49. *Ibid*, p. 6.
50. VF Corporation 1984 Annual Report, pp. 3, 4.
51. *Ibid*, p. 2.
52. Harold McKemy, interviewed by the author, June 3, 1997, transcript p. 9.
53. VF Corporation 1984 Annual Report, pp. 2, 10, 18.
54. *Ibid*, pp. 2, 11, 18.
55. *Apparel Industry* magazine, March 1985.
56. *Bassett-Walker History*, from VF Corporation archives, March 1993, p. 1.
57. *Ibid.*
58. *Brief History of Predecessor Companies Leading to the Organization of Bassett-Walker, Inc.*, unpublished manuscript, author unknown, p. 2.
59. *Apparel Industry* magazine, March 1985.
60. *Brief History of Predecessor Companies*, p. 3.
61. *Bassett-Walker History* from VF Archives, March 1993, p. 1.
62. *Ibid.*
63. *Bassett-Walker History*, from VF Corporation archives, March 1993, p. 2.
64. *Ibid.*
65. *Ibid*, p. 3.
66. *Brief History of Predecessor Companies*, p. 3.
67. *The Martinsville Bulletin*, Progress Edition, February 19, 1995, p. 14.
68. VF Corporation 1985 Annual Report, p. 8.
69. *Reading Eagle*, September 7, 1986.
70. VF Corporation 1985 Annual Report, p. 8.

71. *Reading Eagle*, September 7, 1986.
72. VF Corporation 1985 Annual Report, p. 10.
73. *Reading Eagle*, April 27, 1986.
74. VF Corporation 1988 Annual Report, p. 8.
75. VF Corporation 1986 Annual Report, p. 5.
76. *Reading Eagle*, May 18, 1985.
77. Mackey McDonald, interviewed by the author, December 10, 1996, transcript p. 5.
78. *Reading Eagle*, September 7, 1986.
79. *Ibid.*
80. *Ibid.*
81. *Ibid.*
82. VF Corporation 1986 Annual Report, p. 6.
83. *Reading Eagle*, November 9, 1986, p. 26.
84. VF Corporation 1988 Annual Report, p. 5.
85. VF Corporation 1988 Annual Report, p. 7.
86. VF Corporation 1989 Annual Report, p. 7.
87. VF Corporation history, as contained in achives.
88. VF Corporation 1987 Annual Report, pp. 3, 5.
89. VF Corporation 1988 Annual Report, p. 2.
90. VF Corporation 1988 Annual Report, p. 3.
91. VF Corporation 1989 Annual Report, p. 4.
92. Bob Cordero, interviewed by Catherine Lackner, December 23, 1997, transcript p. 5.
93. *Reading Times*, April 19, 1989.
94. *Ibid.*

Chapter Eight Sidebar

1. Tim Zeigler, interviewed by Susan Shelly, November 13, 1997.
2. *Ibid.*
3. *Ibid.*

Chapter Nine

1. *Wrangler*, unpublished history, author unknown.
2. *Pioneers*, Supplement to the *Daily News Record*, New York and Los Angeles, July 1, 1986, p. 18.
3. *Wrangler History*, Wrangler, Inc., Greensboro, North Carolina, 1994.
4. *Ibid.*
5. Story related by Linda Bell, Wrangler achival employee, January 14, 1997.
6. *Wrangler History.*
7. *Ibid.*
8. *Blue Bell, Inc. – Its History*, author unknown, April 1980, p. 2.
9. *Wrangler History.*

10. *Ibid.*
11. *Sanforization: Spark for Progress*, unpublished manuscript, author unknown, pp. 2-3.
12. *Ibid.*
13. *Wrangler History.*
14. *Sanforization: Spark for Progress.*
15. *Blue Bell, Inc. – Its History*, author unknown, April 1980, p. 2
16. *Ibid*, p. 3.
17. *Wrangler History.*
18. *Wrangler*, p. 2.
19. *Wrangler History.*
20. *Wrangler*, p. 3.
21. *Ibid.*
22. Bill Hervey, interviewed by the author, November 4, 1997, transcript p. 8.
23. Gilchrist, William and Manzotti, Roberto, *A Visual History of Jeanswear: American Originals*, Sportswear International, Zug – Switzerland, 1992. p. 97.
24. From Wrangler archive material, Greensboro, North Carolina, gathered by Susan Shelly, January 14, 1997.
25. Donald Laws, interviewed by Catherine Lackner, November 14, 1997, transcript p. 3.
26. From Wrangler archive material.
27. *Wrangler History.*
28. Hervey interview, transcript p. 10.
29. Bob Coppage, interviewed by Catherine Lackner, November 7, 1997, transcript p. 19.
30. Mark Clift, interviewed by Catherine Lackner, November 10, 1997, transcript pp. 22, 23.
31. From Wrangler archive material.
32. Gilcrist and Manzotti, p. 89.
33. From Wrangler archive material.
34. *Wrangler History.*
35. *Ibid.*
36. *Ibid.*
37. *Blue Bell, Inc. – Its History*, unpublished manuscript, author unknown.
38. *Wrangler History.*
39. *Blue Bell, Inc. – Its History*, author unknown, April 1980, p. 5.
40. Blue Bell, Inc. 1983 Annual Report, p. 29.
41. *Blue Bell, Inc. – Its History*, p. 6.
42. *Ibid.*
43. *Ibid.*
44. *Ibid.*
45. *Ibid.*
46. *Wrangler History.*
47. *Ibid.*
48. Hervey interview, p. 20.

Chapter Nine Sidebar

1. Bill Hervey, interviewed by the author, November 4, 1997, transcript pp. 15, 16.
2. *Ibid.*

Chapter Ten

1. Lawrence Pugh, interviewed by the author, December 11, 1996, transcript p. 5.
2. VF Corporation 1986 Annual Report, p. 20.
3. Dave Reklau, interviewed by the author, June 2, 1997, transcript p. 10.
4. *Ibid.*
5. *Ibid.*
6. *Ibid.*
7. *Ibid.*
8. *Ibid.*
9. *Ibid.*
10. Bill Hervey, interviewed by the author, November 4, 1997, transcript p. 12.
11. Reklau interview, transcript p.15.
12. Mark Clift, interviewed by Catherine Lackner, November 10, 1997, transcript pp. 11, 12.
13. John Johnson, interviewed by the author, December 11, 1996, transcript p. 7.
14. Blue Bell, Inc. 1983 Annual Report, p. 29.
15. *Ibid.*
16. *Reading Eagle*, November 18, 1986, p. 26.
17. Hervey interview, transcript p. 14.
18. VF Corporation 1985 Annual Report, p. 4.
19. Biography of Marithe Bachellerie and Francois Girbaud, unpublished manuscript from Girbaud archives.
20. *Ibid.*
21. *Ibid.*
22. *Ibid.*
23. Clift interview, transcript pp. 7, 8.
24. *Red Kap History*, from Red Kap Industries Advertising Department, p.1.
25. *Ibid.*
26. *Ibid.*
27. *Ibid*
28. *Ibid.*
29. *Ibid.*
30. *The Columbian*, and *"A Brief History of Jantzen, Inc.,"* contained in VF Corporation archives.
31. *The Columbian*, December 20, 1995.
32. *A Brief History of Jantzen*, unpublished manuscript, author unknown, from VF achives, p.1.
33. *Ibid.*
34. *Ibid.*
35. *Ibid.*
36. *Ibid.*
37. *Ibid.*
38. *Ibid.*
39. *Ibid.*
40. *Ibid.*
41. *Ibid.*

42. *Ibid.*
43. Dan Mac Farlan, interviewed by the author, October 9, 1997, transcript p. 7.
44. *Ibid*, p. 2.
45. *Ibid*, p. 4.
46. JanSport History, contained in VF Corporation archives, April 1993.
47. *Ibid.*
48. *Ibid.*
49. *Ibid.*
50. Skip Yowell, interviewed by Susan Shelly, April 1, 1997.
51. "A Pack on Every Back," by Debra Prinzing, *Outside Business* magazine, p. 43.
52. *Ibid.*
53. *A Brief History of Jantzen*, p. 2.
54. *Ibid.*
55. Lawrence Pugh, interviewed by the author, December 11, 1996, transcript p. 6.
56 *Ibid.*
57. Pugh interview, p. 5.
58. VF Corporation 1987 Annual Report, p. 3.
59. *Reading Eagle*, January 17, 1987.
60. Lori Tarnoski, interviewed by the author, June 3, 1997, transcript p. 5.
61. *Reading Eagle*, February 22, 1987.
62. Steve Lehmann, interviewed by the author, December 10, 1996, transcript p. 18.
63. Mackey McDonald, interviewed by the author, December 10, 1996. transcript p. 13.
64. Reklau interview, transcript p. 30.
65. Tim Lambeth, interviewed by the author, September 15, 1997, transcript p. 2.
66. Clift interview, transcript p. 4.
67. Bob Coppage, interviewed by Catherine Lackner, November 7, 1997, transcript pp. 2-3.
68. VF Corporation 1989 Annual Report, p. 4.
69. *Ibid.*

Chapter Eleven

1. *Reading Eagle*, February 21, 1993.
2. *Ibid.*
3. *Ibid.*
4. VF Corporation 1989 Annual Report, pp. 2, 25.
5. *Ibid*, p. 21.
6. *Ibid*, p. 7.
7. VF Corporation 1990 Annual Report, p. 7.
8. *Ibid*, p. 2.
9. *Ibid*, p. 15.
10. VF Corporation Minutes, Volume VII, April 17, 1990.

11. VF Corporation Annual Report, Special supplement on MRS.
12. *Reading Eagle*, February 21, 1993, p. 11.
13. VF Corporation 1991 Annual Report, p. 2.
14. *Ibid*, p. 8.
15. *Ibid*, p. 9.
16. VF Corporation 1990 Annual Report, p. 9.
17. VF Corporation 1991 Annual Report, p. 11.
18. VF Corporation 1992 Annual Report, p. 5.
19. *Ibid.*
20. VF Corporation 1992 Annual Report, p. 6.
21. VF Corporation 1991 Annual Report, p. 3.
22. *Reading Eagle*, October 7, 1992, p. A14.
23. Tim Lambeth, interviewed by the author, September 15, 1997, transcript p. 15.
24. Mackey McDonald, interviewed by the author, December 10, 1996, transcript p. 9.
25. *Reading Times*, November 2, 1990, Business Section p. 23.
26. VF Corporation 1991 Annual Report, pp. 18-19.
27. Nathan Miller, miller@net-connect, Garth Brooks Career Chronology, 1996.
28. VF Corporation 1992 Annual Report, pp. 6-7.
29. VF Corporation Annual Reports, 1989, 1990.
30. *Ibid.*, 1990, p. 13.
31. *Reading Eagle*, February 17, 1991, Progress section, p. 15.
32. *Ibid.*
33. VF Corporation 1990 Annual Report, pp. 13, 14.
34. Feldman, Elane, *Fashions of a Decade: 1990s, Facts on File*, New York, New York, p. 12.
35. McDonald interview, transcript p. 18.
36. *Ibid*, p. 19.
37. VF Corporation 1990 Annual Report, pp. 2, 9, 19.
38. VF Corporation Minutes, Volume VII, October 15, 1991.
39. VF Corporation 1991 Annual Report, p. 3.
40. Bob Coppage, interviewed by Catherine Lackner, November 7, 1997, transcript p. 5.
41. Peter Velardi, interviewed by the author, May 14, 1997, transcript p. 22.
42. VF Corporation 1990 Annual Report, pp. 18, 19.
43. *Ibid.*
44. VF Corporation 1992 Annual Report.
45. *Ibid.*

46. *Ibid.*
47. VF Corporation 1992 Annual Report, p. 11.
46. *Ibid.*
47. VF Corporation 1992 Annual Report, pp. 12, 13.
48. *Ibid.*
49. *Reading Times*, July 9, 1991, Business section, p. 23.
50. David Reklau, interviewed by the author, June 2, 1997, transcript p. 40.
51. VF Corporation Minutes, Volume VII, October 15, 1991.
52. *Ibid.*
53. VF Corporation 1992 Annual Report, p. 9.
54. *Ibid.*
55. *Ibid.*
56. Feldman, pp. 48-49.
57. VF Corporation 1992 Annual Report, p. 11.
58. VF Corporation 1992 Annual Report, pp. 6, 8.
59. VF Corporation 1992 Annual Report, p. 26.
60. Michael Jonchere, interviewed by Jon VanZile, November 3, 1997, transcript p. 3.
61. Jonchere interview, transcript p. 6.
62. VF Corporation 1992 Annual Report, pp. 16, 18.
63. Pere Prat, letter to author, November 5, 1997.
64. *Ibid.*
65. VF Corporation 1992 Annual Report, p. 14.
66. *Ibid.*
67. *Ibid.*
68. *Ibid.*
69. *Reading Eagle*, September 25, 1991, p. 24.
70. VF Corporation 1992 Annual Report, p.14.
71. *Ibid.*
72 VF Corporation Minutes, Volume VII, February 18, 1992.
73. *Reading Eagle*, March 14, 1992, p. A1
74. *Reading Eagle*, February 21, 1992, p. A11.
75. *Ibid.*
76. Feldman, p. 56
77. *Ibid.*

Chapter Eleven Sidebar

1. VF Corporation 1989 Annual Report, p. 3.
2. VF Corporation 1990 Annual Report, Special supplement on MRS.
3. Bill Pike, interviewed by the author, May 14, 1997, transcript p. 11.
4. VF Corporation 1990 Annual Report, p. 5.

5. Lawrence Pugh, interviewed by the author, December 11, 1996, transcript p. 10.
6. *Reading Eagle*, February 17, 1991, p. 17.
7. VF Corporation Minutes, Volume VII, April 14, 1991.
8. Mackey McDonald, interviewed by the author, December 10, 1996, transcript pp. 22-23.
9. Larry Weidenheimer, interviewed by the author, June 3, 1997, transcript p. 18.

Chapter Twelve

1. *Reading Eagle*, September 22, 1993, p. D7.
2. VF Corporation Minutes, Volume VII, October 20, 1993.
3. *Reading Eagle*, September 22, 1993, p. D7.
4. Mackey J. McDonald biography from VF Corporation archives.
5. *Reading Eagle*, August 28, 1995, p. 1.
6. *Ibid.*
7. *Ibid.*
8. Dick Lamm, interviewed by the author, June 2, 1997, transcript p. 10.
9. Donald Laws, interviewed by Catherine Lackner, November 14, 1997, transcript p. 5.
10. Steve Ludeman, interviewed by Catherine Lackner, November 12, 1997, transcript p. 12.
11. Paul Delorey, interviewed by Catherine Lackner, November 13, 1997, transcript pp. 11, 12.
12. Mackey McDonald, letter to the author, January 16, 1998.
13. VF Corporation press release, February 11, 1997, p. 1.
14. *Ibid.*
15. Prakash Bhatt, interviewed by the author, December 11, 1996, transcript p. 10.
16. Terry Lay, interviewed by Catherine Lackner, November 3, 1997, transcript p. 15.
17. Mark Clift, interviewed by Catherine Lackner, November 10, 1997, transcript p. 13.

18. Frank Urban, interviewed by Catherine Lackner, November 12, 1997, transcript p. 8.
19. Tom Payne, interviewed by Catherine Lackner, November 18, 1997, transcript p. 3.
20. *Ibid.*
21. VF Corporation 1995 Annual Report, pp. 6-8.
22. VF Corporation Minutes, Volume VIII, February 13, 1996.
23. *Reading Eagle*, February 12, 1993, p. B11.
24. *Reading Eagle*, September 23, 1994, p. A8.
25. John Johnson, interviewed by the author, December 11, 1996, transcript p. 5.
26. *Reading Eagle*, February 7, 1995, p. D6.
27. *Reading Eagle*, March 30, 1995, p. D7.
28. Company history, unpublished manuscript, author unknown, from Girbaud achives.
29. *Swim Insights,* published by Jantzen, Portland, OR, Vol. 1, No. 1, Spring, 1997, p. 2.
30. Steve Ludeman, interviewed by Catherine Lackner, November 14, 1997, transcript p. 7.
31. Paul Delorey, interviewed by Catherine Lackner, November 13, 1997, transcript p. 4.
32. *Ibid*, p. 4.
33. Robert Matthews, interviewed by Catherine Lackner, November 14, 1997, transcript p. 3.
34. Matthews interview, transcript p. 8.
35. *Reading Eagle*, December 22, 1993, p. D7.
36. *Ibid.*
37. Ed Doran, interviewed by Susan Shelly, April 11, 1997.
38. *"A Historical Overview,"* from H.H. Cutler Company files, 1993, p. 22.
39. *Ibid.*
40. VF Corporation Acquisition of H.H. Cutler Company Fact Sheet, 1993, p. 1.
41. *Ibid.*
42. *Reading Eagle*, October 12, 1993, p. A12.
43. *Reading Eagle*, May 8, 1995, p. A8.
44. *Reading Eagle*, December 13, 1995. p. A6.

45. Gary Simmons, interviewed by Catherine Lackner, November 7, 1997, transcript pp. 2, 6, 12.
46. George Derhofer, interviewed by Catherine Lackner, November 14, 1997, transcript p. 2.
47. VF Corporation Minutes, Volume VII, July 23, 1993.
48. VF Corporation press release, October 16, 1996.
49. VF Corporation 1995 Annual Report, pp. 10, 13.
50. Sandy McMullen, interviewed by the author, June 3, 1997, transcript p. 4.
51. *Reading Eagle*, December 15, 1995, p. B6.
52. Cindy Knoeble, letter to the author, January 16, 1998.
53. *Reading Eagle*, December 15, 1995, p. B6.
54. Mike Martin, interviewed by Catherine Lackner, November 10, 1997, transcript p. 8.
55. Pugh interview, transcript p. 12.
56. Mackey McDonald, letter to the author, January 1998.
57. Dan Mac Farlan, interviewed by the author, October 9, 1997, transcript p. 14.
58. Janet Peters, interviewed by the author, transcript p. 5.
59. Clift interview, transcript p. 5.
60. Bob Cordero, interviewed by Catherine Lackner, December 23, 1997, transcript p. 1.
61. Angelo LaGrega, interviewed by Catherine Lackner, November 18, 1997, transcript p. 3.
62. Cordero interview, transcript p. 2.
63. Lay interview, transcript p. 11.
64. *Ibid.*
65. *Ibid.*
66. Mike Martin, interviewed by Catherine Lackner, November 10, 1997, transcript p. 2.
67. VF Corporation press release, October 16, 1997, via Internet.
68. VF Corporation press release, October 16, 1997, via Internet.
69. McDonald interview, transcript p. 24.
70. McDonald interview, transcript p. 24.
71. McDonald interview, transcript p. 27.

INDEX